THE NEW Angling Times BOOK OF COARSE FISHING

Allan Haines &
Mac Campbell
with additional material by
Peter Maskell

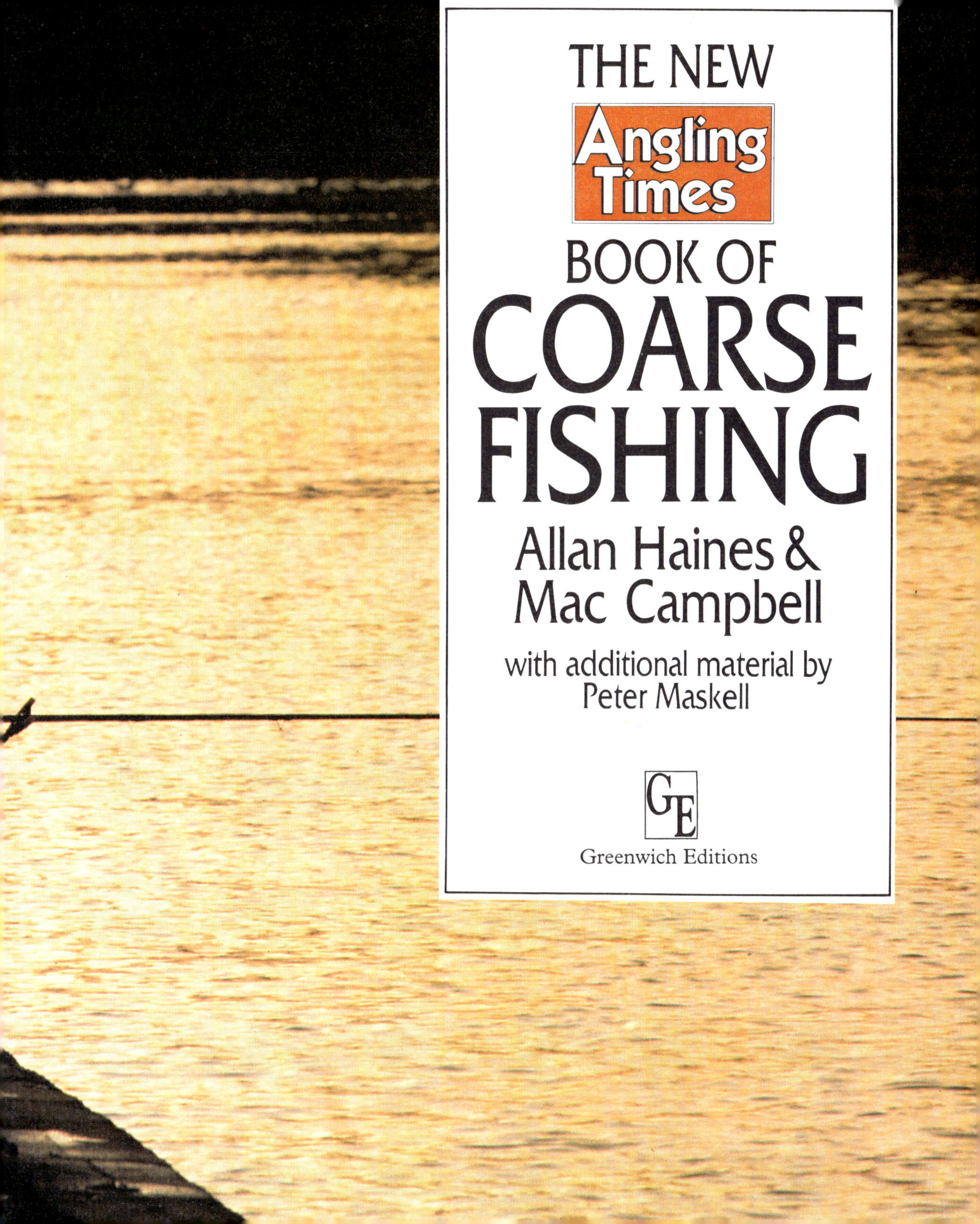

THE NEW Angling Times BOOK OF COARSE FISHING

Allan Haines &
Mac Campbell

with additional material by
Peter Maskell

Greenwich Editions

A DAVID & CHARLES BOOK

First published 1987
Reprinted 1988, 1989, 1991
Revised edition 1994

This edition published in 1996 by Greenwich Editions,
Unit 7, 202–208 New North Road, London N1

A catalogue record for this book is available from the British Library.

ISBN 0 86288 072 6

Printed in Italy
by LEGO SpA, Vicenza
for David & Charles
Brunel House   Newton Abbot   Devon

CONTENTS

INTRODUCTION

There is no short cut to becoming an expert angler. The pathway to the top is long, steep and at times hard. Those who reach its end may be considered 'expert'. But they will only remain expert as long as they continue to learn, either from others or from evaluating their own experiences over the years that follow. Stop learning and the sport of angling will lose its fatal fascination, its attraction that draws us back to the waterside time and time again.

Methods change constantly and it will be those anglers who adapt with progress that will continue to be experts.

Hopefully this book will help you, the reader, avoid some of the pitfalls along that winding road to the top. It will not by itself make you an expert, but it may well make you a better angler.

Both Mac Campbell and myself were luckier than most. In our early days we grew up in the company of some of the very best anglers. Mac learned his fishing on the bream-rich waters of Fenland, long before the threat of zander and pollution loomed on the horizon. The anglers he fished with knew all there was to know about bream, about legering and about how best to beat the windswept venues of their area.

I came from another camp, not far down the road, but in angling terms a different world. My tutors were the float anglers of the Nene, Great Ouse and Welland. They too were great anglers who taught me much, but left a lot of questions unanswered. We found out by experience and long, often fruitless hours, tramping the circuits of the 500 pegger matches that have now long gone.

It was a good apprenticeship that was to be further developed when, years later, we joined *Angling Times*. As journalists we fished with – sometimes against – the best in the world, often in strange countries and on waters such as we had never fished before. The very nature of our jobs demanded we asked many questions. Thankfully we were given most of the answers. And it is those anglers who have made this book possible. It is packed with their ideas – and a few of our own – gathered together over many years. We hope that by reading this book, and turning back its pages again when things go wrong, you will be able to share some of that knowledge given so generously by some of the greatest anglers in the world.

ALLAN HAINES

The smile says it all – a delighted angler and a big carp! But the fish wasn't caught by chance, it was the result of hours of dedication and patience

Longleat in Wiltshire

TACKLE

CHAPTER ONE
RODS AND REELS

Rods

Space-age materials have done much to help the development of fishing tackle. Rod design in particular has undergone considerable changes since the days of Spanish reed, split cane and even fibre glass. With the introduction of carbon, and even more recently, boron and kevlar, overall rod weights have been pruned down to as low as 5oz for a 13ft match rod. Yet this reduction has lost nothing of the strength that heralded the arrival of fibre glass.

High modulus carbon brought with it incredible hoop strength. And as the designer's art developed, so diameters dropped and almost any action could be built into a rod. Another bonus that man-made fibres brought was consistency. Hundreds, or even thousands, of rods can now be made with such accuracy that each joint is interchangeable. Good quality carbon fibre has been further developed with kevlar, a thread-like material, being wrapped around the carbon tube to give even greater strength to a smaller diameter rod. Kevlar is however a heavy material and may add to the overall weight of the rod. The kevlar threads can be clearly seen as a spiral or criss-cross weave along the blank.

Boron is used within the carbon cloth and is less easily seen. Boron is really tungsten threads, only a little thicker than a hair, which have been exposed to boron gas. This treatment makes the threads very stiff and strong so that by wrapping the boron treated threads within the carbon cloth a rod of great strength can be built. Identify boron content by looking at the ends of a rod joint. Within the carbon you should see tiny spots of shiny, steel-like, material. These are the ends of the boron threads that travel the length of the rod joint.

Taking care of these materials is simple. A wipe with a damp cloth to keep them clean is all that's needed. Polish each joint with a spot of furniture polish to prevent rain sticking to them and line will flow better.

But because the designer now has so much technology at his disposal he can build rods for specific purposes. Choosing the right one is not always simple, although the price ticket should be some guide to the true quality. Usually the cheaper the rod the coarser the carbon cloth. It may even have some glass fibres added. If you plan to to buy a cheap carbon check carefully, looking for badly fitting ferrules, cheap rings and even a twist in the blank. Weight alone is not always a good guide to finding the right rod. A rod of 6oz may feel heavier than a similar one of 8oz if the balance is wrong. Remember too that the addition of a reel will make all the difference.

Float fishing

Next thing to consider is the task that the rod will be called on to perform. Fishing a waggler float at long range calls for a totally different action to that required by the stick-float angler fishing close to the bank. And the casting weight of a waggler must also be taken into consideration. For stick-float fishing look for a rod with a tip action. The rod must work within the first half of the top section, giving a rapid strike action. A splice in the tip will often be used to produce this rod. For waggler work a rod able to throw several swan shots and a big float will be needed. The stick-float rod will cope, but at the expense of distance and the possibility of breaking off on the strike. Waggler fishing demands a rod with a more 'through' action. That does not mean a sloppy rod; those are best left on the tackle shop rack. The rod to use will have a sensitive tip but no splice, allowing the action to come down through the whole of the tip section, maybe even into the second section.

The more expensive rods – of high modulus carbon or because boron or kevlar has been used –

Summer action on a carp lake. Note the 'all-through' action of the rod – typical of rods used where big fish are expected. Where a big waggler is being cast long distances the action will extend down the top two sections

will be smaller in diameter. This is desirable in all rods as it helps reduce resistance on the strike and the effects of wind. For most fishing a 13ft rod is preferable.

Choice of rings is a very personal matter. Some anglers prefer ceramic lined ones, while others swear by plain hard chrome. Here again so much development has taken place that it is possible to have lined rings on your rod without adding more weight than would be found with chrome models. The lined rings are kinder to fine lines and have the added bonus of not wearing out after a season or so, as can often be the case with chrome.

Number of rings should also be considered. There is a growing trend to add more and more rings. The effect is to slow down the rod, even to the stage where it becomes tip heavy. At the other extreme too few rings will mean that line sticks to the rod when it is wet and bows will form making it difficult to keep in touch for a quick strike. There is no golden rule on ring numbers but a rough guide is at least a ring per foot of rod. Tip rings should be as small as possible so as not to interfere with the fine tip action.

Legering

The next to consider is a rod for legering. Here we are looking for a rod that will serve for most species such as bream, medium-sized chub, small carp and tench. The big fish rods are a totally different thing. A good leger rod is around 10ft in length. Some even longer rods are now coming into favour and certainly they do help if long-distance casting is likely to be called for.

Although some heavy fish may be caught, chances are that small hooks will be employed. This must be taken into consideration when choosing the rod. One that is very powerful is likely to pull a small hook from the fish long before it reaches the landing net. Go for a rod that is 'tippy' in action but one that allows power to come through to about midway. This is one area where glass fibre is still popular with some anglers, due to it having a slightly more forgiving nature. Quivertips certainly work better if made from glass rather than carbon. And it is often glass that is spliced into the tip to create a sensitive bite indicator.

For casting big leads or heavy swim feeders a steep taper rod is best. That means a butt section thicker than usual, tapering down quickly to a normal tip.

Care

No matter which rods you select they can be broken if used carelessly. Don't lay them on the bank behind you; even the best will not withstand a clumsy foot. Far better to position a rod not in use along the bank or vertically behind you on a rest.

Keep whippings in good order by drying after use and ensuring the varnish is maintained in sound condition. If chrome or stainless rings are used, check them for wear; for once grooved it's only a matter of time before lines start to break and fish are lost.

Reels

In order to make the most of the high-quality rods now available to coarse anglers, reels must also be selected with care. As in rod design, a number of new materials have been brought into play – tungsten, carbon and a variety of light alloys. Bale arms on fixed spools can be automatic, manual, or a mixture of both. Even spool design has been improved almost to an art in order to ensure the best possible line lay.

By far the most popular reel is the fixed spool. It makes distance casting easy and provides rapid line retrieve – vital for match fishing situations.

A snowy morning on the River Wensum near Norwich, Norfolk. Tackle dealer Tom Boulton is using a typical stick float rod, with the action almost all in the tip

Proof that fish can be caught even with snow on the ground – Tom finished with this lovely catch of roach and bream

Fixed spool reel

When selecting a fixed spool there are a few points worth remembering. A spool should be as large in diameter as possible in order to give the best line lay and prevent 'bedding' of fine lines. Depth should be noted too. For most general purposes and match fishing a shallow spool capable of taking 100yd of 2lb to 3lb line is all that's needed. A spare spool is essential and most good reels provide one as standard equipment. But if one doesn't come as part of the price ask your dealer if he stocks them. If he doesn't, buy a different reel!

The spool itself can be either a conventional type or skirted. A skirted spool fits over the bale-arm carrier rather than inside it. This skirted

Skirted spool reel

system certainly helps prevent line getting beneath the spool and into the works when fishing in a difficult wind.

Go for a push-button release spool. You do not want to fiddle with a screw every time a spool wants changing. A carbon spool is possibly the lightest but this is of minor importance after finding the right design. There should be no roughness to the spool lip. On some cheap models it's easy to feel moulding seams where the two edges of the mould meet; avoid those like the plague. Bale arms usually have some sort of roller fitted, which is supposed to help reduce line wear. Make sure it actually rolls. Far too many are nothing more than copies that serve no real purpose other than to look expensive.

The drag system also needs thought. The rear drag system is possibly the easiest to operate while playing a fish. But the frontal drag, operated by a turn of the thumb screw located on the spool, can be very positive. A good drag should not need extra pressure to get it moving. Once set it should operate smoothly at all times and allow for very fine adjustment.

The option to swap from right- to left-hand wind is often used as a big selling point. In truth it serves no purpose. You are either right or left handed and unlikely to change.

When you feel you have the right reel try it on your rod. Check that you can actually reach the spool rim with your index finger. Open and close the bale arm a few times. It should close crisply every time but not with the force of a rat-trap spring. A well designed reel will have no places that line can be caught. Sharp corners and protruding knobs and screws are a menace. Even the push-button release needs to be flush on the spool front. One that protrudes will, sooner or later, end up with line wound around it. Turn the handle fast. If the reel has been properly balanced it will not wobble about. Some form of counter-weight will have been attached to compensate for the off-balance caused by a fast rotating bale arm.

So far we have considered only a conventional fixed spool reel, but many anglers favour one of the closed face variety. And certainly such a tool has its uses. Benefit of a closed face is that it can be used with a facing wind in order to reduce the chance of line blowing back and tangling. Closed face reels are also handy for stick-float fishing on fast-flowing water. Because they rely on a small pin to pick up line rather than a bale arm that would have to be closed, there is no delay or bump between striking and the handle being turned. But nothing comes free in this world. The efficiency and speed they provide is outweighed by the fact that closed face reels usually have narrow spools. These tend to cause bedding of fine lines and upset the free flow of casting and trotting. To summarise; a good reel but one that has its limitations and should be used only when conditions demand it.

Finally the father of all reels – the centre pin. Although considered by many to be old fashioned there is nothing more pleasant than fishing a flowing river with a centre pin. It takes skill to operate one well, but experts claim they are as fast as a fixed spool, and keep the angler in closer touch with float and end tackle. A good centre pin has a fairly wide drum, is light, yet of large diameter and of course very free running. Centre pins come into their own on running water which needs to be fished with heavy tackle. Such a river is made for a centre pin, leaving the angler free to concentrate on bite detection rather than on feeding line off a fixed spool.

To get the best from a centre pin only the minimum amount of fine line should be loaded. Anything more than 30yd will be wasted and do nothing more than bed in, causing sticking as line is pulled off by the float travelling downstream. Try to load the bulk of the line to one side of the drum, using the other side to hold only the line that will actually run off while fishing. The outer edge of the drum should be exposed so that the left hand can 'bat' it hard to retrieve line. Some reels are even made without handles in order to allow the rim to be used at all times. When a big fish is hooked it can be played by inserting a finger into one of a series of holes in the drum's side.

Design points to look for are firstly smooth operation due to good bearings. Is the drum accessible to the hand for delicate control? Can the drum be removed from the backplate easily? Weight and the presence of a line guard are also worth considering.

Treat a good centre pin with care. Keep it well oiled and clean. It's a precision tool that is easily damaged.

Closed face reel

Centre pin reel

CHAPTER TWO
BALANCED TACKLE

Most anglers could dramatically increase their catches if they were to use finer tackle. That is not to say a specimen hunter should try to land big carp and tench on ultra fine gear. Of course big fish such as those demand the use of strong tackle. But for the average angler a day's sport is all about getting bites and catching a good net of fish. To achieve this usually means fine lines and small hooks; and it is possible to land some very big fish on tiny hooks and frail line.

There is a secret to making fine tackle work for you rather than against you – it's called balanced tackle. Line must be matched to the rod – modern fine-tipped carbon rods will go well with lines of 1lb and hook lengths of 12oz breaking strain. Such fine tackle will make for better presentation and yet cope with quality fish without trouble. The reason why the fine line can take so much load is that the rod tip will bend a long way before the breaking strain of the line is reached. The rod is acting as a shock absorber. With experience the angler will be able to detect the line actually stretching and will be able to have a good idea how much load is being applied.

Every angler must have confidence in his tackle and at first it may seem almost impossible to fish with such delicate equipment. So start by running a little experiment. Assemble your rod – which we will assume is a 13ft carbon rod suitable for general coarse fishing – and attach the reel, loaded with 1lb breaking-strain line, threading up the rig as if you were about to fish. Then tie the end of your line to a fixed point, such as the garden fence. Next stage is to apply pressure as if you were playing a fish, remembering of course to keep the rod tip at a steep angle. The rod tip will go right over and eventually you will fear for its safety.

Having tried that little test you will see there is little point in using lines of say 4lb breaking strain on a rod that is only capable of applying a few ounces of pressure. Try the same experiment on an older, glass fibre rod and you may find the 1lb line can be broken. That is because the test curve of the rod is higher.

The test curve of a rod is the amount of pressure, in pounds, needed for the rod to form an arc that makes an angle of 90 degrees between

A typical through-action rod, used by specimen hunters after big fish

You don't have to be experienced to catch carp. They now abound on most of our canals, and young and old alike have a chance of catching them on simple float tackle, using light gear . . . provided it is balanced

tip and butt. Test curves, however, are really intended to be used on specimen rods rather than match type rods which tend to have all the action in the top section. In such cases the test curve has no real value. But for the record, a rod that shows a test curve rating engraved on the butt will need a line of between four and five times that breaking strain. For example a rod with a test curve of 1lb would be well matched to a rod of between 4lb and 5lb strain. The lesson to be learned is always use the finest line possible but at the same time ensure it is well matched to the rod.

So far our test has only considered line that is being subjected to a gently increasing load. In actual fishing this may not be the case. For example, a very hard strike may be too much for the rod to absorb before the line is stressed and broken. So assuming your 1lb breaking strain line was able to pull the rod tip right down during the experiment, you may wish to build in a slight safety margin by adding an extra few ounces, perhaps a line of 1¼lb or 1½lb would be a good choice.

The hook length will of course be finer than the main line, to ensure that if a breakage occurs it is as close to the hook as possible. And the reel line will be subjected to more load than the hook length during casting. Keep fine hook lengths at least 2ft long to give them maximum stretch factor. Short, fine hook lengths will not be able to cope with a sudden shock loading.

Although what is said here is intended to make the reader aware of the need and advantages of fine line, it must also be remembered that it is important to use tackle matching your ability. If you are a complete novice don't expect to land 4lb chub on 12oz bottoms and size 22 hooks. Until confidence and experience are gained, be prepared to step up tackle in relation to your expertise.

Also you must be prepared to step up tackle to cope with a particular swim as well as the size of fish likely to be caught. For example a densely weeded swim would need stronger tackle than a clear, open stretch of water. But in order to make that extra strength work to the full even the rod would, in an ideal world, need to be stepped up.

Like most things in angling there are short cuts and rules that can be broken. Always keep in the back of your mind a number of options to try if your first line of attack does not work. Apply the principles and you will become a better angler. You'll learn when to increase hook size and line strength and when to scale down. There is always a fine dividing line between getting bites, not getting bites and losing a big fish as a result of unbalanced tackle.

A tip-actioned rod, used mainly by matchmen requiring a quick strike when using light tackle, and usually with a stick float

CHAPTER THREE
HOOKS

With so many hook patterns and brands to choose from, selection is bound to be a matter of personal preference. But once you have found a hook that suits you it is best to stick to it. Don't buy a certain type just because it's the one your local match star favours. That's what so many anglers unfortunately do, creating a supply and demand situation that may bear no relation to the hook's quality.

Hooks are of two basic types – forged and fine wire (see main Fig 1). A forged hook is easy to spot at a glance because of the flattened heel which sometimes extends up the shank. This gives a cross-section that is difficult to straighten out. Stressed to destruction it will break rather than bend. For a given size, a forged hook is bulkier and stronger than its fine-wire counterpart. But hooking potential of a fine wire pattern is greater because it is slimmer in profile, therefore that's the one to use with fine lines and delicate baits when presentation is important.

With both forged and fine-wire hooks there are two main patterns – round or crystal bend. A round-bend hook with a wide gape can be crammed with bait, but the wider the gape the less the hook can be an extension of the line and the more leverage there is at the point.

Hook size must be matched to that of the bait, but the old rules of thumb – size 18 for double maggot, 20 for single – are made to be broken. Shop bought maggots vary greatly in size. One day a 20 may be right for a single maggot, another time the bait will perhaps be a fraction smaller and a 22 will be needed. In contrast there are times when fish are not in the least bit hook shy and then you can step up the hook size considerably, even changing from fine-wire to forged pattern at the same time. It may not look balanced to the eye but it is still the right thing to do so long as bites continue to occur at the same rate.

But the number of fish hooked on the strike has as much to do with the bait as with the hook. Maggots are fleshy and even the softest offers some resistance. An ideal hook and bait combination is a caster and a maggot on, say, a size 16 – a bait with movement but no impedance on the strike (Fig 2). Another favourite is double caster on a 16. This is capable of dealing with most fish. One caster is hooked and slid along the shank, the other almost covers the point. On streamier water however double-caster baits can spin on the retrieve, kinking the line. To overcome this, hook the first caster through the blunt end, the second through the sharper end (Fig 2). This will always come away on the strike.

Having sorted out the pattern and hook size you prefer, chances are your next choice will have to be how the hook is actually attached to the line. Apart from eyed hooks, which are usually preferred by big fish specialists, the usual method is by means of a spade end. This is simply a slightly flattened, spade-like end to the shank which acts as a stop, preventing the line slipping off the shank. There are some excellent ready tied spades available, but it is far better to tie up your own. By doing so you will be able to choose exactly what breaking-strain line is to be used as a hook length, how long it is to be and even the brand. It is thus possible to produce a hook that is ideally suited to the situation on the day.

A few rules should however be applied. For example, carry fine hooks in size 14 down to 26 but never tie for example the 26 to 2½lb line because the hook will bend long before that breaking strain is reached. On the other hand a size 14 forged pattern would be an ideal hook to go with a line of that breaking strain. It's all a matter of common sense and balance of line to hook strength (Fig 3).

And before starting to tie your spade ends take a few minutes to check the spades. Frequently they are far too large. It is often possible to reduce

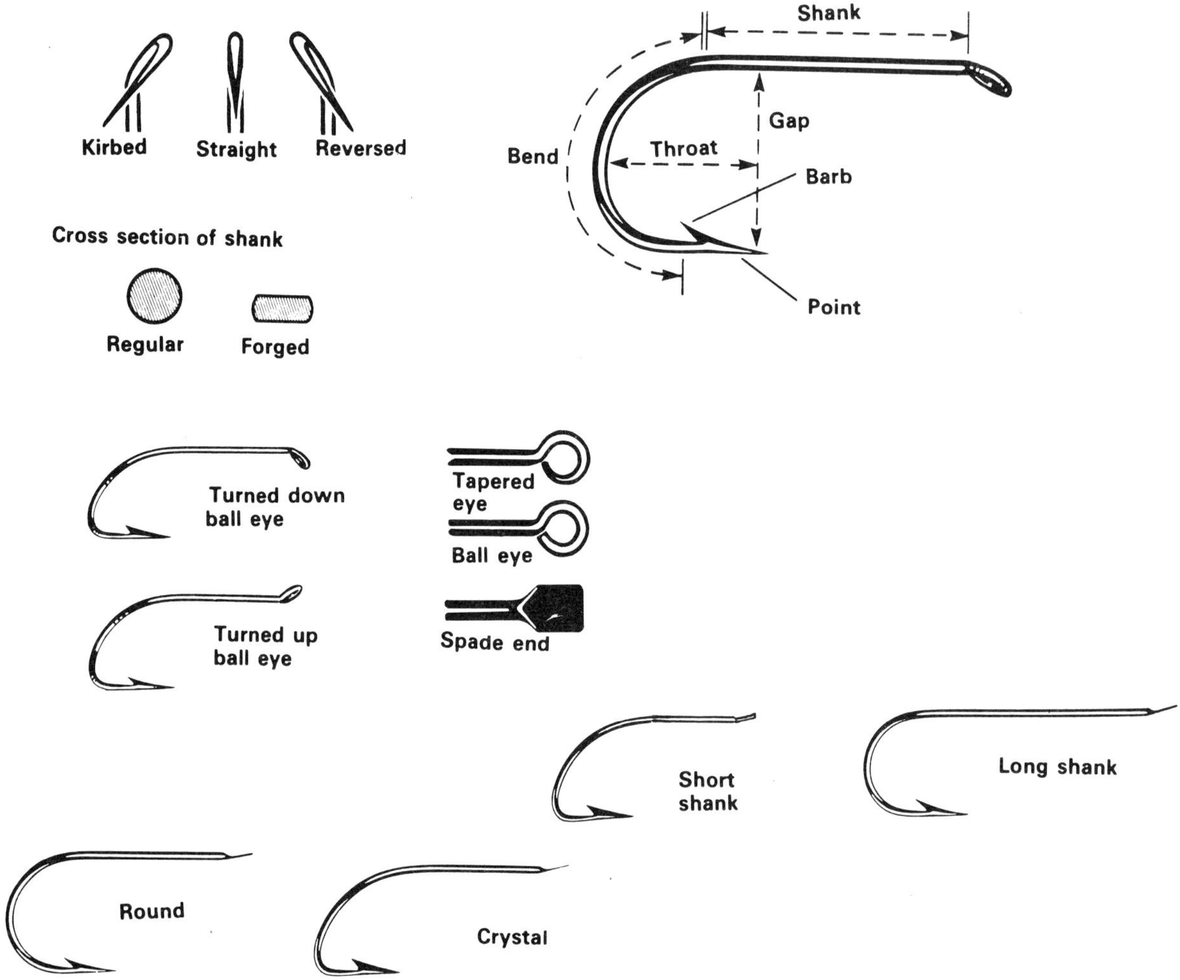

Fig 1 Hooks are produced in many shapes, and from different wires. These are the main ones likely to be encountered

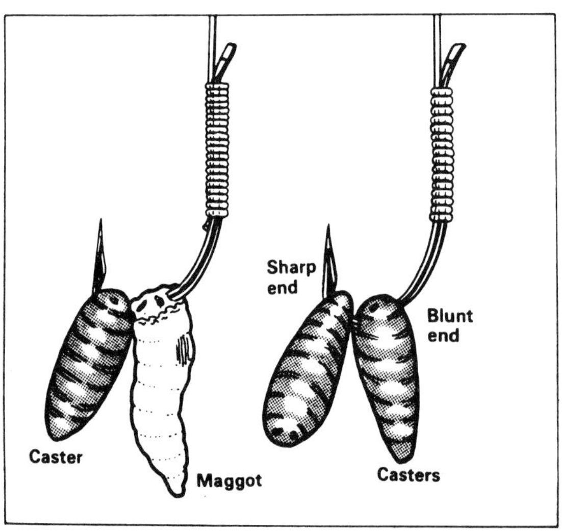

Fig 2 A maggot and caster combination (left) can prove extremely effective. To stop two casters spinning on the retrieve hook them in opposite ends (right)

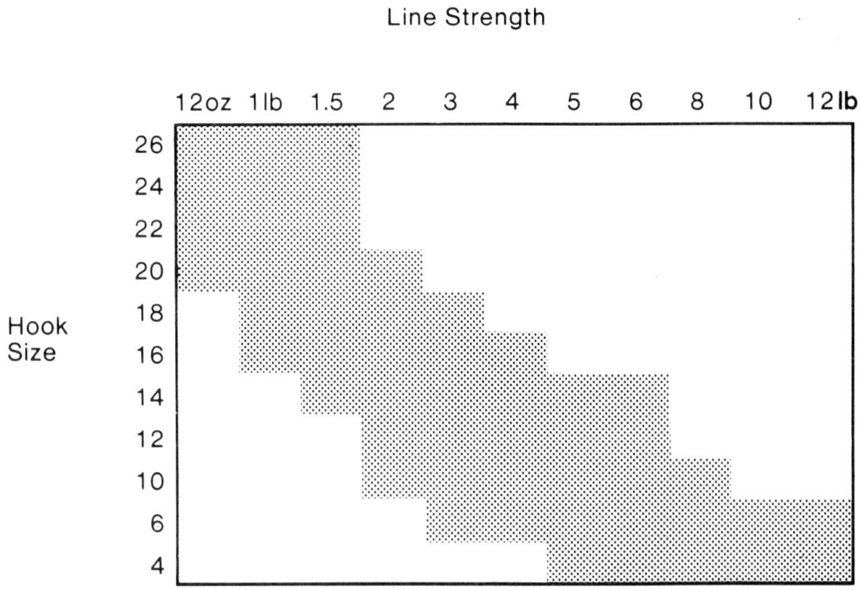

Fig 3 Hook size must be matched to the correct strength line. This chart is a guide to the suitable ranges

the size considerably by carefully stoning them down, but make sure you stone off any rough edges that may be produced. By reducing the shovel-like lump of metal from the shank end you will have an even better hook and the finished knot will be just as strong.

Once you have mastered the spade-end knot (Fig 4) pay attention to detail. The actual number of turns on the knot is something of a personal choice, but too few and the hook will spiral back on itself during the retrieve. Put on too many turns and there will not be enough space in the throat of the hook to hold the bait comfortably. Aim to get a knot that ends at an imaginary point in line with the hook point. And also check that line comes off the spade on the point side of the shank, as shown.

Finally give the points a tone up with a fine oil-stone – a vital operation on some forged patterns. And when you are happy that your hook is perfect add a very small dab of Vaseline to prevent it from rusting. Store a supply of hooks on winders or better still in photographic negative bags, usually 2¼in square, that are sold by most photographic shops and even some of the better tackle shops. Mark each bag with hook size, pattern and breaking strain of hook length.

Of course all hook lengths should be of the same length so that when one is replaced there is

Fig 4 The way to tie a spade-end hook

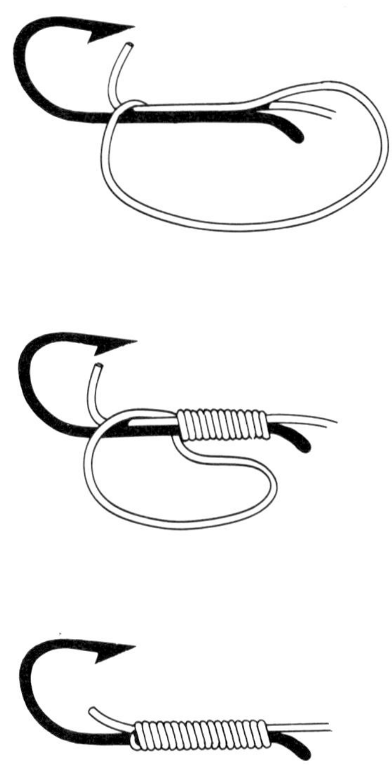

no need to make other adjustments to keep fishing depth constant.

Although you have by now decided on the patterns of hooks best suited to your fishing there is one other factor to consider – the barb. Try to select hooks with low profile barbs rather than ones that protrude a long way. While most hooks have barbs, some anglers now use barbless versions for almost all styles of fishing. A barbless hook has better powers of penetration, is easier to remove from the fish and makes for much faster fishing when in a match.

If you do not wish to go to the expense of tying up barbless hooks in addition to your normal patterns it is a simple operation to carefully squeeze down a barb with a small pair of pliers so that it lies flat against the surrounding metal, making little more than a slight bump.

There are a number of ways to go about tying your own spade-end hooks but the most reliable knot is the one shown (Fig 4). It is tied without the use of any special tools and an evening spent tying will provide enough hooks to see you through many outings.

Fig 5 A guide to the sizes of hooks used with the most popular baits

	HOOK SIZE										
BAIT	26 24	22	20	18	16	14	12	10	8	6	4
BLOODWORM	●										
CASTER			●	●	●						
PINKIE	●	●	●								
MAGGOT	●	●	●	●							
HEMP			●	●							
TARES				●	●	●					
PUNCHED BREAD			●	●	●	●					
SMALL REDWORM				●	●	●	●				
BREAD FLAKE				●	●	●	●	●	●	●	
LOBWORM								●	●	●	●
CHEESE							●	●	●		
LUNCHEON MEAT							●	●	●	●	

CHAPTER FOUR
FLOATS

The waggler

Walk into the average tackle shop and it's odds on you will be absolutely baffled by the array of floats before you. Wagglers will make up a large proportion of the choice on display and you will probably buy two or three. Unfortunately once on the river bank it may soon become obvious that they are almost useless. They may cast awkwardly, take nowhere near the shot loading printed on their sides and, in a nutshell, be totally inadequate. The sad fact is that wagglers, all too often, catch more anglers than fish. So before handing over that hard earned cash, be sure you know what makes a good float.

Start by considering when and where to use a waggler. The most obvious place is a lake or still water – no place for a stick float here since there will not be a flow against which it could be made to work. It is easy to decide when to use a waggler – when fishing is to be carried out more than six rod lengths distant or when conditions are very bad, eg in a very strong downstream wind.

As floats go the waggler is probably one of the easiest to master as long as it is correctly balanced and shotted in a manner that will prevent tangling. Don't confuse yourself with hundreds of different types. Just two materials are worth considering – peacock quill and the clear plastic ones introduced by ace float designer Peter Drennan. A peacock waggler should be straight. This will ensure that it casts true, like a dart, and will ride well in the water.

Two materials then and maybe two or three patterns: a straight waggler without a tip insert, a straight float with a thin tip insert, and finally a bodied version that is used for long-range fishing in shallow water. The body will prevent the float from diving too deeply as it hits water at the end of a cast, a vital thing to watch when fishing for chub right up on the far ledge in water no more than a foot or so deep.

Two types of waggler float. The two on the left have tip inserts of smaller diameter material, making them more sensitive

The inserts are for use on very slow or still water when bites are shy or fish are expected to be feeding higher in the water and likely to take a bait 'on the drop'. Inserts will not work in moving water that has any pace. They are too sensitive for this fishing and will pull under if the hook as much as touches bottom.

On peacock there is no better material for an insert than another, thinner piece of peacock. It is buoyant and light and will not affect the overall balance of the float. The worst material for an insert is cane or other heavy material. If the insert is heavy it will make the float cast badly and land untidily. As a general guide an insert of about 2in long is what to look for, but when fish are feeding on the drop a little longer one may help bites to be seen more easily.

The clear plastic materials are thought to be very good when fishing in clear water since they cast less of a shadow along the bottom. The theory seems to work, especially on hard fished waters where fish may have learned to connect a shadow with danger.

Wagglers come in a very wide range of sizes and as experience is gained your box will fill with many different sizes of the same few patterns. Biggest of the wagglers could, more than likely, have a shot load of five or six SSG shot. But for general fishing something between two BB and three SSG will suffice.

Attaching wagglers to the line is best done by means of an adaptor. Which you choose is very much a matter of personal choice but most top match anglers go for the soft silicon type. These allow the float to find its own path in flight and collapse on the strike to give a direct line through to the hook. By using this style of adaptor a float can be changed in seconds without the need to break down any of the rig. The adaptor is locked to the line by means of shot which should be squeezed either side of the adaptor without leaving any gaps. It is best to use two shot beneath, and one above, the adaptor to prevent slipping.

Wagglers are always attached bottom end only and the line should be sunk beneath the surface by plunging the rod tip under and winding the reel handle several turns. Anglers tighten up in this manner and then give the rod tip a few quick flicks until the line goes under. Soaking the nylon in washing-up liquid helps it to sink.

Wagglers, like all floats, can be shotted in many different ways but at first two basic patterns should be followed. When fish are proving tricky, often in winter, a small bulk of shots works well. Something like three No 4 shot or three No 6 go on the line in a tight bunch, but always make sure they are below half depth. This positioning is very important in preventing the hook looping back in flight and tangling around the float base. Beneath this bulk group goes a 6, two 8s and a 10, all equally spaced between the bulk and the hook. In summer when fish are more likely to be feeding off the bottom all that is needed down the line is two or three very tiny shot, for example two 10s and a 12.

Casting a waggler is much easier than casting a stick float but in most cases it is a two-handed job. Action of the cast is a 'push and pull' movement. The leading hand, which is on the reel foot and takes control of the line release with the index finger on the spool lip, does the pushing. The other hand goes on the extreme butt end, pulls the rod backwards from the butt as the tip moves forwards and the cast is made. The idea is to throw the line and float in a very high arc-like path, feathering line as the float lands so that the tackle falls in a straight line. Once the tackle lands the tip is then thrust beneath the water and the line is buried as already described.

So far everything may seem too simple to be true. But waggler fishing, like any other method, can be turned into a science and with experience it can become a very versatile method. Indeed some very experienced anglers use wagglers for almost all their fishing needs. The biggest single mistake most beginners make is to choose a waggler that is too small for the job. The one selected may work perfectly for a time but there will inevitably come a moment when there is a need to cast further or fish deeper. And that's when a little extra shot will be needed.

As an example let us take two imaginary anglers, both choosing a float to start a day's fishing. The first angler we shall call Fred Higginbottom (with apologies to anyone reading this book by the same name). The second is a real expert whom we will call Kevin Marks. Now Kevin, for the purpose of this example, does everything right. Fred Higginbottom, to his credit, will arrive at the same answer to the angling problems of the day but only through a process of trial and error. During the day he will lose a lot of fishing time but, like the expert, will finish up with the correct float. Follow the action as the session develops (see Fig 6):

Fred: Starts with a light float. Puts the bulk of his shot under the float (Rig A) quite correctly. Unfortunately he has trouble casting when he finds the better fish are near the bottom and needs more shot down his line (Rig B). So he changes to

Gaily-coloured longboats on the Grand Union Canal. In winter the cover they provide attracts fish from large areas. A waggler is the obvious choice of float to use here, as it can be cast accurately to within inches of the boat

A catch of roach from the Great Ouse . . . all taken on a home-made straw float costing just a few pence

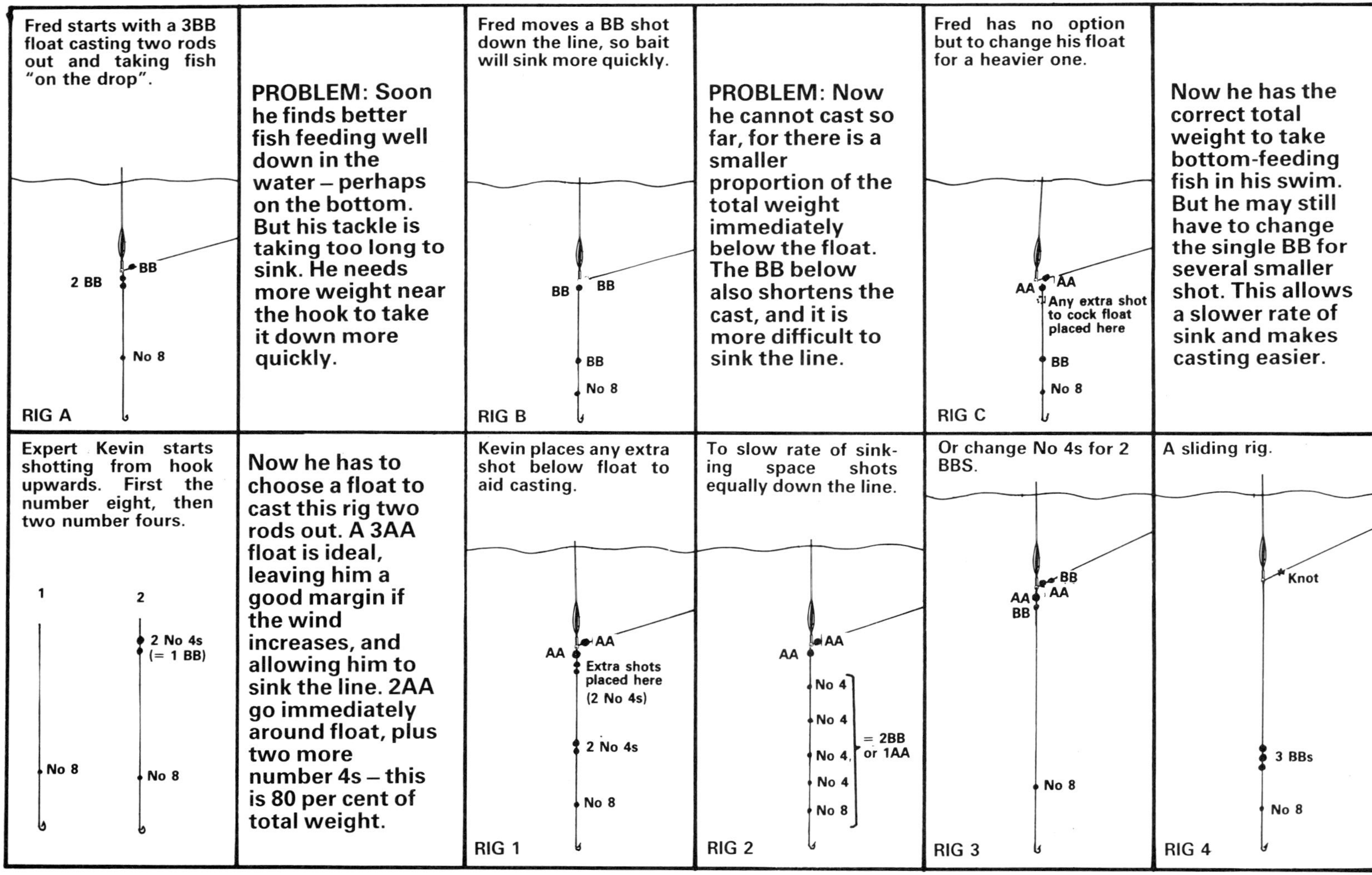

● TOP LINE: Fred Higginbottom – the less experienced of the two anglers. He starts off with a rig that catches fish, but is not versatile enough when he has to fish on the bottom. He eventually arrives at the correct set-up, but has lost time, during which the fish may have moved away. BOTTOM LINE: Kevin Marks – the top-class angler who invariably chooses a heavier float than may seem necessary. He knows, through experience, that conditions may change. NOTE that Fred's original float will work, provided the wind doesn't increase too much, if he uses it as a slider (see final diagram).

Fig 6

a larger float in order to get his bait down faster (Rig C).

Kevin: Decides from the start what he might need in the way of shot near his hook. He then decides what size float he will need to cast this weight. Result, he ends up with a float capable of taking three AAA, knowing he can push all his shot up to the float if necessary.

Both could use a three BB float (Rig 4) if they set up a sliding rig. This allows all the shot to be used in a bulk, will cast easily and gets the bait down fast.

Lesson: It is the proportion of shot immediately below the float that determines how easy it is to cast. The three BB were fine so long as they were locking the float. When they were moved casting distance immediately decreased. As a guide it is best to aim for 80 per cent of the total weight to be used as float locking shot. Note how Kevin has shotted his first rig which has 80 per cent as locking shot. In the second diagram (Rig 2) Kevin has only 66 per cent of his shot around the float but casting is made easier by the fact that the remaining shots are spaced down the line. A single AAA shot down the line would have made things very difficult indeed.

Rig 1 will give a longer casting distance than he needs but it is better to have range in hand than constantly struggle to reach the target. Rig 3 would cast very well and allow the bait to fall very slowly – ideal for catching mid-water feeders.

Fishing the waggler

The waggler float is by far the most popular in Britain today. You will almost certainly be using it if you're fishing a stillwater. It is ideal for beginners too, because it's easy to attach to the line, casts well and is virtually tangle free if correctly shotted. Former world champion Kevin Ashurst gave the advice which forms the basis of this section. Although there are many ways a waggler can be shotted it is best, for a start anyway, to remember the halfway rule. The simple way to remember this is that if there is only one shot on the line it must be more than halfway down the line from the float to the hook, so that if the hook flies backwards during casting it won't catch around the float. It doesn't always work out as easily as that, but it does hold good most of the time. A second shot would go more than halfway

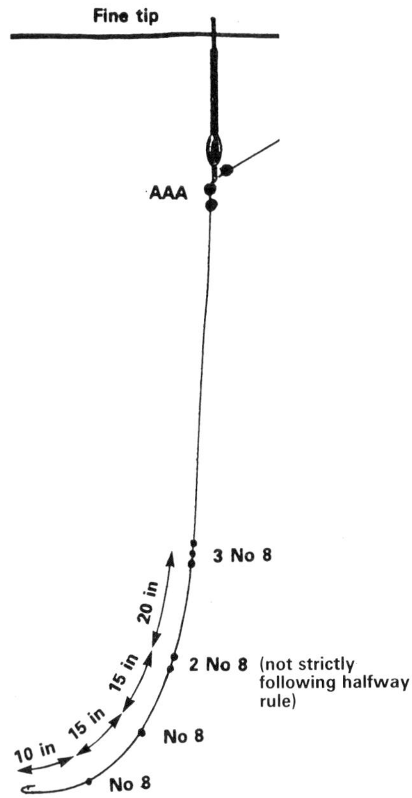

Fig 7 Shotting pattern for fishing on the drop

down from this shot to the hook, so that if the hook flies backwards it can't catch around the first shot. As more shot is added so the rule is applied again and again, each shot going on slightly more than halfway between the one above it and the hook.

Next thing to remember is never put a large shot beneath a smaller one, for this will increase your chance of a tangle. In any case there are very few occasions when this would be needed. On a stillwater the nearer a shot is to the hook the smaller it should be.

When a fish gives a good 'dive away' bite you can't miss seeing it. But if it holds up the bait as it sinks, or lifts it off the bottom, you are relying on that bottom shot to show you've got a bite by the float failing to cock properly, or raising slightly. So it can be seen that the size of the bottom shot must be in the right relation to the float tip. The thinner – and therefore more sensitive – the float tip, the smaller the lowest shot can be.

You really need to know what the effect will be if a fish lifts the bottom shot. This is easily discovered by removing the bottom shot and seeing how much higher in the water the float rides.

As to actual choice of float, there are again, some simple rules to apply. In calm water you are likely to be using a waggler with some form of thin insert, unless you are fishing at long range in which case thickness will be determined by visibility. A No 6 shot will probably be sufficient to show a lift bite. If the water is rougher you'll need a thicker tip for it to be seen easily and not be constantly pulled under by wave action. The obvious choice under these conditions is a straight waggler with about a No 4 shot as a tell-tale, because the extra weight will be needed to move the thicker, more bouyant, float tip.

If at any time you get lift bites which are hard to see, increase the tell-tale shot size slightly. The result will be that the next bite moves the float higher out of the water. It's simple if you think about what is going on beneath the surface.

Fig 8 Bulking most of your cocking shot below midwater, and spreading the rest out in the last few feet, will help stop tangles on the cast

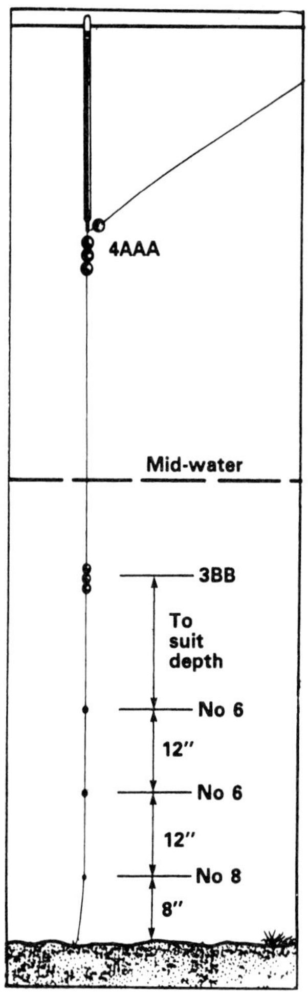

A waggler rig with shots strung evenly down the line shouldn't give too much casting trouble provided you can learn to 'feather' line lightly before it hits water. This slight checking of the tackle's progress through the air will put everything in a straight line. Get it right and bites will register from the surface, all the way down to the bottom. With experience it is possible to bend the halfway rule, but the more it is bent the greater are the chances of tangles.

Once ready to fish, be sure you can actually feed the spot you intend to fish. It's no good casting 20yd into a headwind and then find you can't get feed any more then 15yd out. Start by having a few trial casts to get the feel of conditions. And if you are not confident about your casting ability, start by shotting up a float with all the shot bunched beneath the float and without a hook attached. Try a cast and the float should fly out well. Next push shot down the line, one at a time. As you do this you will find that the more weight used down the line the shorter you will cast. So keep as little shot downstairs as possible and you will cast maximum range.

The easiest rig of all is with most of the weight around the float and only one small shot down the line – below halfway of course and probably between 12in and 18in from the hook. It should be possible to catch fish under most conditions using this simple rig.

Fishing can now start. Cast out and feed an area a few yards short of the float. This is because if the wind strength increases you will need to push the rod tip beneath the surface and wind in a few turns to sink line so that the tackle isn't blown out of position. As your experience increases you will be able to sink line with just a quick turn of the reel and a flick of the rod tip – it's all a matter of practice.

Float sensitivity

Even if you manage to select the correct float there will still be those days when bites are difficult to hit. Your first reaction will probably be to make the rig more sensitive so that bites can be seen sooner. Often this will prove to be the wrong tactic and the tackle should be made less sensitive, giving the fish longer to take the bait into its mouth before the strike.

Theoretically if a fish is confident it will hang on to the bait for a full second or two. Think back to those swing-tipping sessions when you have taken your eye off the tip and the angler at the next swim has yelled out a warning to you. You have struck very late and yet the fish has been on. The trick is to learn when to make tackle sensitive and when to go the other way.

Start by looking at the bait. If you are using maggot and it has been chewed – so that the skin has been broken – you can be absolutely certain that the fish has had the bait well down its throat. For that is where the teeth that grind food are located. Fish do not have chewing teeth near the lips. If your bait is in this state your strike has been too late and you will need to go more sensitive. If the bait's skin has not been broken it is probable, but by no means certain, that the fish has been holding it between its lips only. So allow more time before striking, or make the rig less sensitive, or both. The easiest way to alter a float rig is to move the bottom 'tell-tale' shot upwards to make the rig less sensitive or towards the hook for more sensitivity.

When fishing with caster as bait it is much harder to decide what is going on, for often a slight nip with the lips will enable a fish to burst the bait. It may be worth switching to a maggot in the hope of getting a clue as to how a bite is developing.

Another answer to striking too soon is to use a bigger bait, with more of the float tip left showing. This will slow your fishing down; you won't be tempted to strike at the first indication, knowing you have a larger bait on. Always remember there is no merit in getting lots of bites if you miss them. The idea is to fish for fish, not for bites, and the only fish that count are the ones in your net.

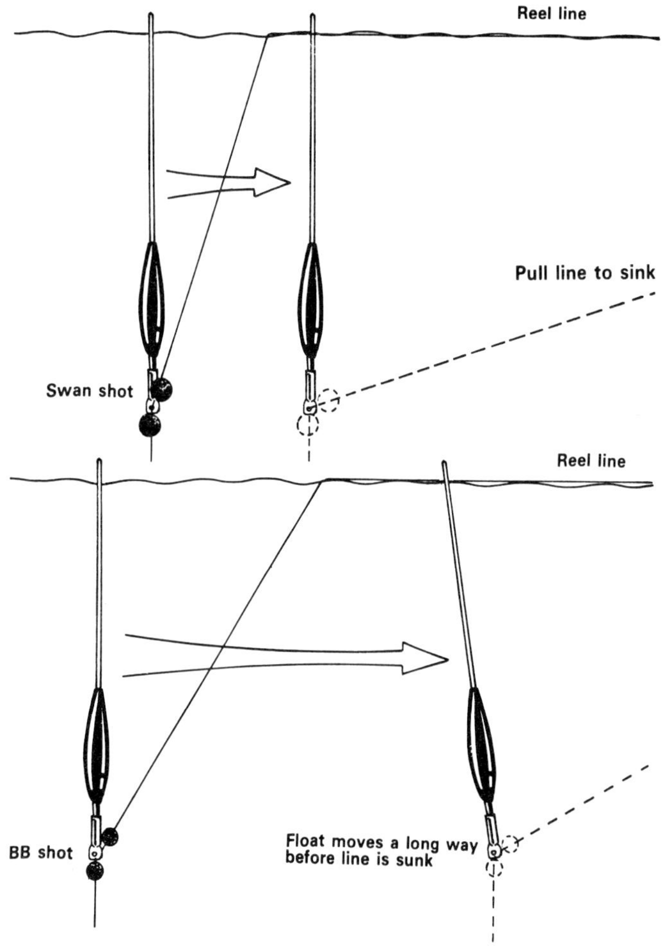

Fig 9 Having a lot of shot immediately next to the float allows the line to be sunk without the float being pulled very far

The stick float

Fishing a stick float can be one of the most rewarding aspects of our sport. It can also be one of the most frustrating. Far too many inexperienced anglers use the wrong float for the job and use it shotted incorrectly. As a result they finish a day's sport with little to show for a lot of effort.

According to most textbooks on the subject, stick floats are for use on running water but only under perfect conditions such as an upstream wind. That myth can be dispelled. The stick float can be used under many different situations provided you use it correctly and remember a few simple rules of thumb. So let us take the stick float through its life in simple stages, starting with conditions and suitable waters.

Two styles of stick float. The ones on the right have wire stems

The first priority for a stick float is moving water where it provides much better presentation than a waggler. When the water is cold it allows the bait to be slowed down, essential when fish are unwilling to chase a bait. The colder the water the more this rule will apply. It is possible to make a stick float do a great deal. With practice it can be made to 'talk'; a waggler will be far more restrictive. Ideally the wind shouldn't be too strong. Direction does not matter a great deal. There are ways around a downstream 'skim' – such as backshotting and using sinking lines.

Stick floats, like most other patterns, come in a variety of shapes and sizes but basically there are two main types – the ordinary and the wire stem. The first type was originally made from cane and balsa. The less buoyant cane was used for the stem with a balsa dome-shaped top. Many anglers still prefer this basic pattern but materials such as lignum, plastic and fibre glass are now being used for stems. These are heavier than cane and are certainly to be recommended for beginners. In fact this is the float to use under most conditions. The wire-stem stick float is more restricted in use but can be excellent in swims with boils as the wire stem is more stable and able to cope well with turbulent water.

Having cleared away the mystique that surrounds these floats the next thing to consider is how they are attached to the line. They can be fixed in the normal manner – double rubber or 'top and bottom' as it is often called – but it pays to give this simple operation a little care and attention to detail. For a start three rubbers, not two, is the correct way. By this method of attachment the third one acts as a safety measure. It stops the float slipping and, should one of the rubbers break, it is possible to continue fishing without having to break down the complete rig.

The bottom rubber should be longer than the other two, overlapping the bottom of the float so that everything is in a straight line and the bottom of the float doesn't knock against the small shot that will be placed underneath as a depth marker.

Next comes the shotting; possibly the most important item in the whole set-up. Tradition suggests a whole string of tiny shot placed at regular distances from float to hook. This is good, but just as good – better in winter – is a small bulk of three No 6 shot with several smaller shot between it and the hook. The bulk should be about mid-depth and, for a start, try No 8s down to the hook. But if the going is tough No 10s will most likely produce more bites. Put a No 8 directly beneath the float to act as a depth marker. If the float slips, it is a simple operation to slide it down again to the marker shot.

So far the rig has been set to fish under reasonable conditions but should the wind be difficult for example downstream, but not too strong, a No 6 shot goes on the line about a foot *above* the float. To make this rather strange looking shot work for you the tackle must be cast further out and a little downstream of the spot where you wish to start the trot. Then retrieve the tackle slightly and start the trot with line beneath the surface. In stronger winds it may be necessary to use three, or even four No 6 as backshot, placed 4in apart above the float. This amount of shot being attached may call for a shot or two to be removed from beneath the float to prevent it sinking too far under the surface.

Having decided on shotting, the next problem to tackle is how deep to start fishing. The short answer is 'at the depth of the water'. Ideally you will catch fish at full depth but in cold conditions an extra foot on the fishing depth and a slight overshotting will enable the float to be slowed down by controlling the speed at which line leaves the reel. This is done by dabs of the finger on the spool rim.

Occasionally with steady feeding, fish will move up in the water to intercept the bait. 'On the drop' bites should always prompt a change of depth. Shallow-up 6in at a time until the feeding level of the fish is found.

With stick-float fishing it is essential to always keep the reel spool well loaded so that line flows off easily when finger pressure is released from the spool lip.

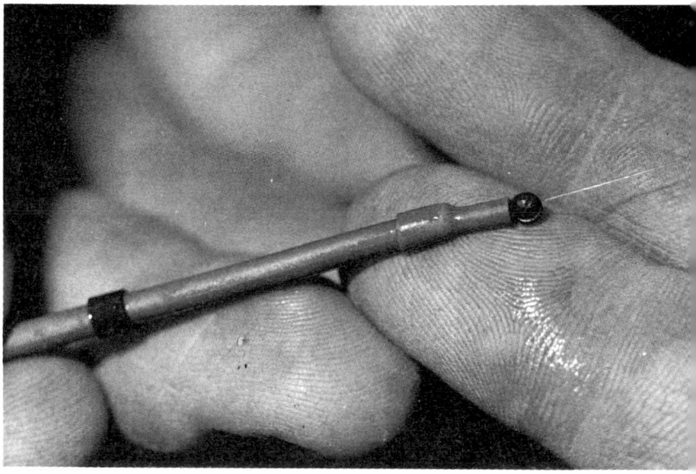

Make sure the rubber at the base of the stem overhangs the end. This will prevent tangles. A shot is placed beneath the rubber as a stop

Fig 10 The two main basic shotting patterns for the stick float. Most popular is the 'shirt button' style (right)

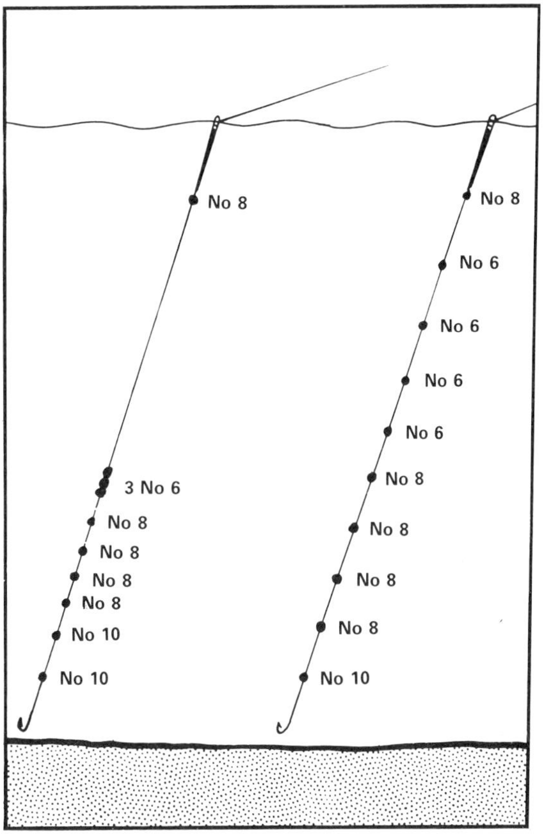

Action on the River Swale in Yorkshire – a fast-flowing river, and obvious stick float water

The result – a big bag of sparkling chub

Casting a stick float can become something of an art, but if you are a beginner you should always start by perfecting a sideways style. This involves holding the baited hook between the fingers of one hand and flicking the rod with the other, letting go of the hook and making the tackle land in the water just downstream of where you are sitting, with the line from float to hook landing in a straight line, also pointing downstream.

Once you have mastered this technique – and it will take some practice – try the overhead cast. It is a quicker method but more tricky. Feather the line as it hits the water or the tackle will end up in one big heap and an enormous tangle. But this is the best cast to use when fishing at maximum stick-float range.

Having mastered casting, the next step is to work out the correct fishing speed. Start the session by letting it run through at the same pace as the current. If bites are slow, try slowing the bait down by careful control with your finger on the reel spool. This will make the float ride out of the water so some overshotting may be needed. In most conditions adding a No 6 shot to the small bulk will do the trick, but if you are holding back really hard as much as a BB may be required.

Range of stick-float fishing is, as a general guide, restricted to about six rod lengths out. But it is important to use a float that is heavy enough to cope with this distance easily. It is far better to use a float slightly heavier than you really need as this will give more control.

Most stick-float problems have now been outlined and hopefully solved. All that remains is to practise until casting and overall control become second nature. As your skill increases, however, you will want to add refinements of your own. Start by considering the type of line to use. One that sinks can be the most useful so ask your dealer to suggest a brand noted for this quality. But to make certain that it sinks, try running it through a tissue soaked in washing-up liquid. In perfect conditions, a floating line such as Drennan floatfish is excellent. That's the sort to go for when there is little or no wind.

Striking when using a stick float will also need some thought. A sideways strike is always best. Forget all the nonsense that has been written about 'up and across'. Pull the rod swiftly, almost parallel with the water's surface.

Finally, as stick-float fishing becomes a major part of your armoury, you will need to develop a trick known as 'mending the line'. This is a way of helping the float to run downriver in a straight line. When your line is on or near the surface, especially in a downstream wind, it will tend to pull the float along at a speed faster than the current and no self-respecting fish will look at a bait doing that. The simple operation to mend line involves lifting the rod tip to take line off the water surface and then flicking it round so that it is once again in a straight line upstream of the float. Again practice makes perfect and you should aim to carry out the whole operation without lifting the float from the surface.

Avon floats made from crowquill and balsa

The Avon float

Angling styles have become less regional than they used to be. Today, for example, no one talks about fishing 'Nottingham style' or 'Sheffield style'. The anonymous waggler and stick float have almost taken over nationwide.

But on the Bristol Avon anglers continue to do their own thing – fishing 'Bristol fashion' you might say. In that part of the country the balsa-bodied crow quill is the king of floats. The 'Avon' however is a float that should be included in every angler's box for it can often make all the difference on those difficult days when something of a change is needed to keep fish feeding. A deep swim, overhanging trees, or simply a large head of bleak that grab every bait that passes their way, can all be beaten with an Avon.

Originally the Bristol anglers tried to find a float to beat the prevailing upstream wind that sweeps along their river. The water is deep and of modest flow so a float and shotting pattern that would allow a bait to move downriver in a natural manner was required. The result was the Avon and a rather awkward looking shotting method. The float worked like a dream, working its way along the river against the wind.

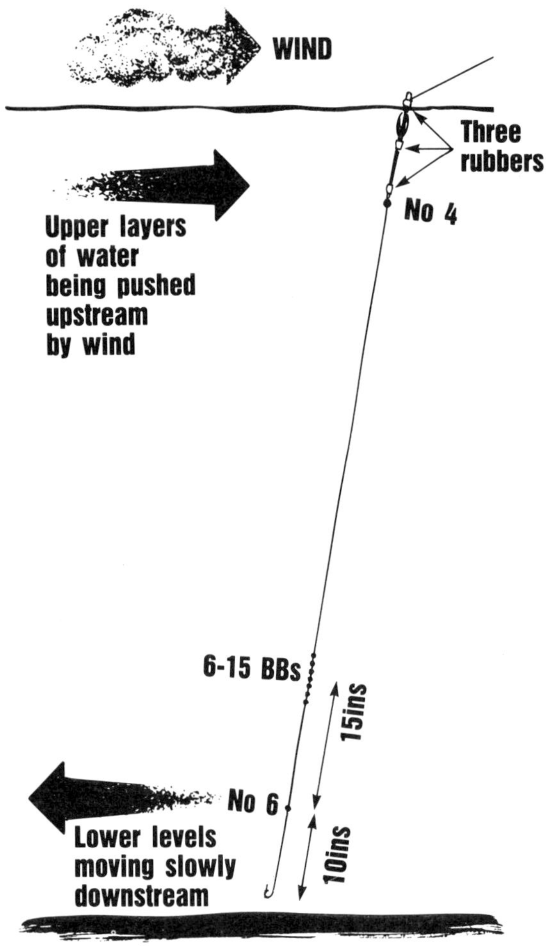

Fig 11 An Avon correctly shotted to carry the tackle through a deep swim against an upstream wind

The principle of the Avon is a buoyant body – usually balsa but sometimes polystyrene – on a very light crow quill. A good one will be lightly varnished and able to carry anything from four to fourteen BB shots. There is no fancy shotting pattern. Nothing goes at the float stem base, but a string of BB go in a long string less than 3ft from the hook. Beneath this bulk a single No 6, or even a 4 acts as a tell-tale.

Strangers to the Avon method may question this bulk method. Why a necklace of BB shot, why not use fewer larger ones? Do shy bites register, and how can you hope to catch fish on the drop? The answer to the last question first – you don't. That is the whole idea of the Avon, to catch fish close to the bottom in anything up to 12ft or 13ft of water. To do that the bait must get down very quickly and with this pattern a matter of four or five seconds will see the float working correctly at that depth. The bulk also acts as a stabiliser, control is perfect and the angler has very effective control of its passage through the swim.

Perfect presentation brings with it good bites. Nine times out of ten the Avon will vanish from sight when a fish takes. But the secret is to get the float balanced then the fish just don't bother about the amount of weight being used. But why AAA do not work as well as the BB string is not really known. Maybe the flexibility of the string of smaller shot is a factor when striking and casting.

Another good thing about this float and shotting method is that it is easy to cast with an underhand swing, something that is essential on the river Avon due to the large number of overhanging trees. With the float right up against the rod-tip ring the cast is made, the string of shot flies outwards and the float follows along the same line.

The method, however, works anywhere. It is certainly not a one-river rig. Most flow rates are taken in the float's stride and deep water really brings out its best. But because the stem is a delicate quill the normal 'top and bottom' double-rubber method of attaching the float will result in breakage. Always use a third rubber at the base of its body. This will prevent the stem becoming bent and also hold the float at the correct depth. Two rubbers may allow it to slip down the line on the strike.

Straw floats

If you fancy making up some very cheap yet versatile little floats, look no further than a packet or two of plastic drinking straws. Floats made from drinking straws will carry a surprising amount of shot, cast well and yet land very lightly, making them ideal for use on shallow or hard-fished waters. They are perfect for many canal fishing situations.

Simplest of all straw floats is a basic straw, plugged at the tip and fitted with a base insert of some kind. A blob of glue on the top and a short piece of cane will serve. But for a wider application, try making stepped up versions by fitting straws of different diameters together. The result

Fig 12 A good basic pattern of drinking straw float – possibly the cheapest float available

will be a superb float and a wide range is possible by cutting the steps to different proportions. If a float with a fine insert tip is called for, use peacock quill – it's the best. There is no place for cane at the top of any float because it will upset the balance.

Because plastic straws are waterproof there is really no need to do a lot of fancy varnishing and painting. But a thin coat of matt paint (non-cellulose) will make them look really professional. Glue the different straws together by using Araldite rapid. If mixed thickly enough it will act as a seal to make up any gaps that may exist between the diameters.

The sliding float

The sliding float was first popularised by the late Billy Lane Jnr during the 1950s. Instead of being fixed to the line, the float slides along it, stopped from going right down to the hook by the shot, and stopped from sliding along the line indefinitely by a knot which, if needed, will glide through the rod rings on casting. The position of this knot is easily adjusted, as it will slide along the line if required.

Theoretically there is no limit to the depth of water which can be float fished with a sliding float. For many years it was used almost solely for the purpose of fishing water greater than the depth of the rod being used; so the deep waters of the Fens, up to 25ft deep, could be fished with a rod of only 13ft. However, Billy Lane realised that once you've got a slider working properly it makes casting much easier in almost any depth of water. And he began to use it to get baits across wide waters like the Witham, Welland and Great Ouse Relief Channel.

The basic shotting for a sliding float is with almost all the shot required to cock the float bunched together 3ft from the hook, the float having already been threaded onto the line. Above that is the knot (there are, now on the market, specially designed rubber stops which are even better than knots), and when the shot has taken the line through the ring of the float the knot jams in the ring and the float cocks in the normal way. Although any float with a small ring will act as a slider, the ideal ring consists of several turns of wire, so the ring is about ⅛in wide. This helps to prevent tangles, which sometimes occur on the cast.

Before the cast, the float sits on the load of bunched shot, and when you cast this acts as if all the shot were fixed below the float. So the float and shot zoom out together a long way. That's another great advantage of fishing a slider – it can considerably increase the distance it is possible to cast against a strong wind, provided you don't require your shot to be strung out down the line. Another advantage is on the strike – the line is pulled through the float's bottom ring and the fish is hit before you feel the float. It is not uncommon to see anglers fishing a float which slides for just a foot, in order to gain the advantage of striking *through* the float ring.

Don't wait until you are fishing water deeper than the length of your rod to try the slider. Have a go in an average swim, say 8ft or so, to gain confidence. A slider can be fished without difficulty in still or slowly moving water, but in faster water it is a job for an experienced angler. And at all times the secret is to get a tangle-free shotting pattern. The wrong pattern can give tangles all

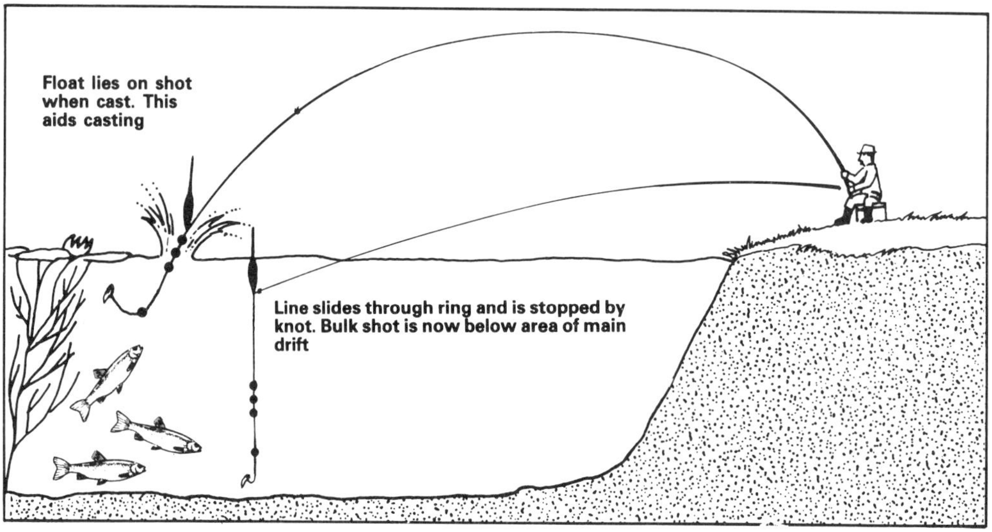

Fig 13 A sliding float rig is the way to tackle deep water. The shotting pattern enables you to cast close to weed beds and to beat top drift

day. So the rule when you are first starting is to keep it simple.

The fact that the float rests on the bunched shot sometimes results in tangles, and many anglers place a No 4 shot 3in above on which the float rests. Then come the bunched shot say 2½ft from the hook, and 18in farther down is a BB. That is the simplest pattern of all, and nine times out of ten it is hard to beat it. However, anglers have inventive minds and naturally want to experiment. Always follow the 'halfway rule', though, by putting each shot, or batch of shots, at least halfway down from the one above.

Plumbing with a slider can be a little difficult, so most anglers prefer to forget a plummet and to use the rig on its own. The easiest way to check the depth is with the basic rig already described. First check the shotting by sliding the knot down to the No 4 shot with the float trapped between them. Cast into water known to be more than 6ft deep (or whatever is the distance from float to hook) and satisfy yourself on how far the float sinks. Aim to have only the top half-inch or so showing.

Now push the knot back up the line, so that the float is well overdepth. Cast out, and if you check the line slightly before the rig hits the water it will help to avoid tangles. As the shots sink, the float will waggle from side to side as it lies on the water. If after half a minute it hasn't cocked, you know your bunched shot are on the bottom. If it cocks, but not fully, the bottom BB is on the bottom. This is why that BB is so important. If you use a smaller shot there you may have a job to decide whether or not it's on the bottom. Move the float down the line a foot at a time (the BB is a foot from the hook, remember) until the float cocks. Now your hook is on the bottom and the BB is off it. Always carry out this process with an unbaited hook to avoid getting false indications by fish holding up the bait as it sinks.

Once you've had a bite or two on this rig, and have gained confidence, you can start experimenting. But don't run before you can walk. You'll get tangled from time to time – everybody does. The most common problem is the bunched shot tangling round the float bottom so that when the float hits the water it cocks immediately. Sometimes a jerk on the line will release the shot and they sink as they should. If not there is nothing else for it but to reel in and often it will sort itself out on the way back!

Sometimes the float will slide back up the line as it flies through the air, particularly if the cast is into a wind. Then the float will cock quite quickly, perhaps closer to you than it should be. Don't confuse this with a tangle; often you realise what has happened because the 'plop' made by the shot is several feet away from where the float lands. One useful tip is to try an SSG shot and an

AAA as the bulk shot, but put the SSG at the top so that the float rests on this. You may get just the odd tangle doing this, but it's worth trying. Also you can split the bottom BB into two No 4s with a No 6 nearer the hook, rather like shotting a conventional waggler. But always push them together when testing the depth, as this gives a much better indication of when they are touching bottom. You can also use weighted sliders, which means there is no need to use so much weight down the line. A swivel instead of a normal ring can help here.

There is one other circumstance which calls for a sliding float, and that is if you are trying to cast to the edge of a weed-bed, perhaps to get a bait to a shoal of rudd. If the water is 4ft deep and your bait lands right on the edge of the weeds, the float will be 4ft nearer to you, and the bait will drift outwards as it sinks. Fishing 4ft from the weeds may be too far away to catch fish. But rig up a sliding float with the bulk shot 2ft from the hook and a small shot 1ft from the hook to keep the bottom length of line straight, and you can beat the problem.

Cast your tackle high up into the air, feather the line with your finger when it's above the spot you want to fish, and let the tackle drop straight down. You should be able to fish a bait only inches from the weeds, and the fact that all the shot is bulked under the float should help to keep your casting accurate. The bulked shot will also help to keep the tackle in place and stop it drifting away from the weeds.

There is nothing magical about using a slider, but once you've got the hang of it it's a very useful tactic to have by you, especially if you want to fish water deeper than the length of your rod and don't want to leger.

Incidentally, the basic rig we've given is excellent for showing lift bites. Bites 'on the drop' are a little more difficult to spot because of the sheer length of time the float can take to cock. But because you are often fishing a fair way away you will probably find the bites you get are bolder because the fish are less scared.

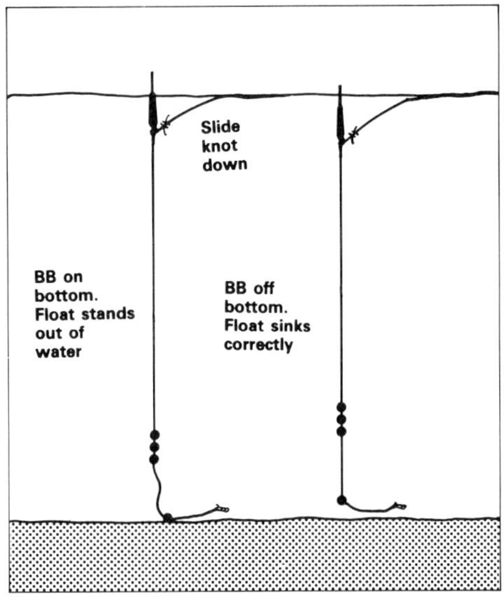

Fig 14 Finding the depth with a sliding float (above). This is easier than using a plummet in very deep water, or where a long cast is needed. (Below) This shows the basic slider rig, but with the addition of a small shot on which the float rests when cast. This helps prevent tangles on casting

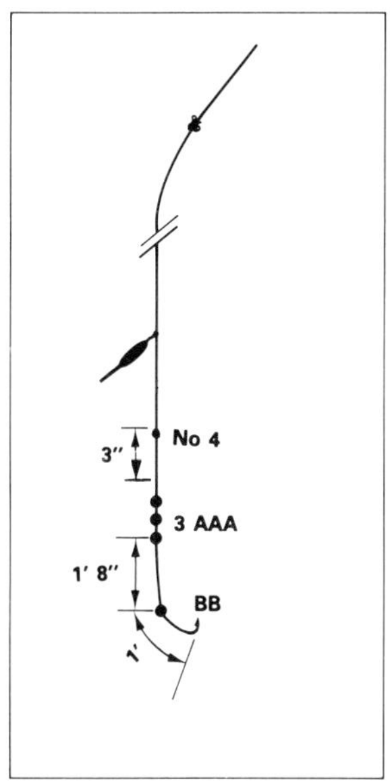

CHAPTER FIVE
ESSENTIAL KNOTS

No angling book would be complete without at least one chapter on knots. Good ones are the angler's friend, bad ones are an absolute nightmare.

Line is the vital link between angler and fish. The latter may be lost through bad luck, act of God or plain stupidity on the part of the angler, yet it is invariably the line that gets the blame. Anglers curse it when it breaks or tangles, and for an enormously wide variety of piscatorial mishaps, yet rarely have a word of praise for it when they land a good fish. It's the most taken for granted item of tackle. Nylon gets subjected to the ravages of sunlight and abrasion. We knot it badly and expect it not to break, coil it tightly on tiny spools and expect it to run out ruler-straight, fish with it long after its useful life is over and yet we react with surprise when it fails.

Good nylon is soft and supple, yet retains a high proportion of its breaking strain when properly knotted. It is fine in diameter for its breaking strain and conforms, within reasonable limits, to the specifications of strength and diameter printed on the spool. Its elasticity is just enough to act as a 'safety valve' yet not so great that the angler feels out of touch with a fighting fish. Bad nylon disobeys all these rules. It may be hard and springy and snap like cotton when knotted. It may be thick for its breaking strain, thicker than the quoted diameter on the spool, and it may be waisted or even oval in places. It may be over-elastic too.

On this last point, some nylons are deliberately made with a very low degree of elasticity and fine diameter for their breaking strain. These are the pre-stretched lines preferred by some experienced anglers for specialist applications, but they are not generally suitable for beginners.

How long does nylon last? So many factors are involved that it is almost impossible to say. One grooved rod-ring can ruin a line in a matter of a few casts, and a brush with a sharp edged underwater rock can cause damage even more quickly than that. In storage a spool left in a cool, dry dark place will last for years, while a spool left on a sunny sill will be suspect as soon as it is put on the reel. In coarse fishing, a line used carefully on a good rod and reel may last half a season, while a sea angler fishing from the shore over rocks or sharp shingle may get through a line in a single session.

How can the average angler get the best from his line? Careful attention to rod-rings and reel is a good way to start. Others include the careful tying of knots and the ability to recognise the first signs of weakness. For instance, if a line feels even slightly rough as it is run through the fingers, it is time to buy a new one. A short section that appears curly will also be weak, and any part of a line that has been trapped in the mechanism of a reel is another potential source of early failure.

Brand new line has a tendency to float, which can be a source of annoyance in some styles of

Fig 15 Universal knot. One of the most useful knots of all for tying on eyed hooks on swivels

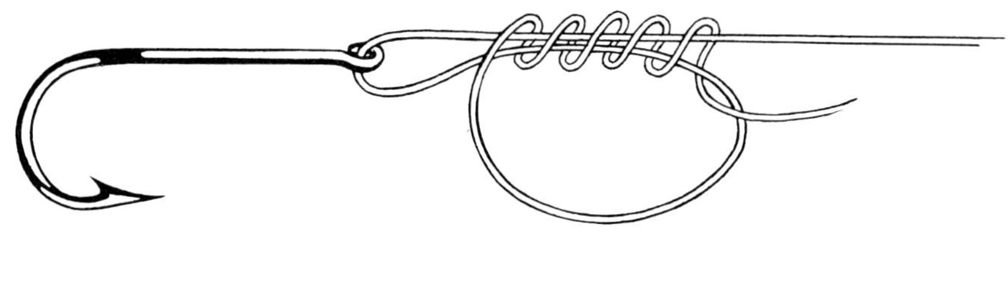

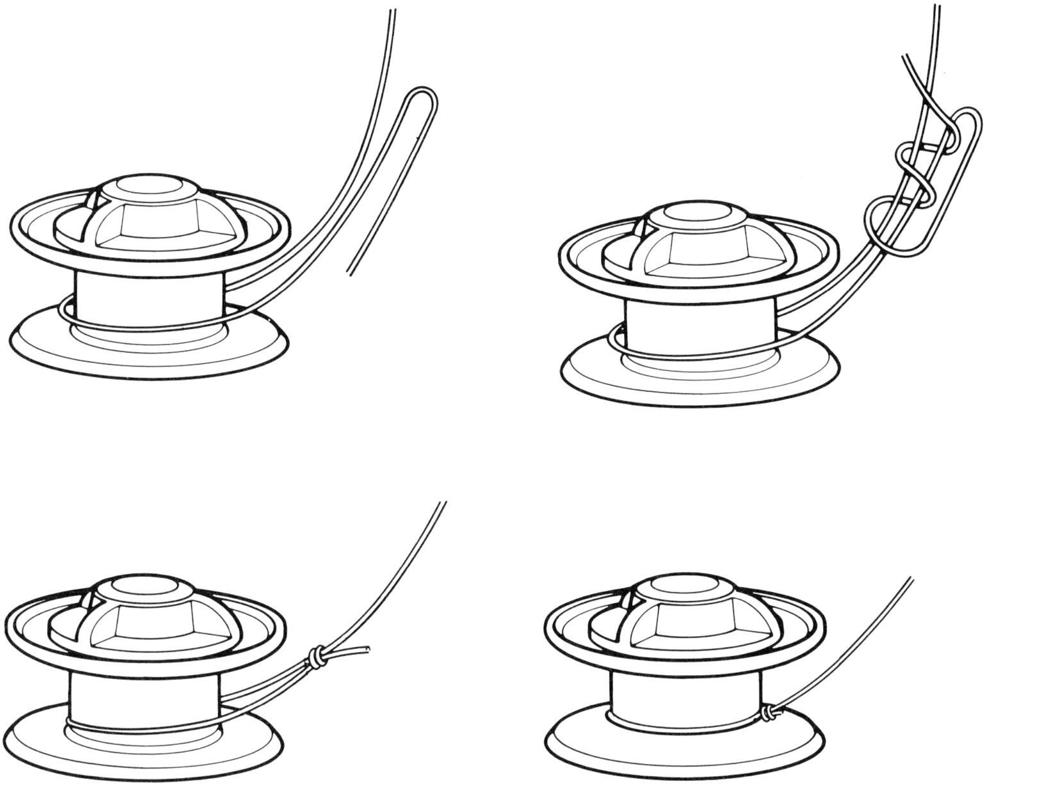

Fig 16 Spool knot. This is basically the Universal knot. The advantage is that it can be tightened, the spare end snipped off, and then pulled tight to the spool. It is exceptionally neat

fishing. You can make it sink by washing it in detergent, while a line that persistently sinks when you want it to float can be made to perform correctly by the application of a little fly-fishing grease such as Mucilin.

Getting the right knot for the job is, without doubt, an essential part of getting the best from any line. Learn the knots on these pages and you will be able to cope with just about every angling situation that demands a knot.

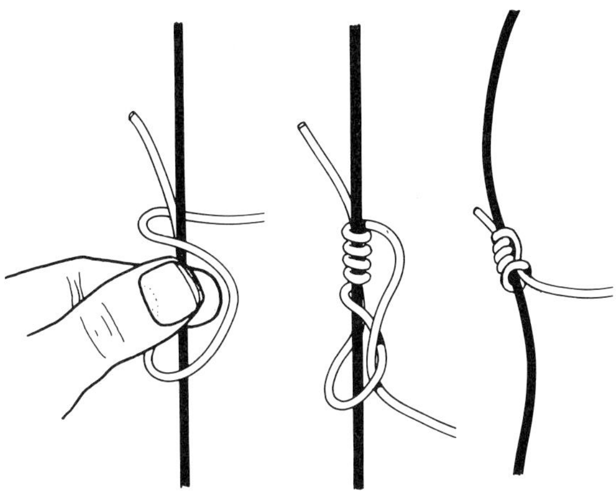

Fig 17 The Stopper knot is used with a sliding float. Wet the main line and the knot will slide, yet remain in place when left

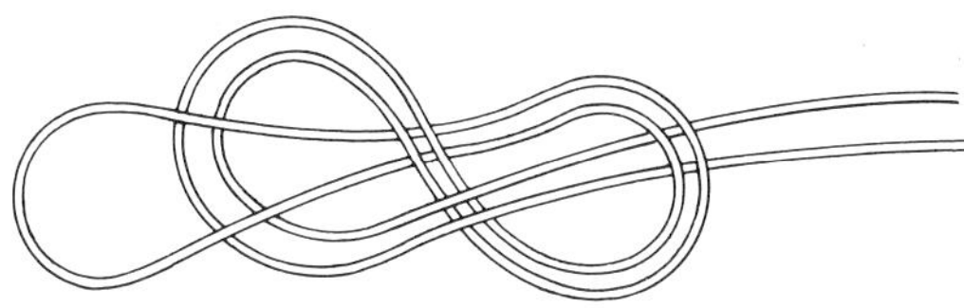

Fig 18 Figure of Eight. In nylon this loop tends to slide under extreme pressure. However, it remains a good knot for Dacron and other lines of braided or twisted multi-strand construction

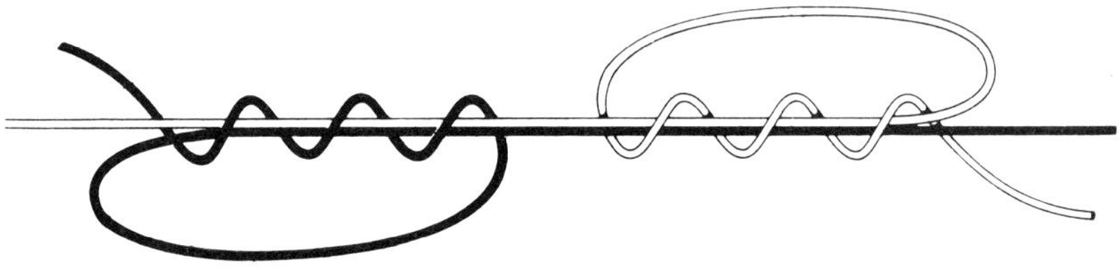

Fig 19 The Double-treble. A good knot for joining lines, and if tightened carefully can join two of different diameters. Very easy to tie

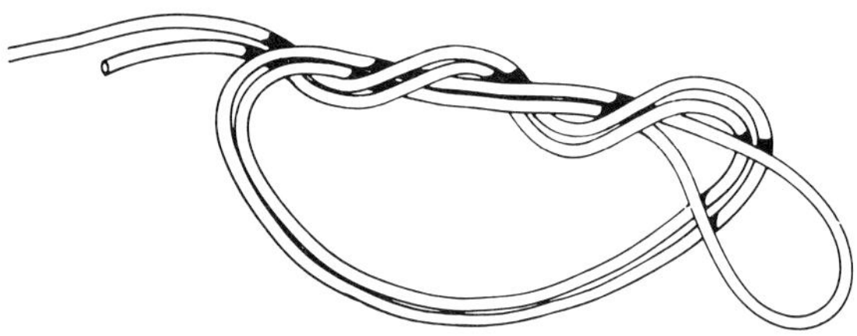

Fig 20 Three-turn Loop knot. This loop knot, based on the Cove or Water knot, is the best of the loop knots for nylon. It is easy to tie and forms a neat, straight loop in light hooklengths

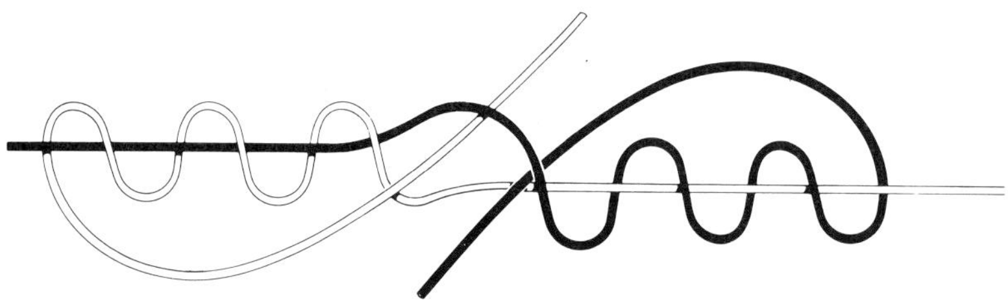

Fig 21 Three-turn Blood knot. Recognised as *the* universal knot for joining lengths of nylon, provided they are of similar diameters. Dangerous when the tails are used as droppers, or where the knot is subjected to a lot of flexing – as in a fly leader. Extra turns can be given for extra security – up to five on each side

BAITS

CHAPTER SIX
CARP BAITS

Boilies are the most popular of modern carp fishing baits. They are versatile, simple to make, can be flavoured and coloured to the angler's own preference and are among the cleanest baits available. One of the great advantages of boilies is that they can be made to almost any degree of hardness. The longer they are boiled the harder they become and thus less likely to be taken by unwanted fish such as tench, roach or bream. By varying the ingredients, boilies can be made up as high, low or medium-protein mixes. And it is a simple task to mix the hundred or so that you will need for a day's carp fishing.

Ready made mixes are available from good tackle shops and specialist bait suppliers but if you prefer to mix one of your own the following ingredients will produce a tried and tested medium-protein recipe: 3oz caseine; 2oz meat-meal; 3oz soya flour; 1oz wheat gluten; 1oz sodium caseinate. These ingredients will normally be enough for a six-egg mix, but do experiment with the number of eggs until you have the right consistency. To sweeten the boilie, you will have to add a sweetener before mixing the whole lot into balls. For the above ingredients about ½oz sugar, or varying amounts of proprietary liquid or powder sweetening should be added. The secret of successful boilie-making is to taste the mix before boiling and then aim for a flavour that is not too bitter but pleasant.

Boilies can be kept almost indefinitely if you fast freeze them, and it's a good idea to make up several batches in one go so that you will have plenty in store for those impromptu sessions when the fishing is good.

To make up a batch of 100 to 120 boilies beat 4 eggs in a mixing bowl. For flavoured and coloured boilies, add ½ teaspoon of flavouring and ¼ teaspoon of red dye.

Flavourings can be any of the commercially available additives or, if you prefer, try a few from the kitchen such as almond, vanilla or strawberry. Colouring can also be done with food dyes or any sold in tackle shops for colouring groundbaits or maggots. Add sufficient base meal to make a soft paste. As already mentioned, for this medium-protein mix, the base meal comprises wheat gluten, caseine, sodium caseinate, meatmeal and soya flour. Make sure the paste is not too stiff, otherwise the boilies will crack. As soon as the paste is mixed, start rolling it into balls of roughly ½in diameter or less. Make sure your hands are damp to prevent the balls sticking to your skin.

Fill a chip pan with water, bring to the boil and add balls of bait in batches of about twenty-five. As soon as they float to the surface they are ready, but if you want a harder boilie, boil for a little longer. Tip the boilies onto a sheet of dry newspaper and leave to cool.

But if boilies are not to your liking there are still plenty of other unconventional baits that may be worth a try:

Dutch Edam This cheese is head and shoulders above all other cheeses as bait for carp. Fish it cut into chunks and loose feed a few smaller samples.
Hempseed Normally used as an attractor and best introduced as a carpet over a hard bottom, where it will attract carp and hold them for a long time. Most bottom baits can be fished over the carpet to good effect.
Trout pellets Normally soaked and mixed with flour or sodium caseinate as a binder to make a soft paste. They need pre-baiting on underfished waters until the carp get used to them.
Bananas An unusual bait that has stood the test of time. Fish pieces at short range and introduce free samples.
Wasp grubs A proven and deadly bait. Fish them six at a time on a size 4 hook. Pieces of empty comb make a good floating bait.
Kit-E-Kat Mixed with breadcrumbs to form a

On cold frosty mornings like this a pink maggot seems to work better than one of any other colour

paste it has accounted for a large number of fish over the years.

Sweetcorn One of the most versatile of all carp baits. It can be fished as a single grain or in bunches of two, three or four at a time. On hard-fished waters the corn may be more effective if dyed and flavoured.

Parboiled potatoes Much overrated yet they remain a traditional carp bait. Possibly their popularity stems from the years when there was little else available other than bread.

Giant American peanuts Simmered for about an hour in water with some sugar added, they make a very good bait.

Maple peas Cooked in the same manner as peanuts they are a first-class bait. But never prebait with uncooked peas as they will swell up inside a carp and kill it.

Lobworms One of the most natural of baits and a very good one to use in coloured water. Fish them singly on a size 6 or 8 hook.

Liver pâté Mix with fine cereal groundbait, cornflour and sodium caseinate to bind.

Slugs Another natural bait. This one is good for taking cruising carp which can be cast to. Fish them singly on freeline tackle.

Munchies An attractor to get carp interested in taking another bait. With care they can be fished on the hook.

Pedigree Chum Mixer, Munchies and Dairy Dinner All very good floating baits if soaked for a few hours in water.

More and more anglers are turning to carp – a species which grows big and fights hard!

The end result, a fine common carp from Linear Fisheries at Milton Keynes

CHAPTER SEVEN
BREAD BAITS

Without doubt one of the best, and cheapest, of all baits is bread. It will catch just about every fish that swims, with the exception perhaps of predators such as perch and pike. And with little preparation it can be made into a variety of different forms. It is capable of being used in very large pieces for specimen carp, or in tiny portions of 'punch' for the most delicate, and hard to catch, canal roach.

Paste

Paste is most likely to be the bait we all started with as youngsters. It is easily made by soaking bread and squeezing it in a cloth. After a little time spent moulding a smooth paste will form. To ensure you get paste right, cut the centre out of a loaf, taking care not to include the drier portions found right next to the crust. If you use these, lumps may appear in the resulting paste. Alternatively use a sliced loaf, but once again using only bread that easily tears from the edges. Wet thoroughly and squeeze in a cloth. Keep squeezing and kneading until it is all about the same consistency, a nice white, soft, but not sticky paste.

Alternatively, Energen rolls have become very popular with paste anglers during the past few seasons. And certainly they are a good source of bait. To prepare rolls for use make a hole in the middle of one or two with your finger when you arrive at the waterside. Fill the hole with water and leave the whole thing to soak in your landing net in the margins. By the time you've tackled up

Fig 22 Typical breadpunch fishing. Fish can be taken at any depth from the surface to the bottom. The rig shown on the left of the diagram is the one to use in conjunction with a tiny cloud of groundbait introduced every other cast. Note the tiny dust shot nearest the hook – this ensures the bread sinks, but only slowly, through the cloud. At the end of every cast strike the bait off. This will groundbait the swim and is particularly good for attracting roach and bream that may be searching near the bottom

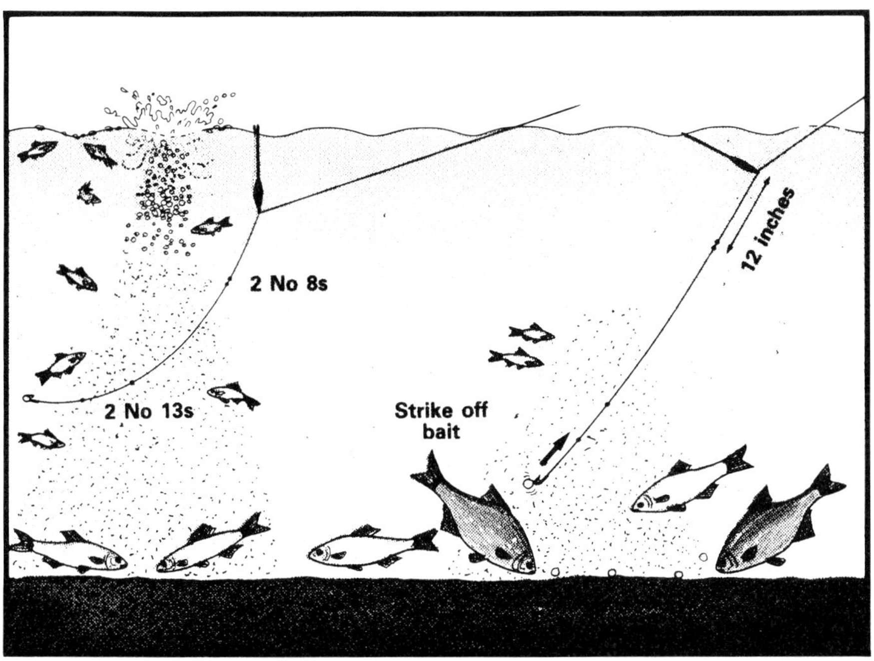

you can empty the water from the roll, wring it out like a wash leather, break open the crust and the inside should be tacky.

A third option is to mix up a stiff mixture of flour with a little water.

As one of the easiest forms of bread to use, paste is very popular with beginners. It is usually moulded around the hook, covering both spade end and point so that none of the hook is visible. It does pay however to make certain that the point is only just covered and not completely buried. The paste must also be as soft as possible. Certainly it should come off every time you strike. If it is too stiff, bites will be missed. If you plan to fish with paste take it along to the waterside wrapped in a piece of clean damp cloth. That way it will stay at the right consistency and will be less likely to dry out. Keep moulding it every so often to stop the outer skin becoming cracked.

The baited hook is completely covered by a bread bait. But be sure to leave the point clear

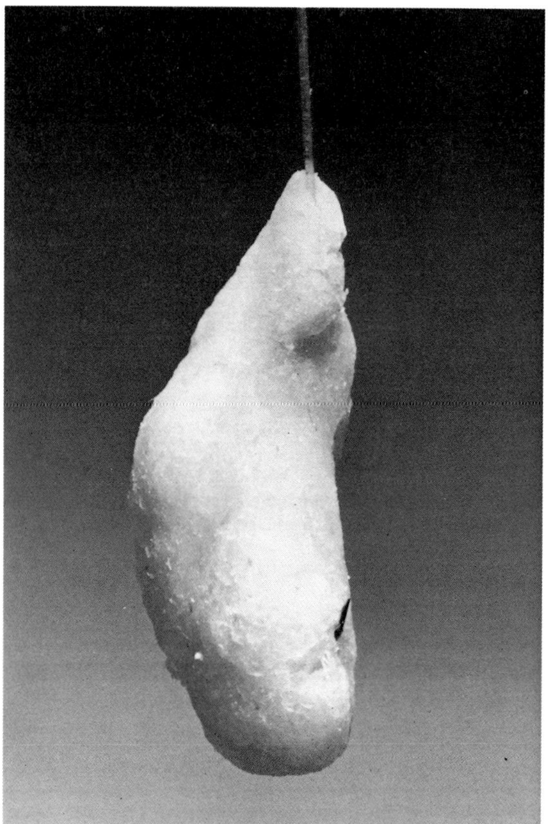

Used without groundbait it is a good bait for roach, tench and even bream. But it will be even more effective if some small pieces can be broken off the ball and fed into the swim as groundbait. The pieces that come off the hook on the strike will also ensure that the swim is kept topped up.

Normal white bread makes up into a good paste but for a change try mixing in a little colouring. Custard powder is a very old favourite for a nice pale yellow, alternatively try a few drops of one of the non-toxic maggot dyes. Flavours can also be added if required, again the commercial additives all work well, or go for something from the kitchen such as honey, cheese or even curry powder. The experiments are endless – and a lot of fun.

But consistency is without doubt the most important factor governing the success or failure of paste, and getting it just right will come with practice. Many anglers swear by new bread, while others prefer to make up paste from bread a couple of days old. As a guide the fresher the bread the more sticky will be the resulting paste. On the whole this new paste is more difficult to handle and for that reason alone start your paste trials with older bread.

Choice of hooks for use with paste is important. If you plan to use soft, doughy paste – the kind you get from a straight flour-and-water mix or from Energen rolls – you can get a tiny smear on a hook down to as small as a size 20. This is a deadly method for canals. But since the whole hook can become covered it is usual to use size 14 to size 10, even larger when fishing for tench, bream and very big roach. Fewer bites are missed with paste than with most other baits, probably because a fish has to take the whole bait – and the hook – into its mouth. There are no loose pieces it can pull at.

Flake

Flake is another way of fishing bread and takes even less time to prepare than paste. But once again getting bread at just the right stage is vital. Very new bread will not pinch into attractive flake. Instead it tends to mould down almost to paste.

Bread about a day old should be about right. It should pinch onto the hook shank to leave a lot of ragged, attractive looking, flakes sticking out. These will swell in water and slowly break off, making a tiny groundbait-like cloud. If the bread you have is suspected of being a little too dry lay a few slices on a plate and cover with a damp cloth overnight. Chances are some slices will have taken in just enough moisture to make good flake. The most common mistake, however, is to pinch flake too tightly. If it is still on the hook when you retrieve your tackle, it is no good.

Flake is not a bait that stands up to a lot of movement; so once you've cast out, leave it put. Try twitching it around and you'll be fishing with a bare hook in no time at all. Having said that, there is nothing wrong with trying one small twitch just before re-casting. This little trick will often tempt a fish that was inspecting a bait.

For a start, just to give you confidence, use the first method of hooking, ie pinching a portion tightly to the hook shank and tipping the bend of the hook with a couple of maggots. Then if your flake is not right you will at least still be left with a baited hook should it fall off. A barbed hook is also a help to hold any form of bread in place.

Two ways to attach flake are:

1 Pinch the flake between finger and thumb and pass the hook through the pinched portion.
2 Bend the flake around the hook and pinch it onto the shank.

Whichever method you use be careful not to pinch too hard. If the bread is new it will form a very hard portion and inhibit hook penetration on the strike.

When baiting up it is usual to leave the spade-end or eye and the point showing. This makes it easy to strike effectively, allowing the hook to pull through the flake better. That so much of the hook is showing when you bait up does not matter very much. Within seconds of casting, flake will begin to swell and become fluffy enough to cover every part of the hook with its soft attractiveness.

Hook size should be matched to the bait being used. Flake is most effective in larger pieces and as such calls for a hook of around size 14. If something smaller is to be used, the best bread would be that from a breadpunch.

Breadpunch

The breadpunch tool is so named because that is exactly what it does – punch out small pieces of bread. It also performs the very important task of holding the tiny disc of bait while a hook is drawn into it. A medium-sliced loaf is best, the bread is then compressed slightly when the punch is pushed into it.

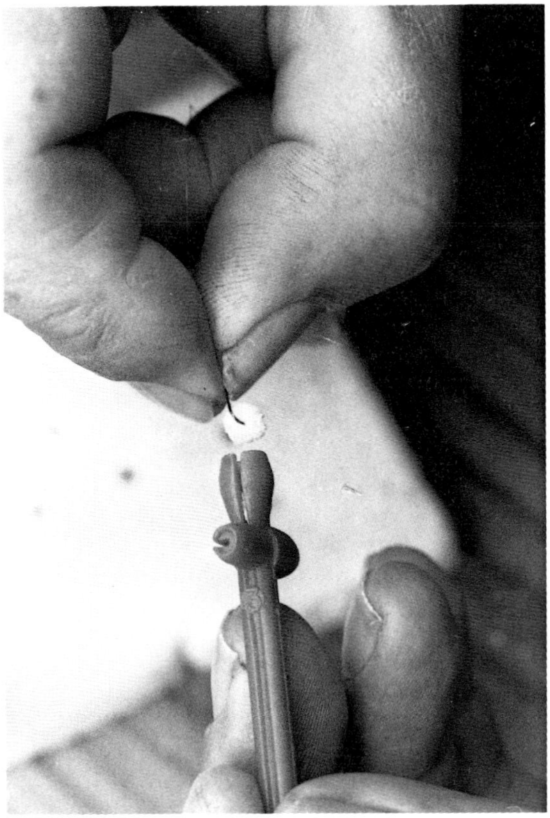

A piece of punched bread is pulled from the punch ready for use

Breadpunches are sold by most tackle shops and are usually available in a choice of sizes and ranging in price from the very cheap but efficient plastic ones up to expensive stainless steel jobs that house a whole host of different sized heads. Buy a punch with a slit in the side of the business end. The hook goes through this, and since the slit stops halfway into the head it ensures the point goes halfway into the bread every time. The hook is then pulled upwards, and the bait comes out already on the hook. Some of the hook will be showing. This doesn't matter since the bread swells in water and makes the hook far less obvious.

Some breadpunch experts steam their bread over a boiling kettle before using it, putting it in a sealed polythene bag overnight to absorb all possible moisture. Some press it with a rolling pin before placing it into the bag. It's a good idea to take each slice to the bankside in a separate bag. That way slices not in use will stay in good condition and not be dried out by exposure to air.

To get a good 'punch' every time is not difficult but you will need a flat surface on which to work. The top of a float box works well if you are not too bothered about marking the varnish. Otherwise a bait-box lid or a piece of wood carried just for the job should be included in your tackle. Place a slice of bread on the flat surface and push the punch into it, turning slightly as you retrieve it. This slight twisting movement will ensure a clean cut round the edges. Next tap down the bread with your thumbnail to ensure it is well compressed within the punch. Once you are more experienced this may not be necessary.

The hook can now be pulled into the punch, through the slit, while holding the bread in place with the other thumb. Both barbed and barbless hooks are suitable. Gently pull the hook through the bread and it should emerge at the top with the point passing right through the middle. It does take a little practice but you'll soon get the hang of it and be able to re-bait in seconds.

Feeding a swim for fishing breadpunch can be a very simple operation. But you will need some very fine cereal; white bread that has been passed through a riddle is the best. In summer, when fish are active, you can expect to get bites anywhere between the surface and bottom, so keep groundbait as fine and lightly mixed as possible. By riddling the crumb before use you will have removed all lumps and large crumbs, leaving the rest to form a very attractive cloud that hangs for a time before settling out on the bottom. Only dampen the groundbait just enough to make it stick together. A well-mixed batch should be capable of being squeezed into a ball but will gradually break apart if held in the open palm of the hand.

Start with a walnut-sized piece and follow with the baited hook. A pole is a very good weapon for doing this, and it will give excellent presentation as a bonus. Introduce another piece before every cast. Fig 22 shows a typical situation in water around 4ft deep – the ideal depth for fishing breadpunch. Because you're not likely to be casting far, it is possible to use a delicate rig, and you don't have to place a lot of shot around the float to give casting weight. But should you need weight to set the float lower in the water, that is where it should go. With just two tiny dust shot down the line, the bread-baited hook will fall in an attractive manner.

After fishing each cast for a time, strike the bait off and rebait. This will act as a secondary means of keeping the swim baited, acting in the same manner as a few offerings of hookbait introduced when maggot fishing.

Crust

Crust is another form of bread that is worth trying, especially if you are fishing a water noted for big roach or surface-feeding rudd. It's a bait that does not get the publicity it deserves, but only because it has fallen from the limelight in recent years in favour of more specialised, but no more effective, baits.

Just about any piece of crust will work provided you can get it to stay on the hook. But by far the best way is to press the end crust from a sliced loaf between two boards overnight. Wrap the crust in a damp cloth and place it between the boards, weighting them down with two or three bricks. This will produce a firm bait which is then cut into strips and finally cubes. Like bread intended for punch, crust is best taken to the water in plastic bags.

New bread from an unsliced loaf can be used but the crust is usually more brittle and it may be necessary to push the hook through the flaky side to avoid cracking the crust unduly.

Crust really comes into its own if the bed of your swim is covered in weed. It is a buoyant bait and will stay a little above the bottom. On rivers crust is usually fished with a bulk of shot down, about a foot from the hook and, generally speaking, rather heavy tackle that allows it to be swung long distances. It is also used as a floating bait for rudd and carp, in which case it is best to ensure that line close to the hook sinks. This will prevent it from making a small wake when moved by wind. It is also less obvious to a rising fish.

Bread punch fishing is easy, clean, and cheap. Here March, Cambridgeshire, angler Dick Pinning swings in a small fish taken on bread punch. Note the slices of bread on his tackle box beside him

CHAPTER EIGHT
MAGGOTS

The maggot

Maggots, millions of 'em – the bait of the masses and now almost the universal bait for coarse fish. But even such a simple bait as a maggot can be used in a manner that will get just those few extra bites that make the difference between success and failure, between a good catch and a poor one.

First let us take a look at the humble maggot or, more correctly, the three main types generally sold in the local tackle shop. The biggest, usually known as the 'hooker' or commercial maggot is the larva of the bluebottle fly – that great big monster that lands with a thud.

Next comes the 'pinkie', a flesh-coloured creature about half the size of a hooker that comes from the greenbottle fly. In fact these maggots are almost white when fresh, turning pink later; so you can judge how old they are when purchasing. It is a difficult maggot to keep under control in hot weather unless you have a fridge, but generally lasts longer than other types. Biggest problem with pinkies is that they sweat very easily and will climb out of almost any bait box – with or without a lid – and as a result have a local name of 'runners'.

Last of the common maggots on sale is the squatt. This is even smaller than the pinkie but it also starts life as an off-white colour, later turning a pale yellow. Squatts are tough little creatures but tend to be less active than other types. It is a greatly underrated bait but sometimes a little expensive and not at all easy to keep in good condition.

Squatts usually come in a dark brown, foundry sand and are sold for use on canals or waters where there are a lot of small fish. They are also a great feed bait for bream since they tend to lie on the bottom and not bury into the silt like other, more active baits. They are also excellent for feeding in groundbait as they keep still and do not cause balls to split in mid air. Once in the water they sink slowly and are ideal for use when catching fish 'on the drop'.

Other maggots not usually sold by dealers include the 'gozzer' which is a very soft maggot loved by bream anglers and the 'blackfly' which is a thin, tough but weedy looking character that all too often makes its appearance in a batch of normal maggots as a result of a rogue fly finding its way into the breeder's fly house.

That's a run down on the types of maggots you are likely to encounter. Now, if you would like to improve your catch rate by as much as 20 per cent, all you have to do is choose the right maggot for your hook. Take the normal hooker as sold by your dealer. Just looking at them they will all look alike, but put them on a hook or hold a few in the palm of your hand and you will soon see there are actually two completely different types. The best sort for using as hookbait are those that hang 'long' on the hook (Fig 23). Others will 'squat up' and these tend to be heavier, making them very good for use as loose feed since they sink faster. They are much less effective as hookbait. This is not imagination; it is absolutely true. Anglers in general do not pay enough attention to the bait they put in front of their fish and this is a very important factor to consider, especially in winter.

So just how do you go about finding the best maggots? The answer is so simple. Fresh maggots will have a blackish feed spot clearly visible moving about at the pointed end of their bodies. The ones to use as hookbait will still have a spot but it will be harder to see. These will most likely have been bred on fish and the spot will be almost translucent – a sort of light greyish-red. They feel soft and silky and will keep wriggling after you have hooked them or when placed on the palm of your hand. The ones to avoid will have been bred on red meat and will 'squat up' when hooked or handled.

To sum up, choose the long, soft type as

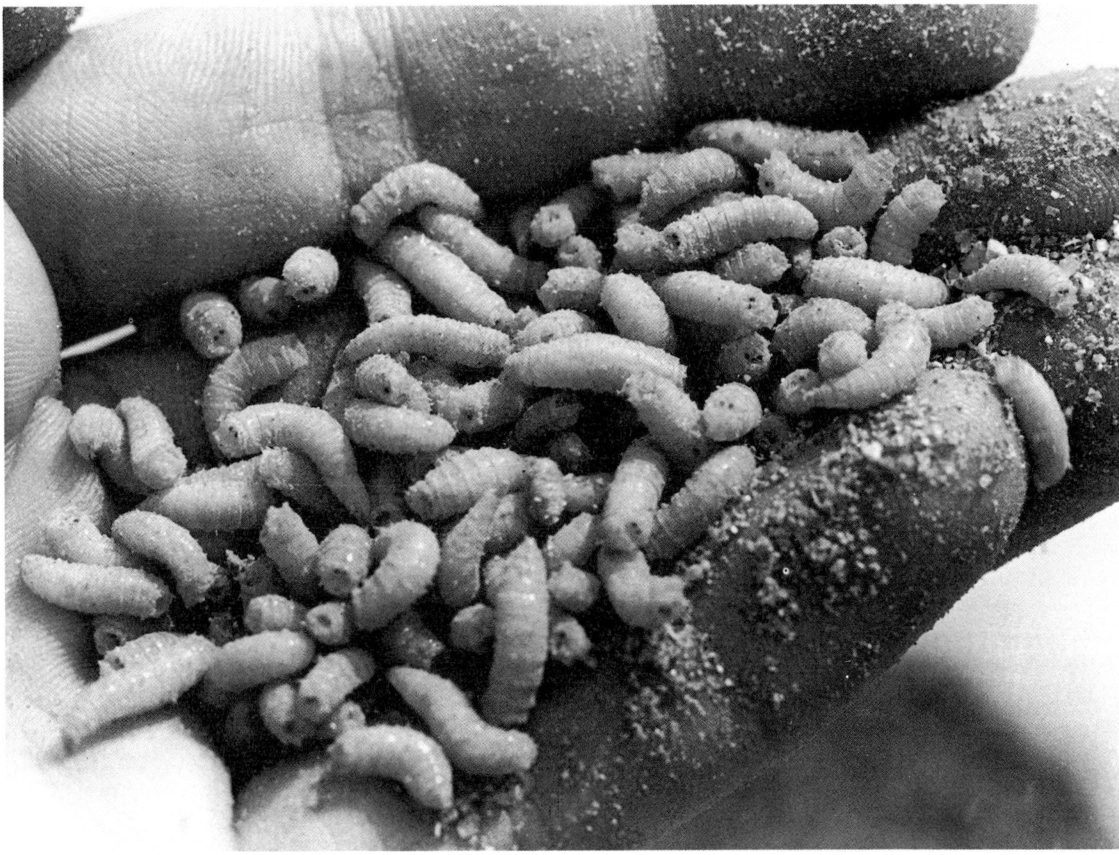

Good quality hook maggots, cleaned and grease-free

hookbait or for feeding on still or slow moving waters. The heavier, meatier sort are fine for loose feeding on medium or fast flowing rivers, still using the long type as hookbait. But always remember that it is no reflection on the dealer if he hasn't the sort of bait you want. After all he has to take what is available at the breeder's farm.

Even with the very best maggots in your box it is vitally important to put them on the hook properly. Yes, everyone knows the hook goes through the blunt end. But there is even a right and wrong way of doing that to get best results. Always hook a maggot so the hook point shows outwards and is not masked by the blunt end of the bait. If a fish takes in the bait and spits it out there is a chance the point will catch its lip (Fig 24).

A small hook is essential – a 20 or even a 22 – and the bait must be hooked so as not to injure it and allow its juices to be lost. Hook it through the small fold of skin at the edge of its blunt end. After all the great advantage a maggot has over

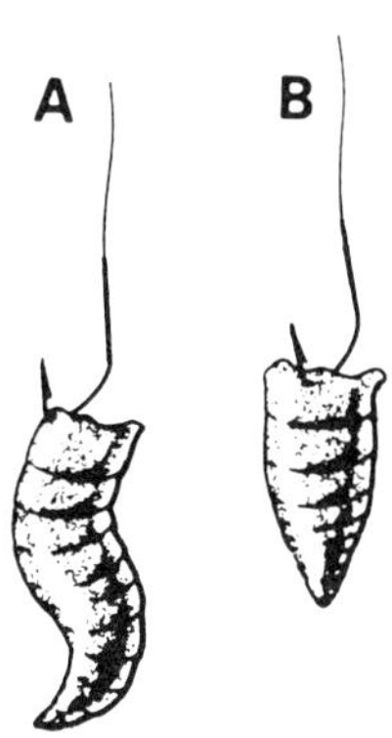

Fig 23

A: The ideal hook maggot – long and lively, even when hooked.

Notice the small, black feed-spot in the pointed end.

This grows smaller as the maggot gets older and indicates its freshness.

B: Some maggots go "squat" when hooked – not the ideal hook bait.

This also happens if the maggot is not hooked properly – as in this diagram – or if it is old.

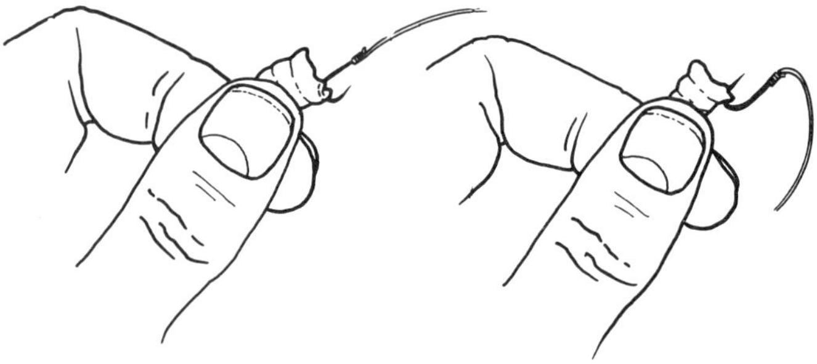

Fig 24 The correct way (left) and the wrong way to hook a maggot. The point should face out from the bait

other baits such as casters is that it moves. Don't lose that attractive wriggle by killing it with the hook!

The reason for using such a small hook is that there is less metal showing to the fish. Even more importantly it allows the maggot to fall more naturally than with a large hook. Remember too that if fish stop biting a change down to an even smaller hook is the first thing to try. Often the switch will bring life back to the swim.

Breeding made simple

Even if you have never even considered the possibility of breeding your own maggots don't be tempted to skip this section. Home breeding is a lot easier than you might think and certainly well worth the small amount of effort it will take. Any fresh maggot will improve your chances of a good catch. And the home-bred maggot doesn't even have to be a gozzer. The gozzer is a super-soft maggot usually bred on chicken, pigeons or hearts and comes from a certain fly that lays its eggs in dark places. Just about any maggot that's bred at home will be a vast improvement on the shop-bought item.

One of the easiest ways to get your own bait supply is to buy a piece of frozen chicken from the supermarket on a Friday. Allow it to thaw overnight and then hide it in a corner of the garden on Saturday morning until it has become fly-blown. You'll know when that has occurred by the tiny white eggs laid in neat rows. Next stage is to pack the chicken into an old tin – a biscuit tin is ideal – with some clean bran. Yes that's all there is to home breeding. The tin can be left at the bottom of the garden. But keep the lid on and ensure that rain cannot find its way inside. By the following Friday evening everything should be right and with a bit of luck there will be little of the chicken left and the bran will contain some big, soft maggots.

By following the weekly cycle your maggots will be tender and slightly grey when you first see them. They should still be feeding on the remains of the chicken and may need to be shaken off. But by Sunday they will have gone much whiter and will be so soft that if you squeeze one too hard it will burst. This method of breeding creates hardly any smell and you will finish up with a hundred or so maggots – more than enough to use as hookbait for a full day's sport. Armed with your 'super bait', you can go to the waterside with the confidence that few anglers will have anything better.

Although home breeding of hooker maggots is really that simple, follow the pointers listed below to ensure your efforts result in perfect baits every week. Often it can be difficult to get a 'blow' until the meat has been outside for several hours. A good way around this is to boil it or give it a couple of minutes in a hot oven. Flies seem to find it more acceptable that way and will probably 'blow' it almost immediately.

If you get too many maggots on your piece of meat and they appear to be in danger of eating the whole lot before reaching full size, don't be afraid to drop an extra piece into the tin – ensuring it is fully thawed of course. And if you want to quickly increase the size of your maggots in the final stages just transfer them to a fresh piece of meat. Some old hands at the game will tell you it is not possible to get maggots to feed on a new piece. Don't believe them, it's a myth.

As your own expertise increases you will be able to gauge exactly how long to give the maggots before taking them off their feed. In hot weather they will feed more vigorously and grow quickly. In winter, even if you can get a 'blow', they could take many extra days.

Keeping maggots

Ground maize is very good for keeping maggots in prime condition. But for those super soft home-bred ones a sprinkling of bran is best in order to protect their delicate texture. For shop-bought ones, maize is ideal because it soaks up the grease from their skins, appearing on the surface as small lumps of furry material. Maize is also good in so much that it helps to remove other smells from the bait, such as tobacco if you happen to be a heavy smoker.

Some anglers keep their maggots damp in the belief that this keeps them softer. But it is a very bad mistake to make with any maggots other than out and out hookers. Damp maggots will actually float and it's not difficult to imagine what happens if they find their way into your groundbait or loose-feed. The best way to keep hook maggots is in a fridge. Try to find a cheap secondhand one that can be kept in the garden shed just for bait; it will save you pounds over a season.

Always give stored bait plenty of room and air space. They are best stored dry in maize or even sawdust, with the lids off their containers. Use shallow, wide containers rather than slim, deep ones.

A rare moment of relaxation for co-author Mac Campbell, who hooked this carp on maggot bait while on a feature on a Gloucestershire lake. The fishery owner, Peter Mohan, looks on

An even rarer event . . . this was *Angling Times* photographer Bob Atkins' first ever fish. He caught the 6-pounder while on the same Gloucestershire feature, also using maggot – the universal bait for British anglers

CHAPTER NINE
CASTERS

Producing your own casters is a good way of making use of left-over bait. It can save a lot of cash and supply you with an alternative for next weekend's outing. Casters – the next stage in a maggot's life cycle – are a tip-top bait which seems to attract the better quality fish from a shoal.

Casters bought from a tackle shop are usually expensive, often of dubious quality and certainly nowhere near as good as the ones you can obtain at home. This is no reflection on dealers, simply a case of mass-production calling for speed and less attention to detail. In turning out a pint or two a lot more care can be taken and a top quality bait produced as a result.

To begin the process you can either keep left-over maggots and turn them into casters or, if a larger quantity is needed, buy large hook maggots from your dealer. A gallon of maggots should produce at least 6 pints of first-class casters. Always try to use maggots from the same batch. Mixing different ones can lead to problems in the final stages of 'turning'. A single batch will tend to turn in a much shorter time, making production easier and ensuring the freshest possible casters. Follow the illustrations for a complete step-by-step guide to home production.

1 Very little equipment is needed to produce casters, simply a riddle with a mesh size of 4 to 5mm, a large container and a bait bucket. A good supply of clean sawdust is also essential.

2 Riddle off any old groundbait, sawdust, bran or maize and allow the maggots to work through the riddle into the large container. This will leave any dead ones and rubbish behind. Always ensure that dead maggots are removed.

3 Place the clean maggots in a large bait bucket and add a good quantity of clean sawdust. Provide about equal amounts of sawdust to maggots. It helps prevent shrinkage if the sawdust is slightly damp. Now store them in a cool place or in a refrigerator. Check daily that the maggots have not begun to turn into casters. And in any case start caster production on Thursday evening for the weekend ahead.

4 Removed from the fridge your maggots will start to turn quickly. Keep a close watch and at the first sign of casters forming tip the whole lot on to a riddle, allowing them to work through into the large container.

5 When all the maggots have worked through you will be left with a mixture of casters and dead maggots. Carefully pick out the skins, dead maggots and any others that look stretched and in danger of dying.

6 The clean casters that remain on the riddle can now be tipped into an airtight plastic bag. These early casters will need to be stored in a fridge until more are run off next day.

7 As your caster supply builds up it will pay to transfer them to a suitable bait box. Casters are living creatures and as such need air, but not too much otherwise they will continue their development and become floaters. Fill the box right to the top with casters then cover with wet newspaper.

8 The wet newspaper will prevent floaters forming, but to ensure that the box lid remains airtight – there will be enough air to keep them fresh – cover the newspaper with a piece of plastic bag, folding it down over the sides of the box.

9 The full box can now have the lid pressed home and the whole lot placed back in the fridge. It will stay fresh for a couple of days.

10 Casters on the left have been allowed to continue their turning progress. They have gone dark and will float. Prevent this by correct sealing of the box and bags and by using a fridge. The dark casters however should be kept to one side since they make first-class hookbait. On the right are perfect casters which should be kept wet once at the waterside. They will remain in good condition throughout the session.

1

2

3

4

5

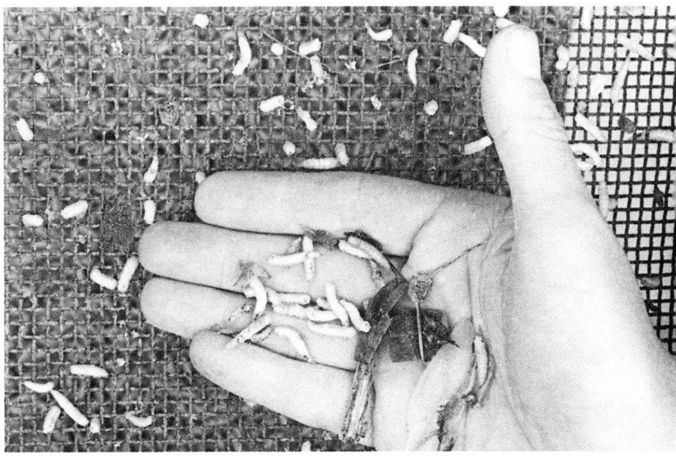

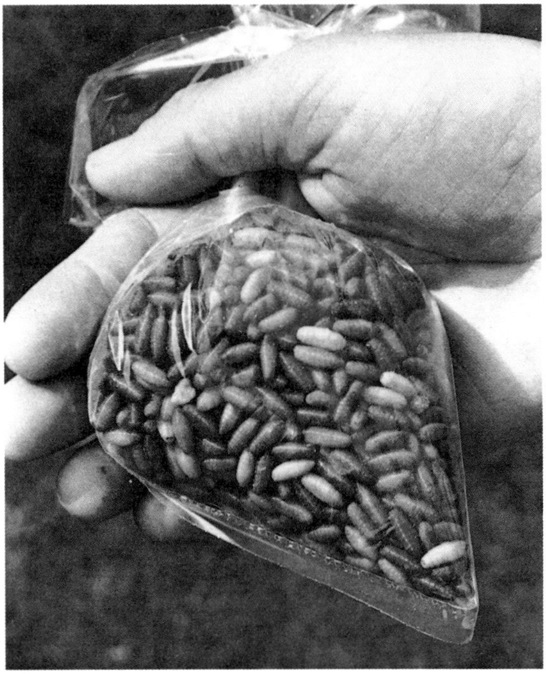

6

7

8

9

10 

Casters are a great bait but they must be looked after with care. Neglect them and they will deteriorate very quickly. Follow the twelve golden rules to keep them fresh and deadly:

1 Keep casters in a refrigerator, or as cool as possible, when not in use. Use them fresh and never if they smell 'off' when the shell is crushed.
2 Use only the sinkers (see rule 8). To check bait at the waterside fill your groundbait bowl with water, drop in the casters and skim off any that float.
3 Floaters are best for the hook, as they sink slowly when the hook is inside. Use them dry, as wet casters tend to flatten out as the hook is pushed inside.
4 Always keep casters out of the sun.
5 Don't leave a bag of casters undone. Take out a few and re-seal the bag, or keep them all in water.
6 If you keep casters in water keep the container out of the sun; the water will otherwise get hot and ruin all your bait very quickly.
7 During mild weather the average caster will become a floater if left in the air for as little as two hours – maybe even less – so always keep an eye on any left in the open.
8 Floating casters can be good for surface-feeding fish such as bleak, chub or rudd.
9 Trim the knot on a spade-end hook as closely as possible. This will allow easy penetration when trying to bury the hook inside a caster.
10 Feed fewer casters than you would maggots. Casters don't wriggle away and will stay on the bottom all day if not eaten.
11 Always feed casters before maggots. A swim fed with maggots first will be hard to get going again with casters. Maggots will get fish pre-occupied.
12 Use a long-shank, fine-wire hook if you intend to bury it inside a caster. This pattern will go in easily and not damage the delicate shell.

CHAPTER TEN
WORMS

Lobs, reds and brandlings; all different names for species of the worm, never one of the nicest baits to use but certainly one of the most effective. Yet for all that it remains neglected. 'I can't go fishing today; I've got no maggots', is a common excuse. Rubbish! A few minutes' work in the garden can produce enough bait for an all-day session, sometimes with surprising results. Often large and wary fish will take a worm – fish which would have ignored a maggot.

Lobworms

This is the largest worm found in the British Isles, and an excellent bait, used either whole or in part, in coloured and moving water. It has the triple advantages of being large and therefore easy to see, smelly, and heavy so it stays in place on the bottom in all except the fastest of swims.

The sheer weight of a lobworm will enable you to catapult it to a distant swim without the bother of mixing up a ball of groundbait to carry it. The tail is traditionally good bait for quality roach in winter.

Collecting lobworms

The tried and tested method of going to your local park or even your own lawn on a moist, mild evening after dark, can't be beaten. Take a torch and a tin for the worms. You'll find them lying on the grass, or on the earth in flower beds, their tails just inside their burrows.

Approach quietly and avoid shining the bright centre spot from your torch directly onto the worm, otherwise it will withdraw, quick as a flash, into its burrow. A heavy footfall will have the same effect. Place a thumb on the part of the worm next to the burrow and hold it down while you grab it with the other hand. Hold it firmly until you feel it starting to come out – it can take fifteen seconds or more.

If you can't find any showing you will have to dig for them. Any moist non-gritty soil should hold them (worms don't like sand or any grit on their skins). Best area is in the ground around the outside of a rubbish heap. Lobworms won't climb far from ground level like redworms will, but hang around a heap absorbing the goodness which leaches down from it.

Keeping

Lobworms won't keep in good condition for long in a tin unless you give them plenty of room and lots of compost. Without some sort of keeping medium they will quickly produce a froth and die.

The best plan is to put your unused ones back in the garden or into a *big* container full of compost. In summer expect to keep them in a normal maggot tin for a maximum of a week before they start to go soft.

When one dies it will affect all the others very quickly. Check your tin every day if you are trying to keep some.

Tackle

You must use a decent-sized hook, even with part of a lobworm, because they are so thick. A 6 is the best all-round size. Usually you will be legering a lobworm because you'll need a huge float to support the weight of the worm.

Tips

In summer, water the lawn and flower beds thoroughly two hours before dark if you're hoping to gather lobs. Then go out two hours after darkness has fallen.

Ways of getting worms to the top in daylight are to water with dilute washing-up liquid or to stick a fork into the lawn and waggle it around. The vibrations can cause worms to come to the surface. Try both methods to see which works in your own garden.

Redworms

Redworms are smaller than lobs, but can grow to several inches in length. Many tackle shops sell them, or they can be gathered from old compost heaps or bred in large polythene bags at home. They are a super bait for bream all season round, though not so popular in summer because they attract too many eels.

It can be difficult to distinguish the redworm from the brandling, because the two can inhabit the same areas. Of the two, the redworm is more popular. Brandlings have a series of bright yellow bands around their bodies and give off a bitter fluid which is thought to be disliked by fish.

Bloodworm anglers sometimes use small redworms, up to an inch long, on the hook while groundbaiting with jokers.

Collecting redworms

It's best to have your own purpose-built compost heap, but it is possible to find old manure heaps containing redworms. Don't waste your time turning over the new deposits of compost; red-worms like stuff that has started to decompose and is six months old or more. Turn over the surface lightly with a fork, and if you see a single

Fig 25 In winter look for worms in the south-west corner of a wormery or compost heap, as this is warmest. In summer search the north side, as this will be most moist

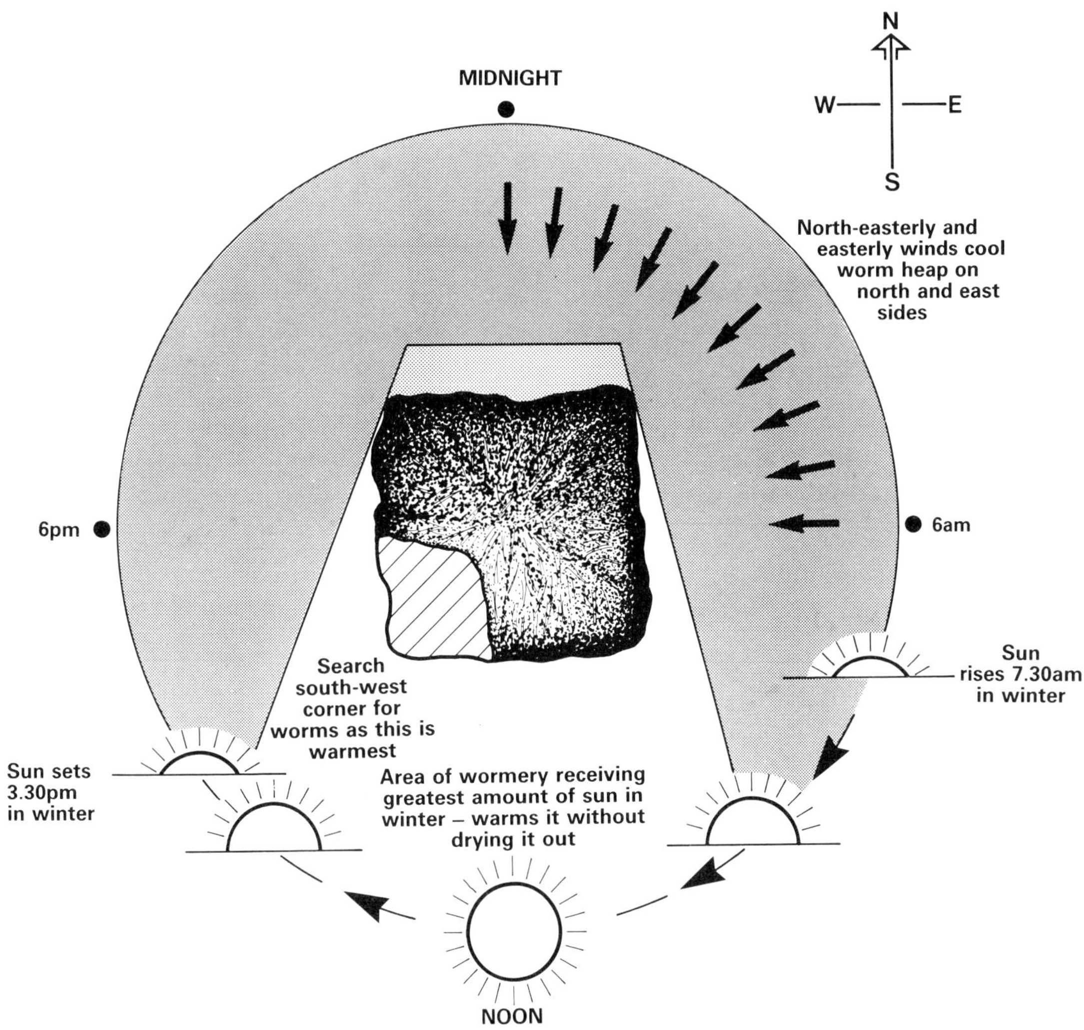

This angler is attached to a big bream on one of the many Fenland drains where casters are a 'must' for most anglers after bream

And this is the sort of fish you may be lucky enough to catch yourself if you are careful and patient, for a shoal of bream can be easily frightened

Opposite An angler reaches for a grayling hooked on Yorkshire's River Wharfe. One of the best baits of all for this beautiful fish is a small redworm

worm work slowly around that point, and downwards. Disturb as little of the heap as possible, for it takes time for them to recolonise the areas you fork over.

In summer look for the moist areas on the north side of the heap, remembering that the wettest part will usually be at the bottom. If you have regular access to the heap, water it thoroughly and lay down some sacking which will help retain the moisture. With a bit of luck you'll find redworms lying just underneath the sack when you lift it up on your next visit.

From October through to March it's more difficult to find redworms. Start your search in the south-west corner of a heap, which is sheltered from the cool north-easterlies but warmed by any afternoon sun.

Keeping

Redworms will keep well provided they have some moist, rotted vegetable matter to feed on. However in summer it's advisable to empty your small tin of worms back into a large container, taking them out when you next need them. In winter they will keep in a small maggot tin (with compost) for weeks on end. But make sure the tin doesn't freeze in your car boot.

In the hottest weather it can help to put your small tin of worms into your maggot fridge. But keep the lid on.

Tackle

A size 12 or 14 hook is about right if you intend to fish a whole, medium-sized redworm. For a portion of worm you can drop to a 16 or 18. Be careful when casting, as a redworm can be ripped off the hook if you jerk it. That's why many anglers always tip the hook with a maggot or caster. Float-fished redworm can be a killing method, and it's one which is badly under used.

Tips

In winter try a tiny piece of worm, about as long as a maggot. The diagram shows the easiest way of doing this. This will attract small roach, gudgeon or ruffe, and is also excellent bait for roach of 4oz or more.

Most old compost, straw or manure heaps will hold redworms.

Few farmers will refuse you permission to search for worms. Remember to ignore new deposits of material, but since these retain moisture beneath them it's worth scraping some aside to find the established stuff underneath.

Worms as groundbait

You'll find that chopping worms up before putting them into groundbait will keep it from flying apart when you throw it.

A better idea, in most situations, is to pack them into a swimfeeder, closed at one end and plugged in the other with groundbait. If the worms are sizeable cut the holes larger. This method ensures they all get into your swim and are quickly washed from the feeder.

It doesn't matter if you get a little earth or rubbish in with worms in a feeder or groundbait, provided it doesn't block the feeder holes. Fish are used to seeing bits of vegetable matter or dirt being washed into the water, and it can make a small cloud. In years past a favourite method of groundbaiting a stillwater swim was to pull up a clump of turf and toss it, grass and all, into the swim. Gradually the worms and insects would fall from the earth, baiting the swim as they did so.

Fig 26 Slipping a caster onto the point of the hook (left) will prevent a worm slipping off. To get a tiny piece of worm on the hook insert the hook near the end and break the worm above it (right)

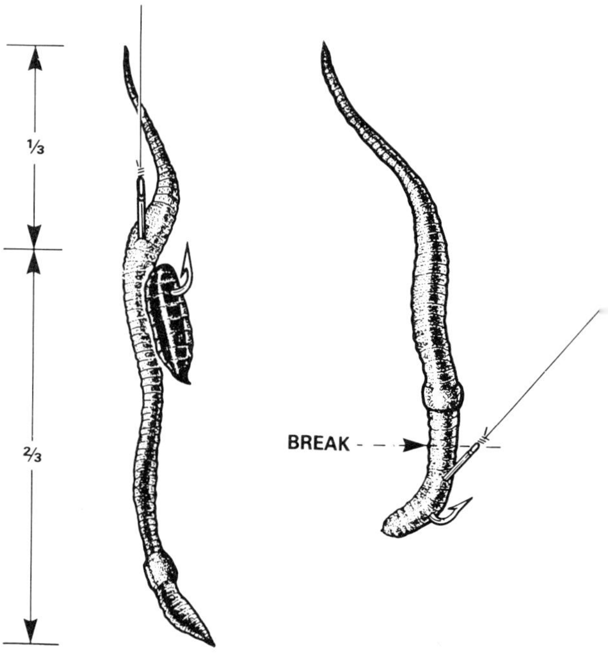

Making a wormery

There is hardly a fish swimming that won't take a nice juicy worm. But how many times have you made a last-minute check on your bait supply only to realise you've overlooked them?

If there are bream about they'll prefer a redworm to almost any other bait. And if you are struggling in a match, a tiny piece of worm, about the length of a maggot, is certain to pick out a small perch if there's one in the vicinity. In winter when the going is really hard, a tiny worm will often mean the difference between a few fish and a dry keepnet. In short, it's a bait you just can't afford to be without.

Getting a regular supply of worms can be a bit of a problem unless you are able to build a wormery at the bottom of the garden. Even then it may take anything up to a couple of years to get it fully established. The system outlined here will ensure enough to keep you going every weekend of the season. It takes little upkeep and, provided you start with the right breeding stock, will produce first-class bait.

The first task will be to get some redworms, either buying them from a tackle shop or finding an established heap. Maybe a friend will come to your rescue with a batch from his own bait supply. Try to get them in varying sizes, not all the huge ones. A couple of hundred will be sufficient to start with if you're only going to rear enough to supply your own needs.

Contents of the wormery are important. Fine grass cuttings are almost the last thing you need in a small one. They matt together and exclude air and water. Straw is much better because it holds air and rots down quickly when wet. Try to get some manure, a couple of handfuls is better than nothing. Pig or horse manure is good but rabbit droppings are even better. Chicken manure is very strong; use it sparingly. Add your kitchen vegetable waste each day – salad left-overs, brown bananas, rotten apples and oranges, potato peelings and even egg shells if some of the white is left sticking to the inside.

1 The heap on the left is too dry. It's covered with grass cuttings and has acquired a 'roof' shape; when it rains the water runs off it like thatch. You need something with sides to enable you to keep the top flat so that it absorbs water. A good idea for a small wormery is the one on the right – nothing more than a plastic pipe, only a

1

2

3

4

5

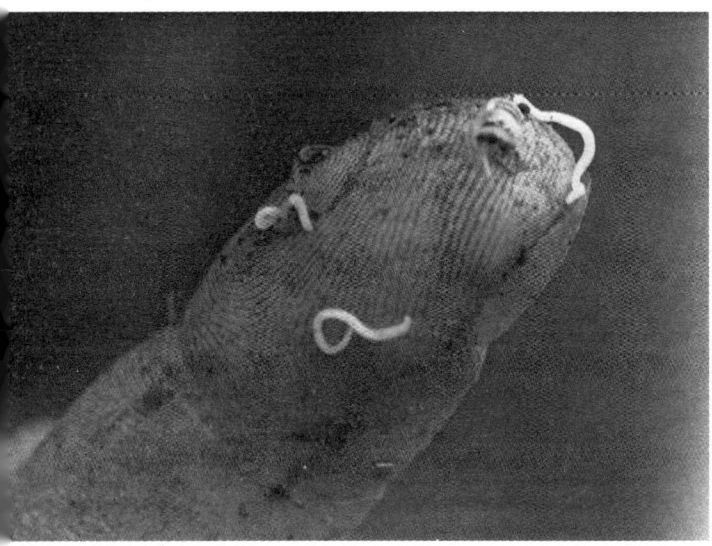

foot high. It is kept covered with newspaper but a good soaking is even better. At all costs ensure that it stays moist. Give it a watering each time you water the garden and you won't go far wrong.

2 Another good tip is to have a wormery in the garage. All that's involved is a large plastic bag which is kept topped up with a spadeful of compost from the outside wormery. This system doesn't smell, and because it's in the garage you can collect worms regardless of the weather, or even at night.

3 Spread newspaper on the floor, tip up the bag, and search with a small fork. Try not to disturb too much earth. It should take no more than five minutes at the most to get enough worms for a day's hookbait. This bag will require less watering than the outside wormery.

4 Lovely juicy redworms; they'll keep for years in your bag provided you keep adding compost, which will act as a food source. A handful of those lawn clippings mentioned earlier will be all right now and again, but far better to use well-rotted compost. Be sure never to use clippings from a lawn that has been treated with weed-killer during the previous six months.

5 If you find these tiny redworms in your bag you'll know things are going well. Often there will be hundreds all matted together. Try not to disturb them anymore than necessary.

6 It's not a messy job searching your bag. The earth can be picked up by the handful and put back, the last lot being poured in from the newspaper. Once it's all back in place push the newspaper into the bag – it's all food for the worms. Just add a milk bottle full of water to start it rotting down.

7 During hot weather it is important to return unused worms to the bag as soon as you return from a fishing trip. This allows them to cool down and get back into good condition.

8 This old margarine tub by the kitchen sink takes all the vegetable waste needed for the wormery. It's sure to get some tea bags too, which are excellent. But be sure to rip open the bags when you put them into the wormery. Use only vegetable matter, no meat.

6

7

8

CHAPTER ELEVEN
HEMPSEED AND TARES

Preparation
Every summer, when water temperatures are at their highest, there is one bait combination that accounts for countless numbers of big roach catches – hempseed and tares. Cheap, easy to prepare and simple to use, these two baits are the angler's dream. They can even be prepared in bulk and frozen until required in plastic bags containing enough for each session.

Tares – small, black, pea-like seeds – are sold by tackle shops and pet food dealers. A ¼ pint or so will be enough for a full day's hookbait, but it's worth doing one good batch and freezing enough for the whole season. Straightforward boiling of tares does work, but it can be an inconsistent method. So try the alternative of casserole cooking. There is no mess, no smell, and after a few trial runs you'll get perfectly cooked tares every time. Follow the step-by-step guide and you will finish up with one of the cheapest and yet most effective roach baits ever discovered.

1 After washing the dry, hard tares under a cold tap soak them overnight. For really dark-coloured ones, which roach seem to like best, add a tablespoonful of bicarbonate of soda.
2 Preheat an oven to gas mark 1 (250–300°F, 120–150°C) and place the casserole dish on the top shelf. Close the oven door and leave for 40 minutes.
3 If a hook can be slid easily through a tare after 40 minutes, it is cooked. Remove the dish from the oven if over half the seeds tested are cooked to this test. If not, replace the dish and leave for a further 10 minutes before testing again. Maximum oven time should be an hour.
4 Allow the cooked tares to cool naturally. The whole point of the casserole method is to allow a gentle heating and cooling through of the seeds so that the skin doesn't split.
5 When the tares are cool, transfer them to a sieve and rinse them under the tap until the water runs clear. Pick out any 'alien' seeds such as corn or maize. Next divide the tares into small amounts – enough for one session. Put into polythene bags and place in the deep freeze.

The prepared tares will be the main hookbait while hempseed is used as loose feed on most outings. But never be afraid to try a grain of hemp on the hook. It is a first-class bait and will often work on days when fish refuse the larger tare.

1

2

4

3

5

To prepare hemp a straightforward boiling method is suitable, and the cooking time is much shorter than for tares. Once again follow the pictures overleaf for a simple guide to good bait. Between one and two pints of hemp will be enough for a day's fishing.

1 First wash the hemp thoroughly. You'll be amazed at the dirt that comes out. Give the seed a good soaking and put it into a saucepan, covering well with water. Soak overnight.
2 After soaking, most of the hemp will have sunk and the actual cooking process will take only about 15 minutes.
3 Bring the hemp rapidly to the boil. A frothy surface will soon appear. Skim this off with a slotted spoon and turn the heat down.
4 Simmer the pan so that only one or two bubbles come up. Hold at this cooking level for about 15 minutes.
5 Now is the time to check the hemp. When the seeds begin to split and their white inside peeps out, the cooking process is complete.
6 Wash the cooked hemp in a sieve. The water

will be very dark and aromatic. It's worth saving this and mixing your groundbait with it instead of with river water.

7 A perfect grain of cooked hemp. The white kernel is just sticking out to attract the eye of the fish. But it has not split too much, so that it is easy for a hook to slide into the crack and stay there. If the seed is overcooked the crack will be too large and the hook would fall out on casting.

8 Place the washed and damp hemp in a clean bait box. It should smell fresh and be a shiny black.

9 Damp kitchen roll or newspaper over the hemp completes the process. The seed must not dry out as this causes it to lose its blackness and makes it liable to float.

2

1

3

4

5

6

7

8

9

Fishing hempseed and tares

Hempseed is now used all year round as groundbait. But it's not an easy bait to fish on the hook. Being small it's rather fiddly to put on. Tares are more popular as hookbait. Being bigger they are certainly easier to handle. But whether hemp or tare is being used on the hook there are likely to be false bites when fish mistake the shot for hemp. Both are normally regarded as mainly a summer bait, and best on those scorching hot days when nothing seems to be feeding. At such times they are unbeatable for tempting big roach.

Old angling books talk about fast, unhittable bites on hemp. Anglers using tares seem to have less trouble, perhaps because fish take them in different ways. Or perhaps as it's a larger bait the fish take more time. Whatever the reason, if you miss bites on hemp a switch to a tare should increase your fish-per-strike average considerably. It may be that fish go for the tare rather than the smaller shot on the line.

When floatfishing either hemp or tares, make a point of laying your tackle in a straight line when you cast. This will enable you to see bites 'on the drop', though if you get several of these you should consider fishing shallower. Even when shot are bunched within 2ft of the hook fish will hold up the bait, apparently not noticing the weight of the shot, in their attempts to grab as much hemp as possible.

The usual practice when pole fishing is to lower the terminal tackle into the water directly under the tip of the pole. But if you're doing that, remember you're missing out on those possible bites on the drop. So swing it out underarm in a straight line. That means using a line the same length as the pole, so you're fishing from the moment the bait touches the water, and you're swinging fish direct to your hand.

Most anglers strive for as much sensitivity as possible when float fishing, but when fishing with hemp and tares it's a mistake to have the float dotted down to water level, or to use a float with a super-sensitive tip. If you strike on the slightest suspicion of a bite you will miss more fish than you hook. Many times you will need as much as 2in of float showing, and then not striking until it all goes under! If you miss bites get more and more of that float showing above the surface – that's the best tip anyone can give an angler fishing with tares. Ignore the taps and dithers, some of which may be caused by fish hitting the line in their excitement, and wait until the float sails away.

Regular feeding with hempseed will result in fish rising to intercept the bait. That's the time when you get bites on the drop, or lift bites. Shallow up immediately. But don't forget that the fish are now nearer the surface and that there are now no longer several feet of water to strike through. The result is often a break on the first strike. Also you'll often find the bigger fish higher in the water, so beware. In fact they will often boil on the top as you throw hemp in. But don't be tempted to fish with no shot at all; you get a lot of short takes and waste time striking. The ideal depth at which to catch your fish is 2ft.

There's usually no reason for finesse if you're fishing for roach with tares in warm water, and if they are feeding well. Use 2½lb or 3lb line through to the hook, and if you're fishing a pole use an elastic. It's not unusual to start catching roach of 1lb-plus on tares on waters where 4oz is normally regarded as large.

Forged hooks of sizes 12, 14 or occasionally 16 are about right for tares. The type of hook is not important, but long-shanked hooks make it easier to hook on the seed and to unhook fish. Hook a tare through the middle. For hempseed on the hook a fine-wire hook is best otherwise you can split the grain when you push it into the crack containing the white kernel.

Though tares can be legered, it's usual to floatfish because you can then carry on taking fish when they start feeding in midwater. It's not unusual to catch roach 2ft deep in 10ft of water.

Beating false bites

The original answer to beating false bite when a fish took a lead shot was to bunch the shot together. That still works, but tungsten flexible tubing provides an even better answer. The side effect is to get the bait down to the required depth as quickly as possible, which saves time. However, it is possible for the hook to catch round the top of a line of bunched shot, or even flexible tubing. The answer is to sharpen the tubing in a pencil sharpener or to use a non-toxic olivette, which is tapered from the top.

The first time

Inevitably an angler fishing with tares for the first

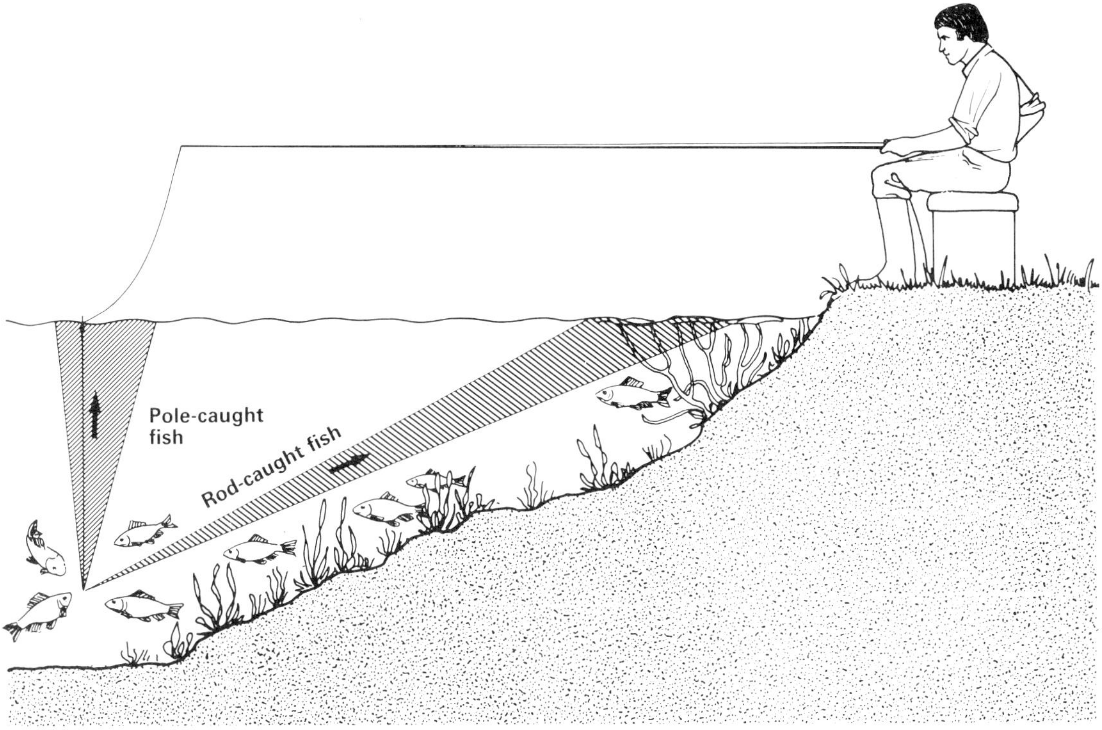

Fig 27 Fish feeding on hemp and tares are usually close in. Using a pole enables you to take them straight out of the swim without disturbing fish near the bank

time may not have much confidence. A useful dodge therefore is to start feeding regularly with hemp – every 30 seconds is not too often – but to use maggot on the hook. Don't put in any loose-fed maggots though.

When you've got a few fish, change over to a tare. If that doesn't work change back to maggot but slip a single shot on the line between the bulk shot and the hook. When you start unaccountably missing bites but find the maggot is untouched, you know the fish are willing to take hemp since the 'bites' will actually be false bites on the shot. Put on a tare, not forgetting to take off the single shot. If at any time you find you need weight between the bulk shot and hook, put at least two shot together – never a single one unless you wish to invite false bites.

Perhaps the hempseed won't stop on the hook. Try artificial hemp. The hook slips through a little hole and it won't come off. Any good tackle dealer should be able to get you some. It is also possible to get fish on a small piece of rubber tubing with a white lining, or a piece of leather bootlace trimmed to shape. Even better is a really black tare (bicarbonate of soda added to the water when cooking will achieve this) and to paint the top of the hook with a blob of white Tipp-Ex. The contrast of black and white seems to attract fish. Don't try any of these unless you're feeding hemp regularly, though.

And at all times remember to keep feeding regularly. A five-minute break can result in the shoal moving away to search for more food, for feeding on hemp seems to make them super-active, and you've got to keep them interested.

Fig 28 Artificial hemp saves a lot of time when the fish are biting well

CHAPTER TWELVE
GROUNDBAIT AND FEEDING THE SWIM

Cereal groundbait

Groundbaiting is an art. It comes only with experience, for there are many points to consider – how much to use, when to use it, when to stop, which species like it and which don't. But the art starts long before the act of throwing it into a swim. For the very best groundbait can be ruined by bad mixing habits. Even details down to using the correct shape of container can make all the difference.

But let's start with a look at the most simple of all groundbait – good, old-fashioned breadcrumbs. Breadcrumb is the basis of nearly all groundbait. It is bread, dried in a low oven, and then ground to a fine crumb. It can be either brown or white depending on the amount of drying it has undergone.

A groundbait made from pure white crumb was once the favourite of top anglers. But that thinking changed years ago and it is now most unusual to see such a mix in use on anywhere but the most powerful of fast-flowing rivers.

White crumb will mix into a very stiff, almost paste-like mixture, that will lie for hours on the bed of the river or lake and as a result have very little attraction to passing fish. It mixes into this stodge simply because its fat content has not been destroyed by the drying process. The very same bread could be dried longer and on a more severe heat, resulting in a brown bread that has been considerably reduced in fat content. This crumb will mix into a much softer, more fluffy bait that will break up almost on entry to the water. It will not however bind together easily and therefore cannot be thrown any distance.

The answer is to balance the two textures of white and brown crumb to give the ideal mixture for the water to be fished.

A mixture of say four parts brown to one of white may be suitable for throwing halfway across a fairly wide river. The white will bind the balls long enough to ensure it gets well down, towards the bottom, before beginning to break up. By reducing the white content the same groundbait will become softer in texture and break up sooner, both before and after entering the water.

On a very shallow canal, where a small piece of groundbait has to be thrown no further than the end of a pole, pure brown may be the thing to use. It's all a matter of getting to know the baits you have at your disposal and how best they can be blended – experience once again.

The very best cereal is pure bread; no rusks, no biscuits or other substances such as dried cakes and even dog biscuits should be used. Shop around and always ask the dealer exactly what the content of the crumb is. Alternatively save up all your waste stale, but not mouldy, bread and dry it for later production of your own groundbait.

Once you have found a good supply of groundbait it may pay to buy in bulk – at least a sack at a time. That way you will have enough to see you through most of the season. You'll get to know that particular crumb and how best to mix and blend it with other ingredients. The white crumb will be used in smaller quantities and is therefore not so important.

All crumb should first be riddled to separate out any large pieces, bits of wrapper and other debris that has a habit of finding its way into the bags. Use a riddle with a mesh of about ⅛in square – smaller if you plan to fish a lot of difficult waters such as canals. The riddled crumb should now be stored in a dry place, well away from the attention of rats and mice. Plastic dustbins make ideal containers, especially if you can get them with the snap-on type of lid.

When it comes to mixing, be sure to have the right container. Groundbait just cannot be mixed correctly in a tall, narrow bucket. Use a shallow tray or bowl that permits all the contents to be worked quickly and the water to spread evenly.

The larger the container the better, certainly it should be as large as possible to fit into your box. Try to get a riddle – one suitable for producing casters is ideal – that fits the bowl to be used; you'll see why later on.

There are two schools of thought on how best to mix groundbait. One says always add groundbait to water, while the other says add water to groundbait. As a general rule it may pay beginners to go for the groundbait to water method as this does tend to give a more even mix. But it is also likely to result in far more crumb being used than is really essential to the day's sport.

If you think you know how much bait is required try the water to cereal approach. Firstly place the crumb in your container, remembering it has already been riddled through in a dry state. Next, using a maggot box, add water, while your free hand quickly works all the cereal around the bowl to spread the water as evenly as possible. Keep working the bait, adding a little water at a time – it's a bit like making a cake – until you think the right mix has been achieved. You should of course have already decided how much white to brown is going to be used and ensured that it was fully mixed in a dry state.

For an average swim of 6ft deep, fairly slow flowing and calling for a fishing range of 10 to 12yd out, you may wish to mix a cereal that will hold together long enough to be thrown the distance and begin breaking up just beneath the surface. Such a cereal should be mixed just wet enough to mould into a ball but so that when held on the palm of your hand it can be seen moving very slightly as it expands from inside. Get to that stage and only a few drops more water will be needed to keep it from drying too much during fishing.

Soft and fluffy groundbait like this is ideal for still or slow-moving water. It will break up quickly to form a cloud

Assuming you are happy with the addition of water it is now possible to move to the next stage – a final riddle. Once mixed to satisfaction, a good groundbait can be greatly improved by a few moments spent on the bankside doing this. Tip the mixed groundbait onto a plastic bag, old cloth or into a second container. Place the riddle over the mixing bowl – now you can see why a riddle of the right size is a help – and run all the cereal through the holes, working it with the flat of your hand to break up as many lumps as possible. Having done this the groundbait will have taken on a really nice fluffy texture and will mould up into balls much better. It also improves the action in water, making it more attractive but less of a meal to feeding fish.

At this stage the groundbait is ready for use. But there is still a lot that can be done to further enhance its attraction and improve its overall versatility. Let's look at making it more attractive

For distance work make balls firm and round. Wet hands will form a nice skin to prevent the feed breaking up in mid-air

for a start. Assuming we are fishing for skimmer bream and roach with maggot as bait, we should be looking towards adding maggots to the cereal mix. But large hook maggots mixed with groundbait will cause it to break up very quickly. The balls will probably fly apart in the air and as a result any fish present will be scattered all over the swim by the free food. Pinkies are a better bet, but even these will burst open a ball of feed if too many are introduced at a time. For the very best effect use squatts. These are smaller than the other maggots and tend to keep still, thus allowing the feed to be thrown with more confidence that it will arrive in the right place.

Casters, being a still bait, are also first class for adding to cereal. But in all cases don't tip in large amounts. It's far better to add just enough to make up the next ball. A good trick is to keep a bait box alongside your groundbait. You will then be able to take out the required amount of maggots or casters, drop them into the cereal in one corner of the bowl, give them a quick stir and make up the ball.

If you are tempted to tip the whole lot into the feed at one go it's worth remembering that wet maggots float. Maggots left to crawl around in damp cereal will absorb water and when introduced to the swim will work against you by either floating or at best sinking slowly. The result is fish being drawn away from your fishing area.

Another good thing about using squatts or casters as feed is that they, unlike other types of maggot, do not burrow into the bottom. Squatts will lie on the river or lake bed until eaten, thus ensuring there is always something present to hold the attention of browsing fish.

With all feeding it is important to realise that once you've put it in you can't take it out. So always work on the safe side, feeding too little rather than too much. The whole principle of good feeding is to tempt the fish, just giving them the taste that triggers off an urge to want more.

How much to put in is again a matter of experience. But a simple rule is that feed is best matched to what is being taken out. If you're catching very little, simply piling in large amounts of feed is not going to do much good. Far better to cut down on the size of offerings but ensure that there is always something falling through the water in the hope of attracting new fish to the area.

On a river when you are catching well, feeding can be stepped up in order to ensure that fish do not drop down the swim and out of reach – or worse into the catching area of the angler below you.

On a lake, however, fish feeding hard will probably stay put as long as there is something on which to feed. In this situation keep the feed going in but don't spend so much time making up balls that you miss half the bites you are getting. It's all a matter of common sense and developing a feel for the swim.

Assuming you've been catching well and then bites slow down, as is often the case, you must decide if the reason is too little, or too much, feed. Try increasing the feed rate and see if bites increase. If they don't, cut back and wait a while before deciding on the next move. If you can loose feed the swim maybe that is all it will need for a time.

The next thing to consider is how best to actually get a ball of cereal into the swim, especially if you plan to fish at range. A good catapult will help greatly but it should be one designed just for groundbait. The Whopper Dropper type is one of the best, having an open plastic cup in place of the more conventional pouch. Such a catapult is very powerful and it's possible to fire a well-made ball of feed well beyond your casting range. So get in some practice where it doesn't matter, even if you resort to balls of mud. Don't make balls too big otherwise the catapult will break them up and feed will be scattered over a wide area. Pieces not much bigger than a golf ball are about right.

Another little trick is to keep a container of water close to the groundbait bowl. A ball of feed is made up in the usual way and then moulded a second time after you've dipped your hands in the water container. This will put a sort of skin on the cereal and it will stay firm in flight. Making up a ball of feed is a two-handed job. Don't rush it and try to make each ball round and the same size. That way they fly true and you'll get the right range every time.

Firing a catapult is easy enough but you will need something to aim at if accuracy is to be achieved. Start by holding the catapult with the arm fully extended and pull back the elastic with the other hand, making a mental note of how far it is stretched. Now line up, using the catapult arms like sights, with something on the opposite bank. A tree, bush or even a rock will do. Once you have worked all this out, it's plain sailing to put ball after ball into a fairly small space.

Using a catapult is all very well but if it breaks halfway through a fishing session you'll be in trouble. Always carry a spare, or at least a repair kit containing new elastic and a set of plastic cable ties – they're the self-locking bindings that usually hold elastic to the frame and cup.

Most anglers attempt to put all their feed into one spot. That is not completely wrong, since the whole object is to get fish into a concentrated area. But there are times when it pays to 'spread it around' just a little, for example on a bream river. The idea is to build up a feeding area so that fish can be caught, but at the same time another part of the swim is 'rested'. Using this system it is possible to keep a shoal feeding for a very long time.

Having decided on the 'target' area a diamond-shaped area is fed, putting in balls of cereal at each of the four points (Fig 29). The hookbait is then presented at point C – the nearest of the four fed areas. Only if bites stop, or did not develop in the first place, do you move to the next corner (points D and B). Area 'A' is a sort of sanctuary and should be fished only as a last resort. This last area may produce two or three extra fish once the main shoal has moved off from the other catching areas. By always fishing to the nearside of a fed area you will not be faced with having to bring a hooked fish through the rest of a shoal and thus risk scaring them.

But possibly the most important thing to remember when considering groundbaiting, is where to start. It's obviously no good throwing in feed, only to find that the area you've just baited is right over the top of an unfishable weed bed or some other obstruction. Unless you know the area, never feed before either plumbing the depth well or having a few exploratory casts first. Once you are happy you've got the best spot in the swim, then, and only then, feed.

Finally after you've finished a day's sport be sure to wash out all traces of left-over bait from your bowl. There is nothing like a few bits of mouldy groundbait left clinging to the container to ruin the next mix.

Groundbait left over should not be thrown in the water where it will serve no good purpose and

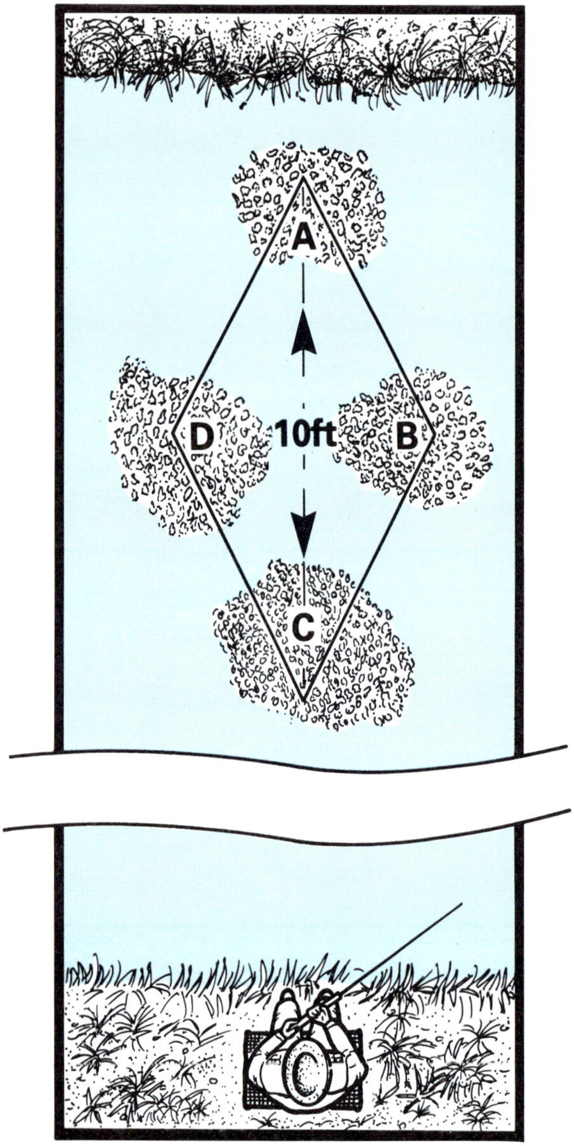

Fig 29 Groundbaiting a bream swim can take the form of a diamond which allows different parts of a shoal to be 'rested'

do nothing more than sour the water. Far better to tip it onto the bank where it will quickly be eaten by birds and other wildlife thankful for a good meal.

The bait dropper

There are occasions when you want to get maggots or casters direct to the bottom of a swim without using a swimfeeder. For instance, perhaps you have a snaggy swim in fast water which you are quite unable to fish with a feeder. But maggots thrown in upstream will be taken through the snags without settling. How do you bait your swim? The answer is a bait dropper – an item of tackle which was once quite popular with anglers in the south. Now it is regaining its popularity, particularly on the Trent, where many matchmen bait their swim with a bait dropper attached to a pole. This makes it possible to lower your bait into the water and release it wherever you wish.

There are two types: those which you jerk to release the bait, and those which release it automatically when the dropper hits the bottom. Some models have an adjustable rod which enables you to vary the depth at which the bait is released. When fish are feeding use the long rod, which allows you to lower the dropper a few feet upstream of the feeding shoal. The initial drops can be made dead on target using the short rod.

The dropper can be hung on your hook, so that you can use it without swopping poles or breaking down tackle. But you can, of course, bait with a pole and then run a float through on rod and line.

Feeding the swim

Once you understand the reasons for groundbaiting a swim, whether it be with cereal or loose feed, you're halfway to getting the best out of that swim. Basically you're intending to do four things:

1 To attract fish to the area.
2 To set off the trigger which starts them feeding.
3 To keep them active and looking for food.
4 To concentrate the fish in one place so that they are easier to catch.

All experienced anglers, whether specimen hunters or matchmen, agree that baiting a swim nearly always holds the key to success. The main exception is when you are stalking a fish you can see, such as a carp, or when you are fishing for just one fish in a known hotspot. This mainly

It's possible to catch chub in freezing cold conditions . . . but you must be careful not to overfeed

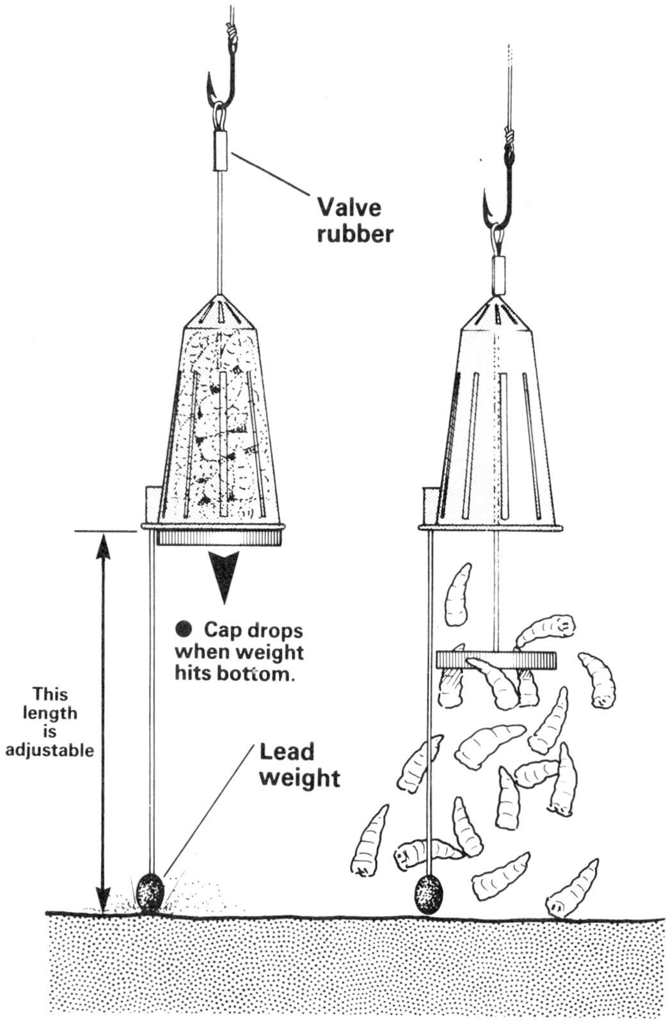

Fig 30 The bait dropper – an item of equipment which used to be popular and is now coming back into favour. There are several different models on the market

applies to pike anglers, who may be roving and dropping a bait in the swims where they think a pike may already be in residence.

For almost all general fishing you will need to groundbait to get the best results. The following covers the four points more fully. Understand the thinking behind them and you should be able to adapt to any situation.

Although most anglers may think the first point is the most important of the four jobs that groundbait does, it is, in fact, the least important. In this country you will have fish in front of you on the vast majority of occasions. Almost every angler will remember times when fish have been rising all around him, yet he has been unable to get a bite. On clear waters you can sometimes see fish swimming around completely ignoring any food you throw to them. So don't assume that just because you can't get a bite, there are no fish in front of you.

However, if your swim is absolutely blank when you start fishing, the only thing to do is to keep baiting it until something comes along. Fish are wild creatures and can spot a morsel of food from a long way away; they have to be alert in order to survive, after all. Thankfully they are also curious creatures and even though they may not be hungry, they may well swim over to inspect your bait. If just one fish does this your groundbaiting has done its first job. But you need to ensure there is food in your swim to attract that fish.

On a stillwater it may be sufficient to put some food on the bottom and wait; that's the main tactic of matchmen when after bream. But for most other species it's better to have a moving bait, as this is likely to excite the fish more than a stationary one. So on a stillwater a cloud groundbait is the tactic to use. Put in a small ball every minute or two to try to ensure that something is dropping through the water at all times.

On a river, when food is being swept away, you may need to feed more frequently. Try to judge when your groundbait has been swept out of your swim, then put in some more. The easiest way of groundbaiting is to put in half a dozen maggots with every cast, assuming the water isn't too fast for this.

If you're using a swimfeeder then you are automatically groundbaiting your swim. Even so former world champion Dave Thomas will still put in a few loose-fed maggots while swimfeedering, because he knows that roach, in particular, like to take a bait before it has hit bottom.

Assuming a fish has come over to inspect a sinking maggot, now comes the important second stage in the process.

Getting the fish to feed

You can't actually force a fish to feed; but you can put temptation in its way.

Any pike angler will tell you that if you

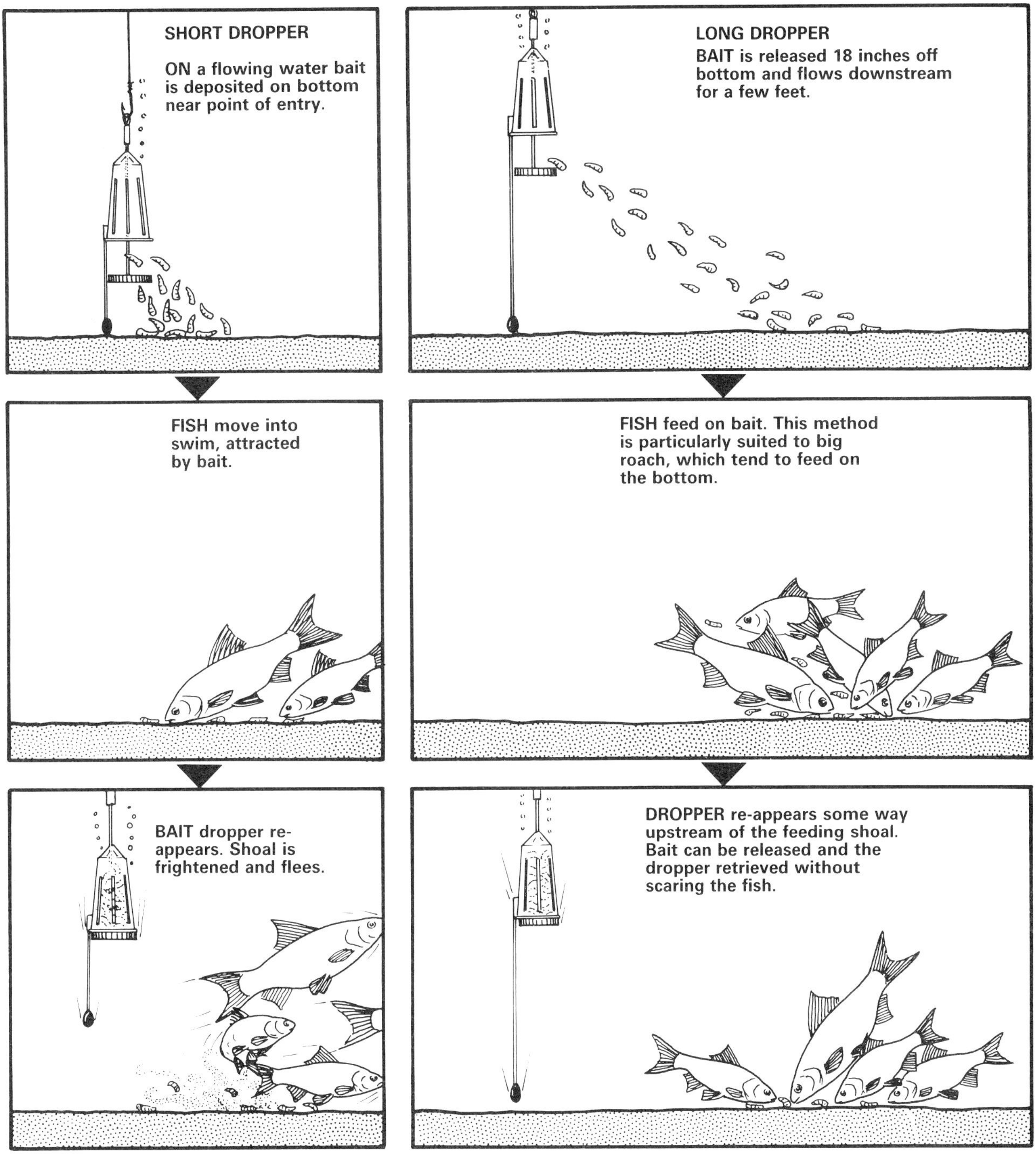

Fig 31 On moving water try to release the bait well off bottom so the shoal is concentrated downstream of the spot where the dropper re-appears

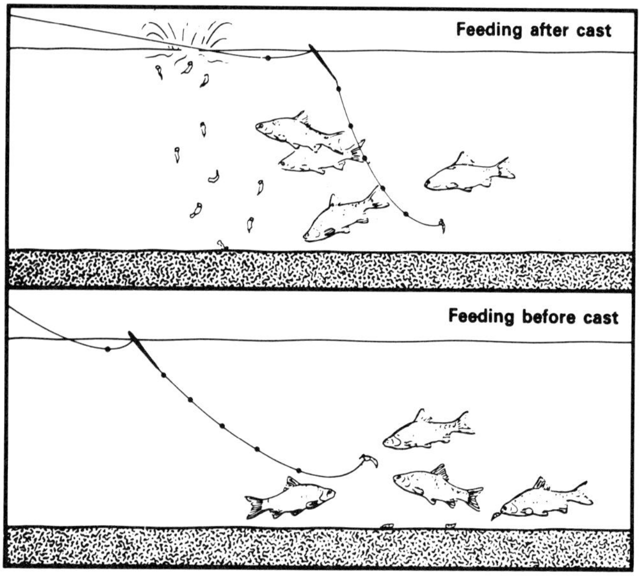

Fig 32 Feed *after* you cast and you risk the fish rushing upsteam to the largest concentration of food and ignoring your hook bait. Feed *before* you cast and your hook bait will come into view just as the fish are looking round for more food

continually pull a spinner past the nose of a pike it's odds-on he'll eventually take a snap at it. Salmon are believed not to feed when they are in fresh water, yet every year thousands are caught on rod and line when they are taking flies, worms or spinners.

Whatever the reason – frustration, instinct, or plain greed to prevent another fish eating the bait – fish will take things into their mouths that they don't intend to eat. So, if there is a fish in your swim and you are continually putting temptation in its way, in the form of juicy maggots or casters, eventually it will probably have a go. Your feeding pattern will be exactly the same as for the first stage. Indeed you won't know there are fish in your swim willing to take a bait until you get a bite. Don't give up too early. So often anglers feed consistently for half an hour, then get bored and go and talk to their mates just when their feeding should start reaping dividends.

Luckily for the angler, fish are very competitive creatures; and one fish taking a maggot may be sufficient to set off the trigger which gets the whole shoal feeding, for nearly all fish in this country go around in shoals. And they are all competitive. Get a shoal of chub feeding and they'll barge each other out of the way to get at a bait. Roach are more sedate feeders, but the same principle applies – when you catch one roach you can be absolutely certain there are others nearby who can be tempted to feed. Getting them to take the bait on your hook is all a matter of correct presentation (see page 161).

Once you've had a bite or two, you know there are fish to be caught, and that will give you extra confidence. The worst thing you can do now is to start ladling in the bait with both hands. More swims are ruined by overfeeding than by underfeeding. For, as with humans, there is a limit to the amount a fish can eat. The secret, as already mentioned, is to keep fish looking for food without actually giving them much. And this is where you take advantage of the competitive spirit which is inbuilt into all wild creatures – the instinct which tells them that they must go out and compete for food if they are to survive.

Imagine a shoal of ten fish, all willing to feed, with an angler on the bank throwing them just two maggots. They will dash after the maggots and devour them. Yet only two fish will have eaten, the remainder will still be waiting. Two more maggots are thrown in and, unless the two lucky fish are full up, they will again join in the dash for the food. All this time they are expending energy, and most times they actually receive nothing. Yet to replace the energy they are using they need – food! So if you can get a shoal of fish competing for their dinner, you are creating a demand for your bait.

The big mistake comes when the angler puts in fifty maggots for those ten fish to eat. With more than enough to go round, the competition for food no longer exists. Those fish might not even bother to go for the maggots, knowing they can have a snack anytime they choose. The feeding pattern has been ruined, and that angler may well stop catching those fish. He will have to start all over again to try to get fish competing for bait, but it won't be easy, Once a fish loses that competitive urge it doesn't come back quickly. If one fish now starts swimming out of the swim the others will almost certainly follow it.

Concentrating the fish

If you place all your groundbait or loose-feed in

one spot, it should take roughly the same route to the bottom. Only an increase or decrease in current will affect this. All you have to do then is to find the spot where you get most bites and concentrate on it. It's that easy – almost.

Sometimes bites dry up and that's when you start searching for the fish. Frequently you'll find them a little closer in, farther out, or farther downstream. The rule of thumb here is to keep feeding the same spot. *Do not* feed farther out just because the fish have moved there. That can have the effect, particularly with chub, of moving the fish still farther out.

On a river there may be underwater eddies taking your loose-feed off line, so that it is a few feet from where you think it is. Or something may have temporarily frightened the fish into diving for cover off the line you have been fishing. Indeed many top anglers will tell you that if you can catch fish off your groundbait the bites are nearly always better – as if the fish thinks it has discovered a bonus feed and wants to dash back to its cover quickly, with its dinner.

This is particularly true of bream, which will apparently circle round a groundbaited spot taking food only from its fringes. With roach, dace and chub, keeping the feed going in regularly seems to give the fish confidence to stop in the same spot. It's almost as if they have a time-clock built into them, and half a minute either way in your feeding pattern can upset them.

Many matchmen have found, to their cost, that taking three or four minutes to play a big chub to the net has so upset their feeding pattern that when they resume fishing their shoal has gone. It's not unusual to see anglers putting in more feed while they are actually playing fish!

Nine times out of ten you will need to keep feeding the same spot once you've had some bites. If the fish are still there and willing to feed, it will concentrate them (though they may move away from time to time), and if they stop feeding you'll need to keep that bait going in to get the competitive spirit going again.

Amounts to feed

The amount to feed will depend on how many fish you think are in your swim, and your only real guide to this is the number of fish you are catching. Nearly all Britain's top matchmen follow the same rule – in summer put in half a dozen maggots or casters with each cast if you're not catching fish. When you start to catch fish regularly (say two fish in three casts) double the number of maggots. Better still, put in half a dozen maggots *twice* each cast.

It's important when loose feeding in moving water to put bait in *before* you cast. Benny Ashurst, father of former world champion Kevin Ashurst, and a top angler in his own right, says this is the best single tip he could give a beginner. Put your hookbait in first, followed by your loose-feed and the fish will make for the biggest concentration of food. Your hookbait can end up well downstream with all the fish swimming towards the head of the swim. But put your loose-feed in first, followed by your hookbait, and the fish will clean up the groundbait first then look around for more. At this moment your bait should come sailing into view.

Don't wait for half a minute after feeding before casting out, though. Fish will often mop up the falling maggots and go straight back to cover when the last one has vanished. The actual spell of feeding may last for only 15 seconds.

In winter try six or seven maggots every few minutes. When the water is cold it's so easy to overfeed fish because they are not so active and aren't using so much energy. Nevertheless it's important to keep something wafting past their noses, even in winter. If only one fish has a go it could be the trigger that sets others off.

Former world champion Dave Thomas won't use cereal groundbait in winter if he can help it. Even if he's swimfeedering he'll loose-feed if he can so that he doesn't have to alter his feeding pattern if he decides to try floatfishing. And he still has the chance of catching a fish on his swimfeeder as the bait is dropping among the loose-feed.

Feeding for fish in midwater

It often happens, especially in summer, that fish come off the bottom to take feed in midwater. Indeed you are more likely to catch rudd in the top half of the water than in the bottom half.

If you want to keep the fish at this depth, where they are often easier to catch, be sure that the amount you feed is small enough for the fish to eat all your morsels before they drop to the bottom. Err on the side of underfeeding. You're unlikely to lose the fish, provided you feed regularly,

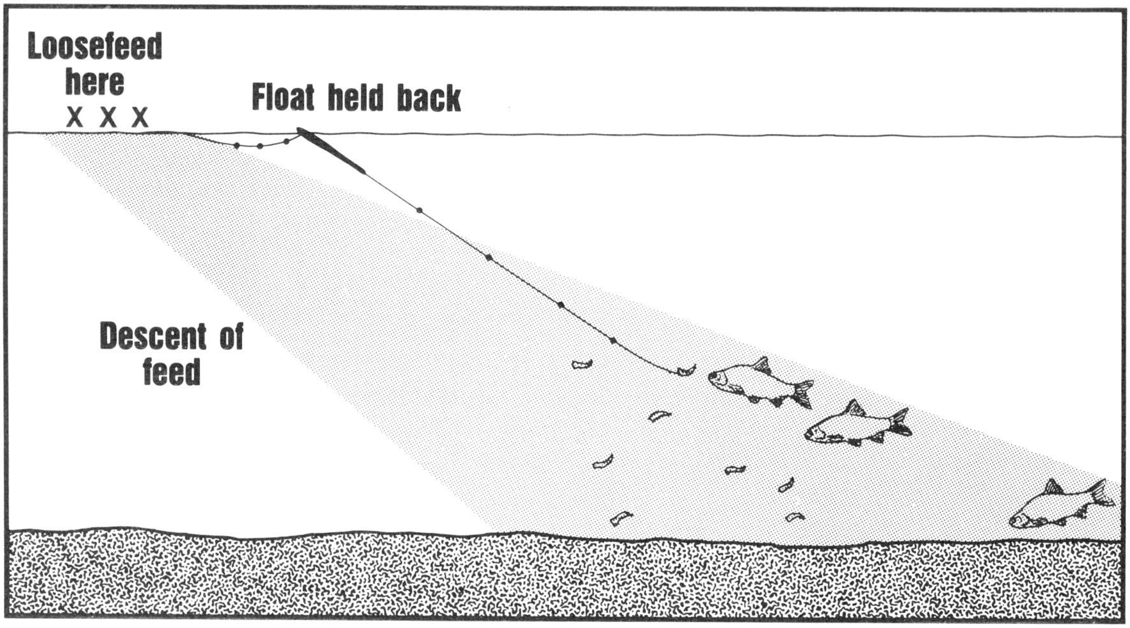

Fig 33 The faster the current the larger area the feed will be spread over. To give the bait a natural fall hold the float back downstream of the point where your loose-feed hits the surface

because if the fish are feeding in midwater they are almost certainly hungry and competing for food.

If, however, you want the fish on the bottom you should put in too much for the shoal to eat in one go, so that fish have to follow your groundbait down to the bottom. But this is a risky operation for the beginner, and most times you will be better off catching the fish where they are feeding naturally. The danger is that you will overfeed the shoal.

A better way of getting them down is to put in some hemp, which sinks quickly. On running water remember to put it in a little downstream from where you have been feeding maggots, because it is heavier.

Feeding for bream

Although a shoal-fish, bream are different from chub or roach in that they are easily frightened. And the splash of a big ball of groundbait on the surface just above their heads is one of the things that scares them most. That is why all experienced bream anglers follow the golden rule often quoted by former national champion Bryan Lakey: '*Never* feed on top of a feeding bream shoal.'

Put your feed in before the shoal arrives, and don't put in any more until bites start petering out. Then you have to play it by ear. This is the rule on almost all stillwaters.

On a river, you have the advantage of being able to put in your groundbait upstream of where the shoal is lying. So you can usually afford to put some in with every cast. Again, remember the golden rule to keep feeding the same spot. If you are feeding in front of you but catching bream 20yd downstream you should be able to keep the shoal feeding. But put just one ball of groundbait down towards the shoal and it's likely you'll scare them. And unlike chub and roach, bream don't often return to a swim once they've left it.

Additives

There is one school of thought that claims there is nothing to beat good, old-fashioned pure bread crumbs as cereal feed. And certainly British anglers have done well enough for many years with nothing more than that in their mixing bowls. But with the continental fishing-style revolution came a new breed of thinking and a whole host of fancy flavours and ingredients.

Some work better than others, but all have a special role to play. So let us take a look at what a few of the better known additives are for, and what they consist of.

Imagine you are walking down a street, not feeling particularly hungry, and you are confronted by the smell of bacon and eggs wafting through an open window. The chances are your taste buds will be stimulated and you will be tempted to eat some. Continental groundbaits play on this human weakness and translate it into fishy terms. Even a non-hungry fish is likely to be tempted to your hookbait if it is attracted by the nutritious smell of the bait you have introduced.

Attracting your fish and keeping them in one spot is half the battle if you want to make a decent net, and continental mixes definitely concentrate fish in a very confined area, from which they are easier to pick off. The multitude of ingredients help you use your groundbait in such a way that by varying the mixes you can feed on the surface, midwater or hard on the bottom.

In fact, there is a lesson to be learned here from the specimen hunters, who have been working along the same lines for some time. They too want to keep one step ahead of the fish and they know that their smelly baits will attract from a fair distance unlike, for instance, breadflake, which will only be taken if a fish happens upon it.

How much feed you put in is a matter of experience and experimentation, but if you've ever seen some of the top Continentals in action – and probably laughed at their bait bombardment at the beginning of a match – you will have some idea of what is wanted. The actual ingredients you will use in your groundbait are all obtainable from a variety of supermarkets, health food shops or specialist bait suppliers such as Bait 78.

The percentages given below are the maximum amounts for each ingredient and are worked out by volume and not by weight. For example the mix will be the same no matter how much you make up in total. A cup used as a measure will give the same result as a bucket, provided you keep the ratios constant. Any of the items listed can be mixed together, but the base meal – breadcrumbs – must be taken into account as a percentage of the total mix. Grind them all in either a coffee grinder or a liquidiser.

What makes blending your own baits so much fun is the wide variety and scope available. The trick is knowing what each one does and how it will affect the overall mix. Some will bind cereal into a very heavy mix while others cause it to break up quickly or to hang high in the water.

Breadcrumb (mix to suit):
This is the base ingredient of all your mixes. Use best quality breadcrumb and riddle through flour sieve to remove lumps.
Rusk:
This is a very fine white powder, available from British Groundbaits. Its prime use is to bind the feed together without adding too much bulk. The quantity to feed is a matter of personal judgement.
Rice (5-15 per cent):
Buy this from a supermarket in 1lb or bigger bags. It is an excellent dispersant. Can be used in all mixes, but usually in surface feeds.
Poppyseed (to 10 per cent):
These tiny seeds have proved excellent attractors of large bream. They are quite expensive but luckily you need only smallish amounts.
Bran (to 20 per cent):
An old English favourite, but the continental variety is much finer. Quite a cheap ingredient to bulk out your feed.
Silkworm (10-15 per cent):
A very smelly additive primarily used for surface feeds for bleak, although it can be successful with gudgeon when used in a bottom mix. Available only to special order from Bait 78.
Powdered eggs (2-3 per cent):
Used for bleak in surface and midwater mixes.
Sunflower seed (5 per cent):
Health freaks will know of these. Prime uses are for surface and midwater feeds. Grind down in a liquidiser.
Potato flakes (5-15 per cent):
For bottom mixes when bream are the target. Very heavy when wet. Use flakes – not powder like Smash.
Broad beans (5-15 per cent):
Excellent for bottom feeds for bream and carp. Use raw after liquidising.
Pumpkin seed (2-3 per cent):
A surface additive primarily for bleak, but also works well in gudgeon mixes. Available from health shops.
Oil Cake (15-20 per cent mix):
This is used to replace the volume of breadcrumb

in a mix. It is mainly used as a dispersant, though it can be very good as a gudgeon attractor. Normally only available from specialist bait dealers.

Chestnut (to 10 per cent):
Primarily used for bream, especially when mixed with coconut. Put in coffee grinder, shell and all.

Linseed (10-15 per cent):
This seed looks like a little tomato pip. When ground down, the mix makes an excellent attractor for small bream. Use with hemp and coconut.

Hemp (to 25 per cent):
This is one of the most important of all ingredients, especially for bottom-feeding fish, particularly roach. It has a lively particle action when first immersed in water after being ground.

It can be grilled after grinding, which improves its powers of attraction.

Maize (to 15 per cent):
A common ingredient in this country. Cook in a casserole or large shallow pan with other ingredients.

Rapeseed (10-15 per cent):
Use in bottom feeds for roach and bream to help bind and give bulk. It is quite oily when ground.

Peanuts (5-15 per cent):
An ingredient with a very high nutritional value and being fairly sticky, it helps bind a feed together to reach the bottom before it disperses. Peanuts are excellent for roach in a high-percentage mix, or bream in smaller quantities. Use either raw, or roasted in a very hot oven, which produces a terrific aroma. Break down in a liquidiser or coffee-grinder to produce a fine powder. A third variation is to mix roasted and uncooked peanuts together.

Pigeon excrement (to 20 per cent):
Widely used in Belgium, this has a very strong, unpleasant smell. It is good for gudgeon and small roach. If using in a mix with hempseed, make the combined total up to 20 per cent maximum.

Coconut (to 20 per cent):
Another high nutritive value ingredient that is an excellent attractor for medium-sized skimmer bream. It is very popular on the Continent and much of the commercial bait produced there for bottom-feeding fish contains it. Frequently used with mollases.

Blood (to 5 per cent):
Dried blood has been used for years in groundbait for tench fishing, but in a continental style application has been found excellent for bigger bream and gudgeon.

Cork (2-3 per cent):
A finely ground powder that is generally used in surface feeds. It will float all day and produces a particle action on the surface.

There are other ingredients that have not been included so far, namely the powders that have special attractive qualities to certain species. To obtain them try either your local specialist bait dealer or health food and Indian food shops. The possibilities are endless but the ones listed have proven fish-catching ability:

Fenugreek: Frequently used in curries, and excellent for roach.
Badienne: Has a similar smell to aniseed and is again good for roach.
Vanilla: A very sweet flavouring, good for bream.
Coriander: Lemon fragrance, good for bleak and roach.
Aniseed: Good for roach.
Fennel: Highly regarded on the Continent – good for roach.

One good method of mixing all these various ingredients is to tip them into a plastic dustbin liner and give the whole lot a really good shake. When you are happy that it is all properly mixed it can be tipped into your mixing bowl and water added. Decide how the mix should end up – stiff for bottom feeding or sloppier for surface and midwater use.

Always try to make mixing your first waterside task, even before you open your rod bag. The reason for this is that the consistency of the feed may change after a short while. The balls that made up perfectly well on mixing, may change consistency as they soak up water. Once you have tackled up turn attention once more to the groundbait, at which stage you can bring it back to the right consistency by adding either more water or more ingredients.

Although the permutations are endless here are two recipes, tried and tested by some of the best match anglers in the country.

Don't be surprised. Lots of girls and women go fishing! And those who find out they like it usually make very good anglers. This lucky fella is a mirror carp

1 **Typical roach recipe** that makes up into 2½lb of groundbait: 1lb breadcrumbs; 8oz maize meal; 4oz sunflower seed; 4oz hemp; 4oz peanuts; 4oz coriander. If you want to feed near the surface, substitute rice for the maize and add more water.

2 **Bream and tench mix** to make up 4¾lb of groundbait: 2lb breadcrumbs; 1lb copra molasses; 8oz poppy seed; 8oz hemp; 4oz coriander; 8oz dried blood.

Modern tackle shops now stock a huge range of commercially-mixed groundbaits which can be used as purchased or with extra ingredients added. These are, almost without exception, very good value for money.

A fantastic double for the fair sex. These are also carp, but scaled all over, denoting that they are common carp

CHAPTER THIRTEEN
THE BLOODWORM

Make no mistake, bloodworm will not make a good angler out of a bad one. They are not the secret formula for success and will not catch fish to order. True they will often get you bites on those days when bigger, more conventional baits such as maggot fail. But badly presented on the wrong tackle they will become just another bait. Bloodworm or no bloodworm the best anglers always come out best in the long run. There is just no short-cut to success.

As a bait, they must rank as the one to have caused the most controversy in recent years. Bans have been imposed – many through no more reason than sheer ignorance. Claims are that it is too expensive and not available to everyone; both claims are without foundation. Many modern tackle shops now sell bloodworm, although they may need to be ordered a week in advance. Mail order suppliers are increasing in number almost daily, and if all else fails it is usually possible to locate a source where they can be collected – absolutely free.

Another myth is that bloodworm are bait suitable for catching only small fish. Skimmer bream just love them and even the bigger bream will take a bunch of four or five. Perch of all sizes, roach, and tench, will all accept bloodworm. In fact they are probably the most natural of all baits, being the staple diet of most fish.

At this stage perhaps it is best to take a look at where these tiny creatures – the larvae of the midge – are found. Here again the humble little worms are surrounded in mystery. In Lancashire you hear many stories of secret bloodworm ponds – secret that is to those anglers who have taken the time and trouble to search them out. In truth there are plenty of waters where bloodworm are to be found, and it can be a lot of fun just hunting for them. The water may be large or small, still or running; if it suits them they will live in it.

Size of the worms will vary from water to water for no obvious reason. One water will produce the very best large worms, while a matter of a mile away a similar water will be full of much smaller ones. Such is the survival rate of these bright-red creatures that it is possible to find a few in long-established puddles or deep cart-ruts that have filled with water. They are tolerant of a high degree of pollution, even to a level that will not permit fish life to exist.

Bloodworm live in the mud that is found on the bottom of rivers and ponds but the actual depth of water over them can vary from a few inches in warm weather to as deep as it is safe to go in chest waders. The colder the weather, the deeper the worms will go. It's rather like following fish from shallows to deeps as the seasons change.

Equipment for gathering bloodworms is simple and easy to make yourself. Firstly you will need a scraper which is best made from a strip of stainless steel about 15in long and 1in wide, tightly bound to a 5ft-long pole with plastic insulation tape. Such a scraper is right for deep water, but you can make up several with different handle lengths for shallower ponds and little streams. The angle between the blade and the shaft is about the same as that between head and shaft of a golf club.

A floating tray will be required into which the freshly gathered worms can be dropped. The best type is really two trays in one, with wooden frames, so that they float without the need for extra buoyancy. One tray fits inside the other, and the inner tray has a coarse mesh bottom that allows the worms to wriggle through but retains bits of weed, twigs and the other rubbish in which the worms live. The outer tray has a bottom of very fine mesh, almost like a tea strainer, so that it retains the worms and very fine peaty material that gets through the larger mesh above. This helps keep the worms, and forms a peaty cloud in the water when you introduce them as feed.

You also need a good pair of chest waders and, for safety, some form of buoyancy aid. A good money-saving tip is to use a couple of 5-litre plastic cans with screw tops, connected to a short length of stout cord. In use the cord is passed between the legs as you enter the water so that one can floats in front of you and the other behind. This rig can serve two purposes. It will save you from a ducking in what can be rather foul and smelly water should you loose your footing, and the extra buoyancy it provides when wading in deep water allows you to traverse very soft pond bottoms into which you would otherwise sink.

The idea of the scraper is that it is pushed through the mud a few inches below the surface. If bloodworm are present they are folded over the leading edge of the blade. The collecting stroke starts by passing the blade in a sweep just through the surface of the mud and continues in an arc until the blade breaks the surface. It will come out covered in mud, bits of leaf and dead weed material and – if you are lucky – bloodworm will be draped along the leading edge. All that's needed now is to wipe the whole lot, weeds and all into your inner collecting tray, and the wriggling worms will do the rest.

At the end of the collecting session the worms are wrapped in damp newspaper, where they will live happily for several days. Keep them cool, but not too cold, and they will stay alive and fresh ready to give you some of the best bait possible for a weekend session.

But having gone to so much trouble to collect this wonderful bait you must make sure that it is used to the best possible effect. They are delicate worms and must be given the right treatment when being placed on the hook. The hook pattern, too, is of great importance. For a single worm a hook of size 22 to 26 is about right. Size is important, but thickness is the critical factor. The wire must be fine; no place here for forged hooks. A good-quality caster hook will be fine, ideally with a small barb or, if you prefer, totally barbless.

Bloodworm, like most baits, can be most effective if hooked in a particular manner. Sink the hook in just anywhere and you will be left with nothing more than a soggy mess of lifeless

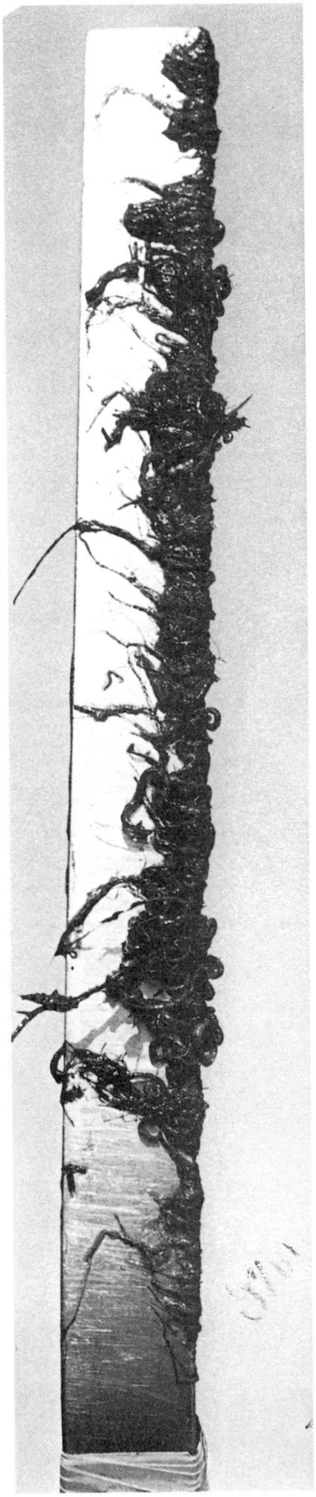

Bloodworms gathered on the leading edge of a scraper blade

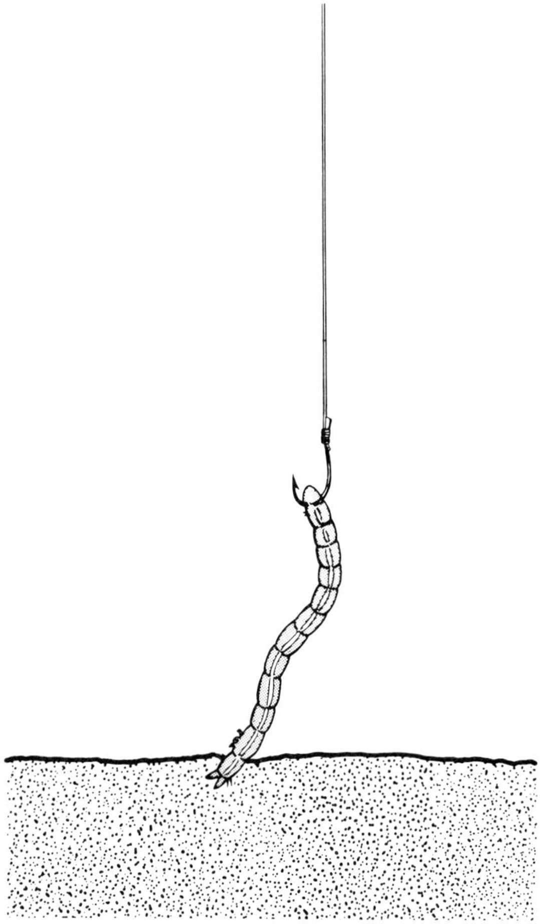

skin. Before hooking your first bloodworm look at it carefully and you will notice that the skin is made up of several segments. At one end, the tiny breathing tubes can be seen, while the other end – the head – has a first segment of much darker colouration. It is this end into which the hook is inserted. But be careful, even at this place the bait is fragile. Pass the point into the very end segment, having first checked that the hook is as sharp as possible.

Having mastered the hooking, the next stage is to present the worm to the fish in the most natural manner, ie with its tail just sitting on the bottom. With a pole rig that is a simple enough matter, but it does need some accurate plumbing. Once the exact depth has been found, simply shallow up ½in and you are in business.

Fig 34 A bloodworm correctly hooked through the first segment of the head. Top bloodworm anglers will endeavour to fish it as shown, just touching the bottom, which is a natural position for bloodworm

ON THE RIVER BANK

CHAPTER FOURTEEN
CHOOSING A SWIM

General advice

The best angler in the world cannot catch a fish if there isn't one in his swim. That statement is obvious enough. But what may not be as clear is just where to fish when you arrive at the waterside.

The inexperienced angler may choose a spot that is comfortable, perhaps with a nice flat bank, with the sun shining on him and the wind at his back. All very pleasant, but not much good if every fish in the river or lake is elsewhere.

Rivers

Let us imagine it is 16 June, the start of a new season, and everything looks so different from when we left the cold damp bankside last March. In those last few days of the old season the best results more than likely came from the deeper, or more steadily-flowing parts of the river. Put that behind you. By 16 June the water temperature will have risen and fish should be more active. When it was cold they didn't move about much, so settled in deep water where they could feed without expending much energy, taking in just enough food to replace the little energy needed to combat the flow. Now they will be recovering from the effects of spawning and will be making for the highly oxygenated water. This means we must fish for them below weirs, or in shallow water running faster than the rest of the river.

Look for a swim that has something 'different' about it – maybe below an outfall or near a ford. Unless you know the river well, ignore those long, deep glides that authors often fantasize about in angling books. Chances are such areas are devoid of fish life at this time of year, unless the water is suffering from a freak flood. On the river Severn, for example, ford swims are the ones to make for. They can be spotted a couple of hundred yards away by the shimmering surface, made as light reflects off the boiling water. And in the height of summer, when sport is slow, fish can be seen turning in those fast swims, some of which may only be a foot or so deep.

Of course the term 'fast' is comparative. On a river like the Severn it may be running no more than a foot deep, with boulders sticking above the surface. On a slower river a 'fast' swim may be several feet deep. So it's really a case of making for the fastest water you can find that is fishable. Look for turbulence on the surface, (Fig A) but remember that it can occur in deep water if there is an obstruction on the bottom.

Such an obstruction may make it a good place to fish at this time of year. In this case it is a sunken log, which provides cover at a time when there is still not much weed growth. But the water is not moving any faster, so don't be fooled. A twig thrown on the surface will be bounced around but probably won't move downstream any faster than the surrounding water. So if you decide to fish the swim shown in Fig B you will need to sit well upstream of the turbulence and trot your tackle down to the obstruction.

It's the easiest thing in the world to miss the hot spot by sitting too near the fish. So be on the safe side by sitting well upstream. The faster the water is flowing the bigger the gap will be between the actual obstruction and the resulting turbulence. This also means that if there are two of you fishing together your swims need to be at least 30yd apart, otherwise the upstream man will not get the full benefit of his swim.

Of course many anglers catch a lot of fish from areas that are not among the shallowest on the river. But if you use the rule-of-thumb, fast-water guide, you're less likely to miss out on the early action. And if you are on a strange river or are not too sure of a water's form, ask an experienced angler. The local tackle shop is always a good source of information.

On the slower rivers of East Anglia, where there are few weir pools or obvious differences between swims, you may have to rely entirely on local knowledge. If you can remember, or can check back in old newspapers, to find out where matches were won last season at the same time, you have a head start on the angler who is going to trust to luck. And even on these slow rivers it will still pay to search out the shallowest water, which is usually at the upstream end of a section between lock gates.

Gravel pits

We look next at gravel pits, to which there has been a big swing in recent years. At the beginning of a season, some species – in particular tench – spend a lot of time in the margins and this is where sport is most likely to be found.

The depth of water close in is not too important, though a spot where it is between 3ft and 8ft is likely to be the most productive. The deeper swims are not so good, they are not rich in weed growth. But in really deep pits, say over 12ft on average, if you can find 10ft it is a good place to start your tench hunt.

Weather plays an important part, and the old adage that tench do not like bright light does not apply to gravel pits, especially if weed growth is sparse. The hotter it is the better gravel-pit tench like it, though bites may come in bursts rather than spread equally over long periods. The reason for this is that gravel-pit tench are cruisers, spending much of their time swimming around. In many pits the traditional dawn start is a waste of time. Chances are greatly improved two hours after the sun has risen, continuing until noon, and deteriorating from then onwards.

This does not apply where bream, roach and chub are concerned, however, for then early, or late after dark sorties are usually better. But fish are unpredictable creatures, and the chances of bream and, to a lesser extent roach, are often good around midday. At such times deep-water swims are usually the most productive, especially if there is not much weed growth. An exception to this is in some heavily weeded pits. In these, roach can often be caught in less than 6ft of water throughout the day, provided the bait is as close as possible to weed.

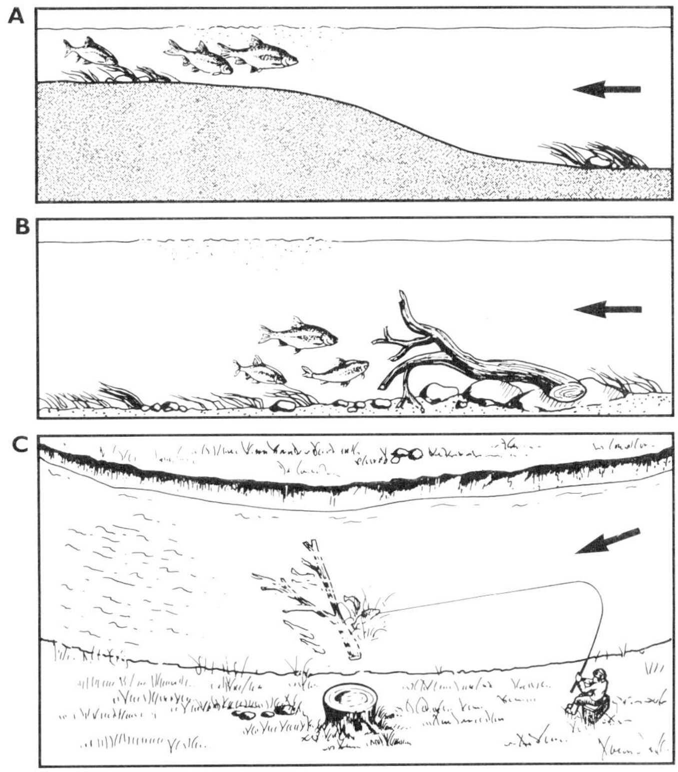

Fig 35 (A) An ideal choice for the beginning of a season. A shallow swim which you can spot by the broken water on the surface. Being shallower it will be flowing faster, and fish will be revelling in this type of swim
(B) Broken water here, also, but caused this time by an obstruction on the bottom. The water below this obstruction will not be flowing faster than the rest of the river, though. This could be a good chub swim
(C) If you fish this swim (middle diagram) bear in mind that the rough water will be downstream of the snag. The faster the river the farther down it will be. So sit well upstream to fish this type of swim: 20 or 30yd may not be too much. Keep feeding and this should draw the fish through the snag, when you will be able to catch them

Natural lakes

Natural lakes can also take some sorting out during the early weeks of the season. Actually picking the right one is the biggest headache of all. So start by selecting one that you know holds fish. Then at least you'll be fishing with confidence on your side.

Most lakes have at least some of the following characteristics and features that will help you to decide where to fish:

An angler prepares to return a barbel to its watery home in the mighty River Severn, one of the best barbel rivers in the country

Bulrush (Scirpus): Usually indicate a gravel or clay bottom and fish will feed right in among the stems. Don't beat all the stems down – they provide cover for both you and the fish. At the beginning of the season tench may be right in among the reeds, which you may spot shaking, even when there is no wind – a sure sign that fish are searching for food.
Reedmace (Typha): Sword-like leaves with big, cigar-shaped seed heads, though these heads will not be present at the start of the season. These plants thrive in soft mud and spread very rapidly, so if a bed of reedmace ends suddenly you can be sure the bottom shelves off quickly or it changes from mud to hard gravel. (Often called bulrush.)

Knowing the difference between the two plants is useful because they indicate a different type of lake bed. Tench, in particular, like the type of bottom bulrushes grow in – a light covering of silt over a gravel bottom. Both the bulrush and reedmace seldom grow in water more than 2½ft deep, so that's a useful indication too.
Waterlilies: Everyone knows what the lily pads look like, and very attractive they are too especially when dotted with flowers. But fishing right against them can often be poor and they are so tough it is almost impossible to drag a big fish from them once it gets among the stems.
Weed beds: Any weed bed will probably be a natural fish-holding area sometime during the day. But the beginner is best advised to avoid areas where weed covers the bottom – usually the shallowest areas.

One advantage the lake angler has over river-based fishing is that during the summer months

The Warwickshire Avon at Twyford. Chub love this type of swim, with overhanging trees and plenty of bankside cover

Autumn sport on the Dorset Stour, one of our very finest angling rivers

fish are usually very active and easy to trace. If possible pay a visit to the lake before fishing it – say the day before – and you will be able to have a good look around and determine where most activity is taking place.

Bream: These roll about on the surface, but the shoals roam about a lot and there is no guarantee that a swim holding bream will still hold them the next day. They tend to have a set patrol pattern, and the bigger the fish the harder they are to find. But their feeding areas are usually the same, so a swim where bream were caught last season may well hold them again a year later. If they are feeding you may see large bubbles rising to the surface and the water will be discoloured. They are likely to be in the same spot for a few hours, so if you see a feeding shoal when you have your tackle with you, take full advantage of it.
Carp: If present, will be one of the easiest fish to locate – they can be seen cruising around near the shore provided they have not been disturbed. A pair of polaroid spectacles will be useful.
Perch: Their holes are pretty obvious – fallen trees or old wooden landing stages; wherever there is an obstruction.
Roach: Will appear almost anywhere during the day but the bigger ones are harder to locate. Late evening or early morning are the best times, for the light is then much softer. When the sun comes up it may pay to go for tench, bream or carp, for they will feed during the day.
Rudd: Given the right conditions they may be feeding on, or near, the surface. They are not difficult to spot and can be tempted with a piece of float-fished bread, a maggot, or small redworm.
Tench: Are likely to produce masses of tiny bubbles. But the idea that they like rooting about in mud is a fallacy. They prefer a harder bottom, which is why they are so often found near bulrushes, not very far from the bank.

The way the wind blows will make no difference to the feeding places of the fish, so there's no sense in fishing into the teeth of a gale. If you have a choice, choose the easiest swim with the wind in your back or to the side. After all you are fishing for pleasure.

Beat the clock
We all suffer blanks. It's part of the delicious uncertainty of fishing. But you can cut down on them if you realise that picking the best time of day to fish is often the key to success. Fish on running waters have to feed constantly to gain energy to combat the flow. But there's no such incentive on stillwaters, and fish here tend to feed only when the temperature and light conditions are ideal. Sun affects fisheries in two ways – it warms up the water and it sends sunlight through it. Both these factors affect the way fish feed and, indeed, whether they will feed at all.

In summer, stillwaters usually cool down during the night. The period just before dawn is often the coolest, and fish may move off the shallows to where the temperature is a degree warmer. For shallow water loses its heat faster than deep water. Yet it also warms up faster, so when the sun first rises it may be sufficient to bring the fish back, if they've moved away. What is certain is that by ten o'clock if it's a boiling hot day, the water may be too warm in the shallows, so the fish move into the cooler, deeper areas for these take longer to warm up. When water is warm it also holds less oxygen, which makes it less attractive to fish. At the same time some species, particularly roach, dislike feeding in bright sunlight. So as a rule of thumb the period before ten o'clock is likely to provide the best fishing.

The one thing which can keep fish feeding all day is a wind which ripples the surface. Not only does the wind usually cool the water, but it cuts down on the amount of light penetrating the surface. If this is combined with strong cloud cover, which cuts down on both light and heat, fishing may be very good.

In late afternoon the water will cool and the sun slowly set until there comes a time when both the water temperature and low light level combine to set fish feeding again. Whether fish feed all night will depend almost entirely on the water temperature.

During winter the water is mostly too cold for fish to keep feeding all day. So you should aim to fish when the water is at its warmest. An early start is often fruitless in winter, especially on stillwaters or slowly moving rivers. It's better to start fishing at noon when the sun is at its highest. The hours between one o'clock and three o'clock are often the best. You have only to see how many matches are won in the last hour in winter.

On faster rivers the effects of temperature and

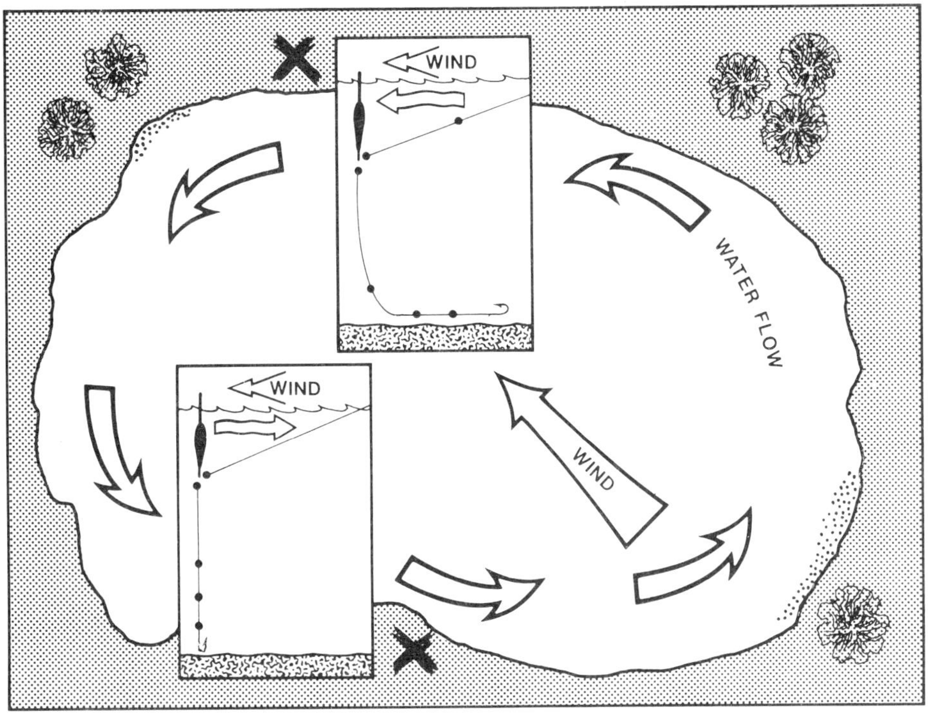

Fig 36 The effect of wind on a lake. If you have it over one shoulder (bottom swim marked X) the drift will be against the wind so you can fish with your bottom shot *off* bottom (bottom inset). However, if you sit facing the wind (top X) the drift and the wind will be working together, and you will need to drag a shot on the bottom to slow the bait up (top inset)

light changes are not usually so pronounced. In summer the water tends to be cooler, so you can hope for fish through most of the day. And in winter, though the overall temperature may be as low as that on a stillwater, the fish, being more used to it, are not so badly affected. And they have to keep eating to obtain energy.

To be more specific as to what happens in a lake: when the whole of the lake has reached 4°C a strange phenomenon takes place. At that temperature water is at its densest, so if the surface cools to 3° it will not sink. The only circulation which now takes place is that caused by wind. Consequently the surface soon reaches zero degrees and freezes. Yet the water at the bottom of the lake is still 4° warmer! That is one reason why it can be dangerous to break ice on a small pond; you are disturbing water at the bottom which would otherwise provide a safe haven for fish in semi-hibernation. In many instances it is the only place where fish will feed. On Britain's deepest lakes, such as those in the Lake District, the water remains almost constant at 4° all year round.

When spring comes, however, the shallow water heats up much more quickly than the deeps, and when it gets warmer than 4°, you are likely to find the fish there. For the same reason you may catch fish for an odd hour or two in the winter in shallow water if there is bright sun and no cooling wind. Best of all is a warm wind, as this affects a much greater area of water in a short time.

In stillwaters, the water in the deepest holes is nearly always coolest in summer; yet in winter it's warmest. The reason is that the sun warms the top of a lake first, but it may take a long time before the bottom waters are warmed because cold water is denser than warm water, and it stays at the bottom. So it needs strong winds to circulate the water. It may be July before the deepest areas start to feel much benefit. That water will almost always be colder than the shallows in summer, and the fish gravitate towards it when the shallows become too hot and devoid of oxygen.

In winter the reverse takes place and the heat is lost from the surface first. This water, now being colder than the rest, sinks to the bottom. No wind is needed, which is why water loses its temperature much more quickly than it can gain it. Within a week or two the water on a lake can have lost an enormous amount of heat – 20 degrees Farenheit or more.

Here are some tips on the conditions fish tend to like. Remember that the biggest fish of most species often refuse to obey the rules, and are often the only ones caught on that day. Frequently they are taken in conditions in which, theoretically, they shouldn't be feeding:

Barbel: Affected mainly by water temperature and less by the amount of sunlight on the water. Feed only spasmodically in winter.
Bream: The most finicky of all the species. Night is often best, but given a ripple and warm wind they will feed all day in very warm water. They always prefer a rising water temperature to one that is dropping. In summer a drop of half a degree can put them off. But in winter, even with the water near freezing, they will sometimes feed in rivers in coloured water if it warms up a degree and holds that temperature for twenty-four hours. Occasionally they appear to break all the rules and feed all day in brilliant sunshine; but almost always when the water temperature is rising.
Carp: Will feed all day and all night, given a reasonably high water temperature. In winter they will feed given a slight rise in temperature, but often for only a couple of hours. Many of the biggest carp are taken at night because this is the time when lakeside banks are quietest. They will cruise the margins all night. Like rudd they will come off the bottom in very warm water.
Chub: Active fish, and although the biggest ones will feed at night the shoal fish of up to 5lb prefer a fair amount of light. They often stop feeding as the light fades. Will tolerate huge temperature ranges and quick drops and falls. But dislike water containing large amounts of suspended silt.
Dace: More affected by the amount of silt in water than by the temperature. But they will feed in most conditions since they are active fish, found

There is excellent fishing in the middle of many English towns. This is the Embankment at Trent Bridge, in the heart of Nottingham

mainly in our faster rivers. Summer is the best time, though, apart from when they are massing to spawn.

Eels: Night time definitely best, with the finest conditions a hot summer's night, as black as possible, with thunder in the air. Tiny little 'bootlace' eels will feed all day. Mainly caught in summer, though occasionally they will feed in high flood.

Perch: A predator which needs a fair amount of light in which to hunt its prey. Most good perch are taken in daytime.

Pike: Generally regarded as a daytime fish, though some anglers hunt them at night. In winter the traditional clear, frosty day is probably good – not because of the frost but because of the light which pike need (like perch) to hunt in. There may be a brief flurry as the light fades, but usually pike stop feeding as the big roach start.

Roach: The better fish will come on as the light fades. If you're after quality roach it's worth stopping until you can hardly see your float. Unlike bream, roach will tolerate a fairly wide range of temperatures. Like bream, the stronger the wind and the denser the cloud cover the better the chance of a big catch. But small ones will feed all day.

Rudd: Will feed in most conditions in summer, staying near weed in bright sunlight and moving into open water as the light fades. If it gets very hot, rudd are one of the last fish to stop feeding. Not so tolerant of cold water as roach, though.

Tench: Mainly a summer fish; they bury themselves in mud during winter. Floods sometimes get them moving, otherwise they prefer the same conditions as bream. However they will continue to feed in bright sunlight for longer after the bream has stopped. In winter on stillwaters they need mild conditions for some days before they come out of their semi-hibernation. Dawn is always a good time to spot the stillwater tench, which puts up large areas of tiny bubbles in shallow water as it feeds.

Finding a carp hotspot

Success at carp fishing depends very much on the amount of energy put into it. There are the easy ways out, taking short cuts by watching other anglers and jumping into the swims that have a good track record of producing a lot of fish. But even if you are lucky enough to find yourself in the 'hot spot' there is still a lot of work to be done in order to get the best results.

The swim may be 150yd or more across and anything up to 100yd wide. Just where you fish in all that water is something you still need to work out. In order to get the best from that swim you may have to concentrate on it for many weeks on end – maybe the whole season. Do that and you will build up a mental picture of what it is like beneath the surface. You will know every gravel bar, how silty the gullies are, where the drop off starts and where each of those gravel bars ends.

A day spent plumbing the depth and mapping the contours will be a day well spent. If it is possible, and allowed on the waters you fish, a boat and a depthfinder can be a great help. When you come across deep gullies, which usually collect a lot of silt, find out how deep that silt is because when a fish passes through the area you are not going to catch it if your bait is buried in a foot of bottom debris.

To find the silt, cast out a heavy lead and allow it to settle, slowly winding back and watching the surface. Silt will show itself by giving off a fine line of bubbles. Actual depth of the silt can be found by marking the end few feet of your line with Tipp-Ex (typewriter correcting fluid), which will go dark as the silt stains the white coating.

Having this knowledge of bottom conditions can also help with groundbaiting. On big windy waters carp move around very fast and the only way to hold them for long in one place is by having a lot of free samples lying around. Again they are no good, if like the hookbait they are buried in a foot of silt. The samples should, in any case, be buoyant enough to rest on top of whatever layers the bottom is made up of.

Fig 37 The key to stillwater fishing in Winter is catching the water at its warmest. This is nearly always when the sun is at its highest . . . between around 1 pm and 3 pm.

Contrast this to a Summer's day, when by 10 am the water is too hot to provide consistent fishing, and often doesn't cool down again until around 7.30 pm.

Note the steep decline in water temperature in Winter – if you stop getting bites, then it's highly unlikely that the fish will come back on the feed.

Fig 38 Carp will move into shallow water during the evening and move out again when the sun comes up. This plan shows roughly where you can expect to find the carp during daylight on a typical summer's day

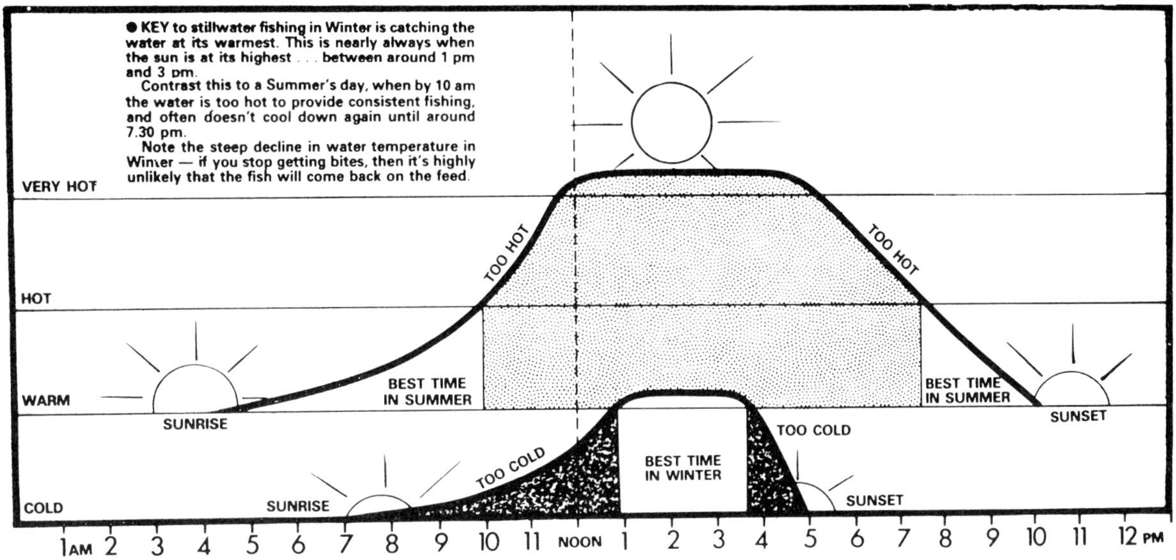
● KEY to stillwater fishing in Winter is catching the water at its warmest. This is nearly always when the sun is at its highest . . . between around 1 pm and 3 pm.
Contrast this to a Summer's day, when by 10 am the water is too hot to provide consistent fishing, and often doesn't cool down again until around 7.30 pm.
Note the steep decline in water temperature in Winter — if you stop getting bites, then it's highly unlikely that the fish will come back on the feed.
VERY HOT
HOT
WARM
COLD
TOO HOT
TOO HOT
BEST TIME IN SUMMER
BEST TIME IN SUMMER
SUNRISE
SUNSET
TOO COLD
TOO COLD
BEST TIME IN WINTER
SUNRISE
SUNSET
1AM 2 3 4 5 6 7 8 9 10 11 NOON 1 2 3 4 5 6 7 8 9 10 11 12 PM

Fig 37

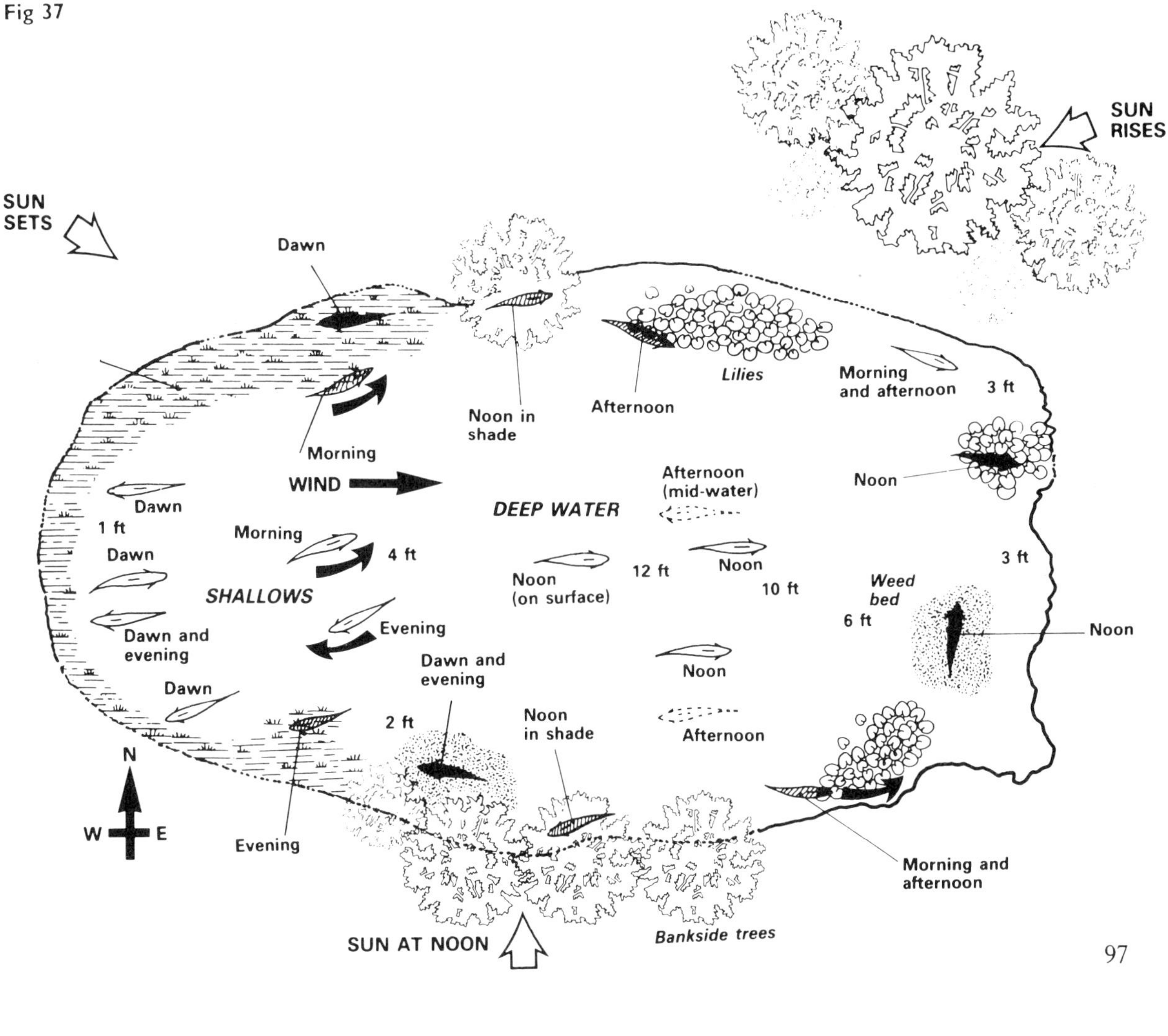
SUN RISES
SUN SETS
Dawn
Lilies
Noon in shade
Afternoon
Morning and afternoon
3 ft
Morning
WIND
Afternoon (mid-water)
Noon
Dawn
DEEP WATER
1 ft
Morning
Dawn
4 ft
Noon (on surface)
12 ft
Noon
3 ft
10 ft
Weed bed
SHALLOWS
6 ft
Noon
Dawn and evening
Evening
Dawn and evening
Noon
Dawn
2 ft
Noon in shade
Afternoon
N
W
E
Evening
Morning and afternoon
SUN AT NOON
Bankside trees

An idyllic summer's day on Norfolk's scenic River Bure at Wroxham

Knowing the ends of gravel bars is very important. In many cases these ends are almost vertical drops beneath which a lot of silt and food ends up. Carp will cruise along the drops, feeding off the sides, generally from the direction of the wind. A bait placed on the opposite side of the bar will not be found. Nor will its flavours attract such fish, because currents run down the gullies and not up and over the bar.

By placing a bait at the drop off where a gravel bar ends the angler is in fact doubling his chances, because it will be encountered by fish whichever side of the bar they choose to feed along. Once again a good carpet of free food offerings will increase your chances. Fish will move through maybe many times during the day, and the longer they can be kept in the area the better the chances of them picking up your hookbait.

SPECIALIST TACTICS

CHAPTER FIFTEEN
LEGERING

Introduction

There's hardly a water in the land that will not, at some time, respond to good legering techniques. Yet all too often the method is looked upon as a 'chuck it and chance' idea to try when float fishing has failed to produce a good catch. Neither is there a fish that cannot be caught on a leger and as a method it can often have many advantages over float fishing. For example, it is less likely to be affected by wind, is less complicated than float rigs, is more accurate, is quicker in that there are fewer false casts, it makes possible a longer cast, and is often the method to locate the bigger fish which so often prefer to take a still bait. The one disadvantage it has is that a badly weeded bottom may make it ineffective.

To the beginner a large lump of lead may look crude when compared with a float rig. In fact nothing could be further from the truth. The bream anglers of Fenland use legers to catch shy, often delicately feeding fish and legering has been developed by match anglers into a fine art.

Swingtips

The greatest step forward came in the 1950s when Boston's Jack Clayton invented the swingtip. That single invention enabled anglers to abandon the normal butt indicator – a method that required a lot of careful setting up – and instead see a bite develop from the rod end where there was no resistance from rod rings and angles formed in the line. But like all indicators the swingtip comes in many forms developed to deal with a range of conditions.

Jack Clayton swingtip The original Jack Clayton tip is still one of the favourites with Fenland anglers. It is 15in long with an extruded link which is part of the main nylon stem. The stiffness of the link prevents the tip twisting round and snagging line, something which happens all too often with a soft link. The Clayton tip is ideal for windy days and can also be made to work in fast water – possibly one of the conditions that is not ideal for swingtipping.

Medium length swingtip Very similar to the Clayton but with a shorter link. This design works well on days when there is very little wind.

Extra fine swingtip A very fine, 12in long tip made from an old quivertip. It is very sensitive indeed and can only be used if there is no wind.

Armed with those three tips you should be able to fish most waters when conditions are suited to swingtipping. But if you find the tip will not stay at an angle steep enough for a bite to register, the chances are a quivertip is the correct indicator to select.

Quivertips

Quivertips, even more than swingtips, come in a very wide range of lengths and strengths. They can either screw into a threaded end-ring of the leger rod or be part of the actual rod tip, a spliced section known as a donkey top.

Use a quivertip when the water is flowing too fast for a swingtip or if conditions are very rough. You can tighten up to a quivertip in a strong wind and still be able to see bites. The quivertip is very good for roach fishing in that if you miss the little knock of a bite moving the tip forwards you get a second chance as it returns to its original setting.

When selecting tips consider the conditions and what they will be asked to do. On slow-moving water a parallel tip will indicate bites best, but when the water is pulling hard a tip with a taper, thinning towards the extreme end, is best. That is the general rule but look at the diagrams on the following pages for a more detailed check.

Springtips

Following development of swingtips and quiver-

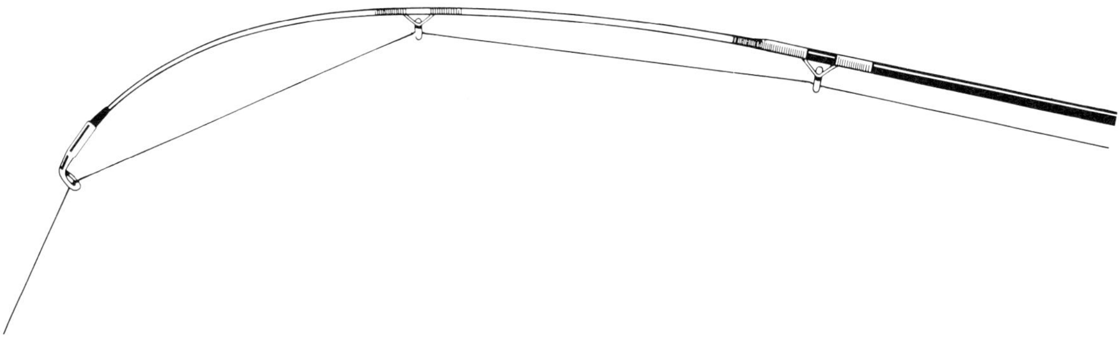

tips the next stage was a combination of the two – the springtip. Main advantage is that, unlike with a quivertip, a biting fish feels no build-up of resistance as it pulls the tip round. This is due to the small spring that replaces what would have been the link on a swingtip or the stiff butt end of the quiver.

Some of the best springtips are adjustable and can be set in many different ways simply by pulling the tip further out from the spring into which it sits. When fully located the tip will stand out straight like a quivertip until a bite develops, at which stage the spring begins to bend.

By pulling the tip out from the spring an angler can effectively weaken the spring tension. This can go on in stages until the springtip almost becomes a conventional swingtip, hanging downwards from the rod at a steep angle. Overall a very versatile tip that will cover almost all legering situations (see Fig 40).

The line itself

The oldest of all indicators must be the line itself and if used correctly it can be very deadly indeed. This system is known as 'slack lining' and the only drawback is that it cannot be used on running water.

No special indicator is used, instead the angler watches the line between rod top and water. A bite is signalled by line streaking away. If you can fish this method it is the most sensitive of all indicators, but as an added insurance try it with a quivertip attached – at least until you are confident enough to go direct to the rod top.

Butt indicators

Finally, no section on legering indicators would be complete without at least a mention of the butt

Fig 39 Quivertip rods have a light, spliced-in section at the tip end designed to show bites. A tapered one as shown will tend to be more sensitive than a parallel one. But a parallel quivertip may be easier to spot bites on as it bends throughout the whole of its length. Experiment to see which you prefer

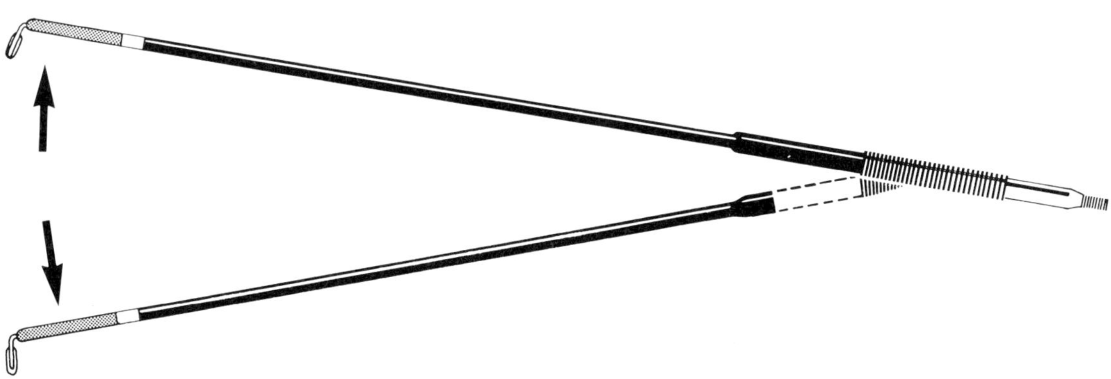

Fig 40 A springtip. The spring bends in the middle when you get a bite. But the quivertip can be pushed down into the spring, stiffening it, and bites are then shown as a bend in the tip

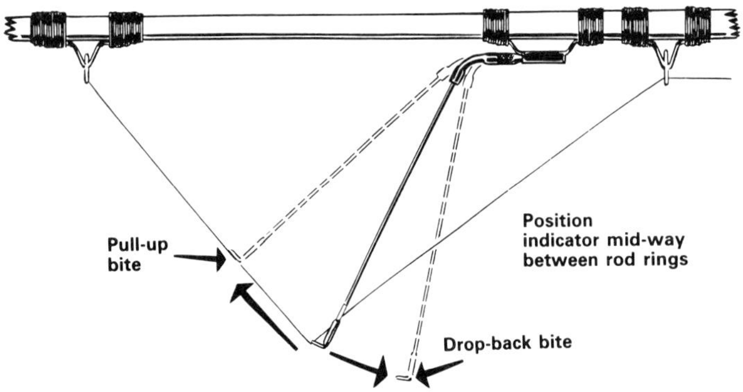

Fig 41 Adjust your bite indicator so that it will show both lift and drop-back bites

type. But compared with the other indicators already covered they are a very poor second, demanding very careful setting. The only time when a butt indicator can really score is when fished under extremely bad conditions. By sheltering a butt indicator behind an umbrella, bites can still be seen; but at all times getting line to point straight down from leger weight to butt indicator is vital.

Target boards

Although bite detection when legering is not difficult, a few simple additions to your tackle can prevent you going boss-eyed by squinting down the length of your rod. Watch a swingtip or quivertip for long enough and your eyes will begin to play tricks. Windy conditions make this even worse. The last time the tip moved was it a bite or just the wind?

What is wanted is some form of shelter for the tip and a marker to which it can be aligned. An umbrella of course makes the ultimate in windbreaks, but there really is little fun in sitting out in the pouring rain while your swingtip enjoys the warmth and comfort of complete shelter. The answer is some form of target board that offers both protection for the tip from wind and also, as the name suggests, gives the angler a target on which to 'set' his eye against the tip.

A simple target is an extra bank stick pushed into the ground or allowed to jut from the bank a few inches beyond the tip. Even an old float set in the ground will be enough to line up on. But a clear plastic board, suitably painted with stripes or lines, is even better. Now both sight and

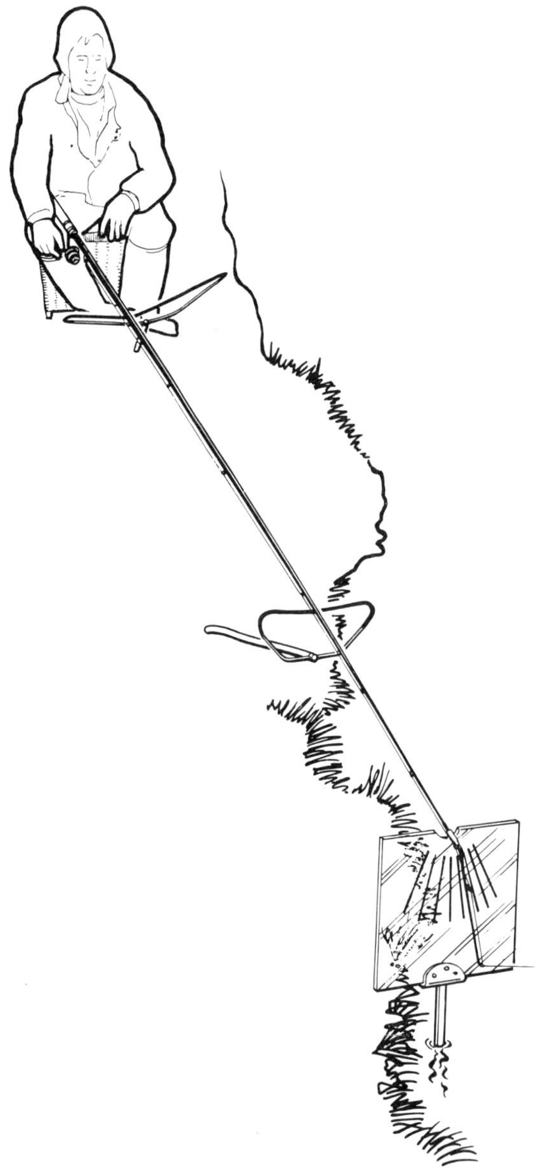

Fig 42 Target boards are popular with swingtip anglers. They shield the tip from wind and enable the angler to see shy bites more easily

One of Britain's top match anglers, Kim Milsom, lands a common carp at Arrow Valley Lakes, Redditch

protection has been taken care of in one go. And if a suitable vee is cut into the board's top edge and a screw fitted to the bottom edge, it will also serve as a rest.

In the case of swingtips the tip is allowed to sit alongside the board, either in front or behind depending on wind direction. With a quivertip it is often best to actually point the tip at the board, placing the target a few inches away.

Although the target board acts as a rest very close to the rod tip, a second rest will be called for some distance back along the rod to prevent sagging. A correctly rested rod should remain straight. If it is allowed to sag in the middle, striking will be difficult.

Striking

One of the most common mistakes when legering is to strike before a bite has properly developed – and that's a statement that is true whether the quarry is roach, bream or barbel. With bream it is vital not to hook a fish and then lose it. For if you do so before the shoal has settled down it will almost certainly move away. Far better to sit with your arms folded while you wait for that first bite. It may look a lazy way to fish, but at least it prevents you from striking too early. If the bite doesn't develop, nothing has been lost. Given time the feeding shoal will get bolder and sooner or later your indicator will register a proper bite.

Of course there will be those days when bites just fail to develop into full blown pulls that send the tip flying round or out straight. And on those tricky outings you may have to take a chance and try hitting a twitch that would otherwise be left. It's a chancy game but the risk is one you will have to calculate for yourself.

However there is another trick that is a favourite with bream anglers; it also works with most other fish when you know they are there but not too keen to feed. Twitching is the thing to try. This involves making the bait move slightly on the bottom so that a browsing fish is attracted by a sudden movement. It believes its next meal is about to escape and may make a grab.

To begin a twitching session, cast as usual and allow the bait to rest in its normal static manner. If a bite doesn't develop, gently lift the rod just enough to move the lead an inch or so, wind up the slack and be ready for a real sail-away bite. Often this is so sudden that a swingtip will not settle back after you've pulled the bomb. Watch out too, for dropback bites which cause the tip to remain slack even as you tighten up with the reel.

Take care on those hard days and you will catch a lot more fish. For example always cast to the nearside of a shoal. Even if you know there are a lot of fish to be caught this little trick will help keep them feeding longer. If, for example, a bream shoal is known to feed along the middle of a river don't start by casting beyond the middle. Instead fish well towards your side and see what happens. Bites may not come, which calls for a slightly longer throw until eventually contact is made. A good indication is a series of line bites. If they occur, shorten again as it means you have gone beyond the shoal and fish are bumping into the line. By fishing from your side of the shoal hooked fish will not be pulled through the others as they feed. It's yet another old trick used by those crafty Fenland bream experts – and it works.

Actual positioning of the rod is critical when legering and with one or two exceptions it always pays to get the tip, quivertip or swingtip, as low as possible to the water surface. On a stillwater you will be best with your back to the wind although of course a swingtip can be fished in almost any position. With a quivertip you should aim to make an angle of roughly 90° between tip and line. So if you cast directly in front of you a quivertip rod will need to be positioned almost parallel with the bank.

On running water however it is important to strike across the current rather than upstream, for the flow of water will assist you in setting the hook correctly into the fish. In order to achieve this the rod will need to be positioned downstream after casting.

The exception is when fishing more or less downstream of your spot. In which case place the rod so that it points directly out in front of you. In this position a strike will pull line directly upstream rather than across it, thus creating the minimum amount of resistance.

Striking should also be a sweep rather than a short sharp snatch. For with legering you have to take the stretch out of the line, get the leger weight moving and at the same time set the hook firmly. With the right rod and correctly balanced tackle it is possible to strike with a follow-through style action and get the fish – especially bream –

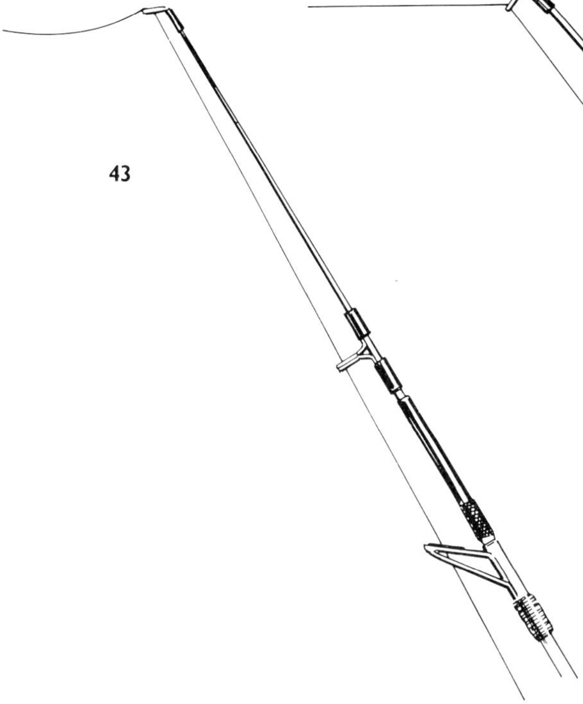

43

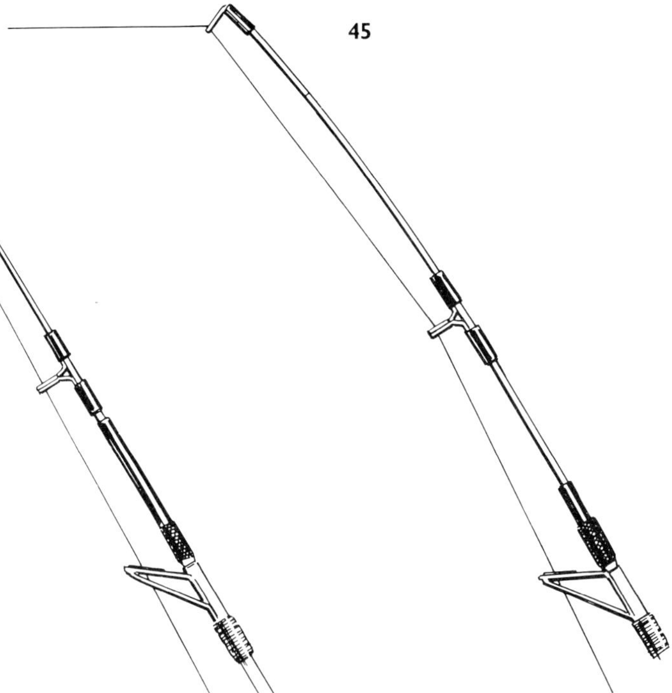

45

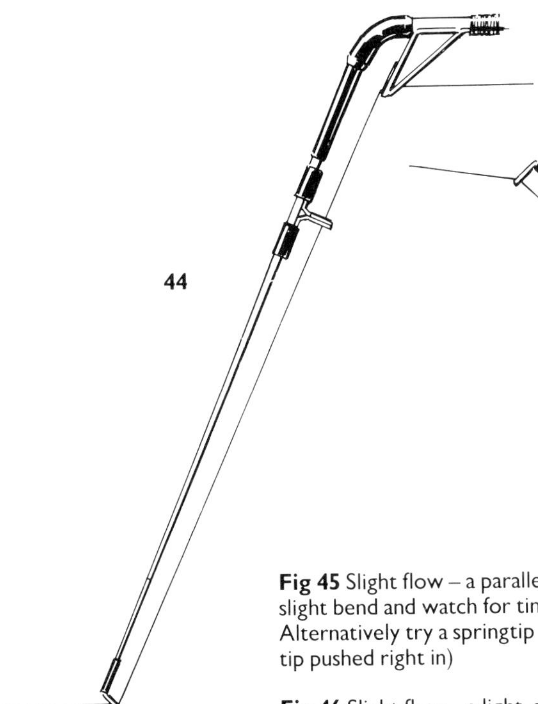

44

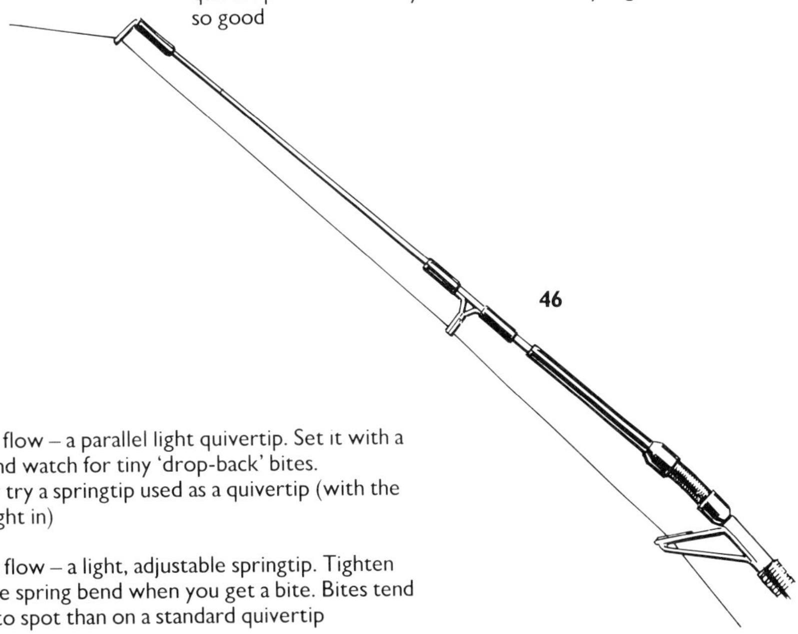

46

Fig 43 No flow – slack-lining (watching the line for bites) but with a very sensitive tapered quivertip as an insurance against the water starting to move or drift

Fig 44 No flow – swingtipping with a broken quivertip pushed into a rubber link. This will be better than a quivertip fished normally for those whose eyesight is not so good

Fig 45 Slight flow – a parallel light quivertip. Set it with a slight bend and watch for tiny 'drop-back' bites. Alternatively try a springtip used as a quivertip (with the tip pushed right in)

Fig 46 Slight flow – a light, adjustable springtip. Tighten and watch the spring bend when you get a bite. Bites tend to be easier to spot than on a standard quivertip

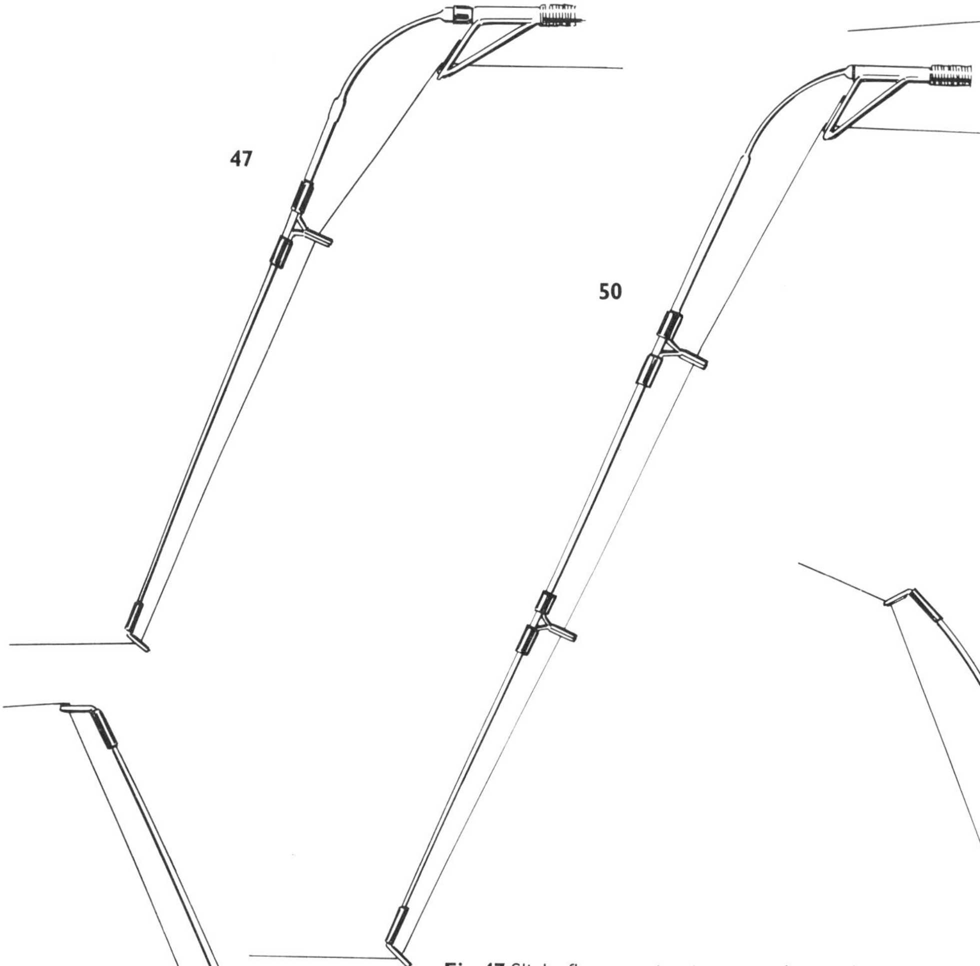
47

50

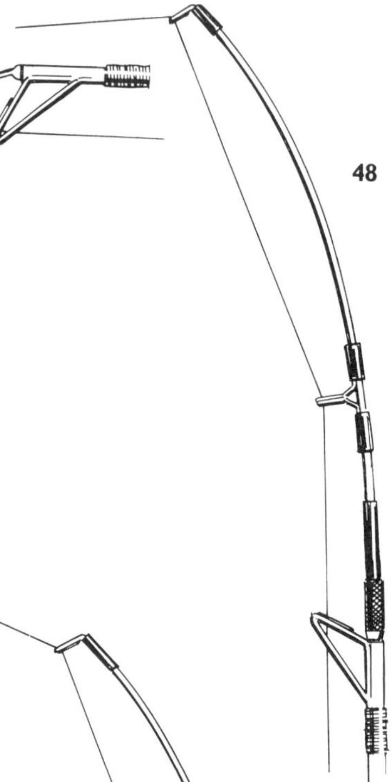
48

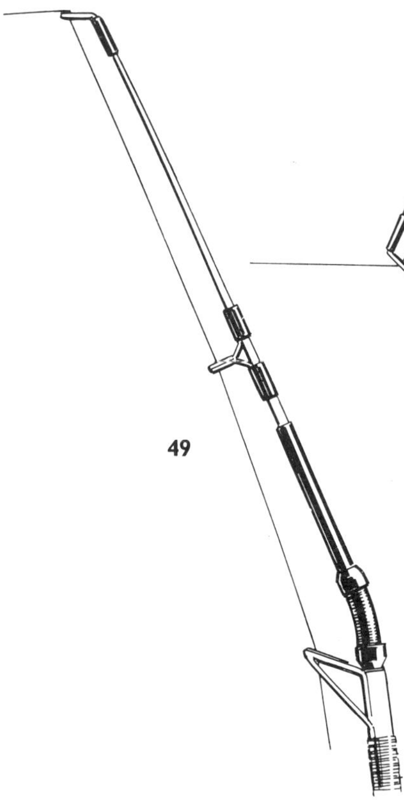
49

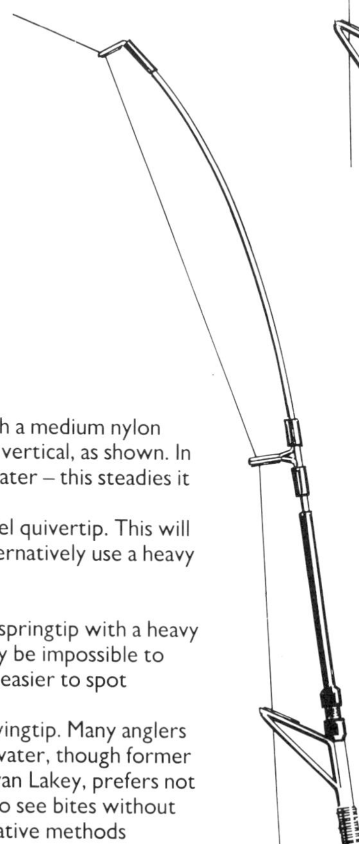
51

Fig 47 Slight flow – swingtipping with a medium nylon swingtip. Tighten so the tip is almost vertical, as shown. In wind let it touch the surface of the water – this steadies it

Fig 48 Medium blow – a heavy parallel quivertip. This will not bend too much in fast water. Alternatively use a heavy springtip pushed right in

Fig 49 Medium flow – the strongest springtip with a heavy spring. If the water is too fast this may be impossible to use. But if you can, you will find bites easier to spot

Fig 50 Medium flow – a long, 15in swingtip. Many anglers wrap wire round the end in flowing water, though former National and Embassy Champion, Bryan Lakey, prefers not to. If conditions are too bad for him to see bites without wire on, he will use one of the alternative methods

Fig 51 Strong flow – a stiff, parallel quivertip is the only answer. Alternatively, a springtip with the stem pushed right in, or a specially-built feeder rod

moving away from others in the shoal. Once you've got a fish moving, keep it going. Reduce the pressure and it will turn back towards the others and maybe panic them into moving off.

Long-range legering

Legering is a method that can often call for long-distance casting – often 50 or 60yd, even more on the big waters where bream are the main target. But as distance increases so do the problems of using fine tackle. A conventional 3lb breaking strain line is just not capable of throwing a leger weight of anything up to an ounce over such ranges.

What is needed is something to absorb the shock without loading up with a much thicker line that in itself will only serve to reduce the distance achieved and create more resistance to a biting fish. The answer is to be found in a 'shock leader'; which is a length of stronger line knotted to the end of the standard reel line. Making up a shock leader is simple, but there are a few rules that need to be followed for best results.

But firstly let us look at the shock leader principle. In fact we are building a strong section into the tackle – a section that can take the initial shock of launching the leger weight on its journey. The leader, while being able to take the shock still allows the main reel line to remain at 3lb or even less in some cases. Remember however that it is always unwise to knot two pieces of line together if they vary greatly in diameter. Any variance of over a 1lb in breaking strain is likely to cause problems at the knot.

Let us assume we are making up a shock leader to a 3lb main line. In such a case a leader of 4lb will be knotted by means of a water knot. Keep the end facing the hook long enough to be used as a link to which the leger can be attached later, while at the top end take special care to clip all loose ends off neatly. Length of the leader is decided by the total of rod length plus the amount of line outside the top ring, plus enough to ensure that half a dozen turns remain on the reel prior to casting.

Once the shock leader is in place it may be beneficial to step down to the hook length by means of a secondary piece of line. For example, if the shock leader is 4lb strain and the hook length required is 1lb, a length of 2½lb would be needed to 'step down' between the two.

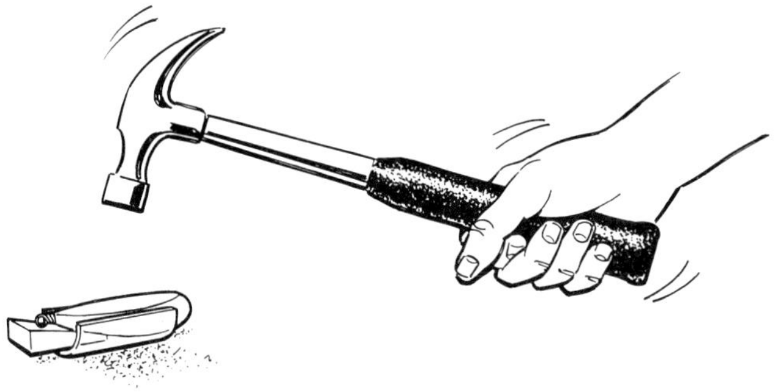

Fig 52 In running water flattening a leger weight helps it hold bottom

Distance casting also calls for accuracy and a leger of reasonable weight. If you are struggling to get the distance with a light bomb you have little chance in maintaining the required accuracy. Far better to opt for a bomb of ½oz or even ¾oz and reach the correct spot with ease. It will also allow you to tighten up much quicker to the bait after it hits bottom.

Correct bomb weight is possibly more important on stillwaters than on rivers. On lakes the bait needs to be cast and stay put; but in the case of running water a bomb that can be eased along the bottom by the current will often prove to be a real killer.

Always be prepared to make minor changes to bomb weight by adding split shot. By carefully adding a little more weight at a time, it is possible to get a bait to gently bump along in a very natural manner. Arlesey bombs were designed by the late Richard Walker for long-distance casting but they have, over the years, become the standard leger weight for almost all waters. Some modifications can, however, be made to enable a lead of a certain size to hold bottom in a much stronger current than the normal-shaped lead.

To 'improve' the lead for this style of fishing you will need a piece of metal pipe cut horizontally into which a bomb can be laid and then flattened on one size with a hammer. Prepared in this way the flat side will settle better on the bottom of the river and be less inclined to get pulled off downstream.

On hard fished waters another little trick is to camouflage leger weights by painting them a colour that matches the bottom. There is nothing more likely to scare a shy bream shoal than a shiny leger weight falling through the water only inches in front of their noses. Choice of colour is not too important, anything black, brown or green is going to settle into the general background.

Float legering

Float legering is rarely used nowadays. Yet apart from giving an angler a float to watch (and that's always more exciting than watching a swingtip or other bite indicator) it can, in certain circumstances, beat straightforward legering hands down.

Take a lake in summer, when banks of weed line the margins and it is impossible to tighten up to your leger weight without the line catching in that weed. If you manage to fish, there's still the problem of seeing a bite. Indeed if the fish feels resistance it will be likely to drop the bait altogether. There's a problem even if the weed doesn't reach up to the surface. It's down there somewhere, and you may feel it as you retrieve. It may even snag you completely. But put a float on and the line can lie on the surface or just under it, away from the weed beds.

Fig 53 The float leger is a very old style of fishing, but useful for keeping a bait over marginal weed without the line tangling in it. Fish well overdepth and tighten the line until the float just shows above surface

The way to rig up is as follows. Set the float well overdepth; in 8ft of water put it at least 10ft from the leger weight. Cast out to your chosen spot, and tighten until the float cocks. A further, minor adjustment will bring it down so that only the tip is showing. The rougher the conditions the more float you leave above the surface. If you are able to do so, put your rod tip under the water as you tighten up, and leave it there when the float is set. You will find the float sets better. Remember that if you lock a float on the line with shot they should be only small, otherwise you can't tell when your line is tight to the float.

Float legering in moving water is more difficult, but on rivers like the Welland in Lincolnshire which flows only slowly and has a lot of marginal weed in summer, this is a killing method. Once you've got the hang of it, substitute the fixed float shown in the diagram for a sliding float. You'll find it easier to cast.

Swimfeeders

Next time you haul out a big catch of chub or barbel on a feeder rig be thankful that Cockney anglers of the 1940's were thinking men. For it was the capital's anglers that did so much to develop swimfeeder fishing from a crude method to a highly skilled art.

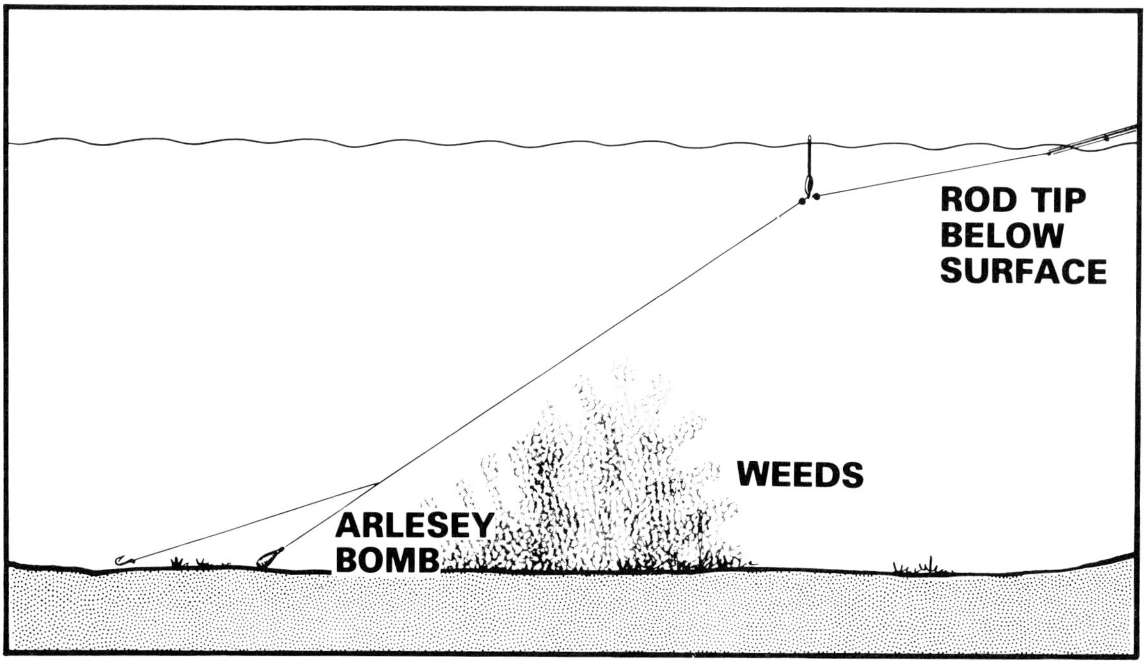

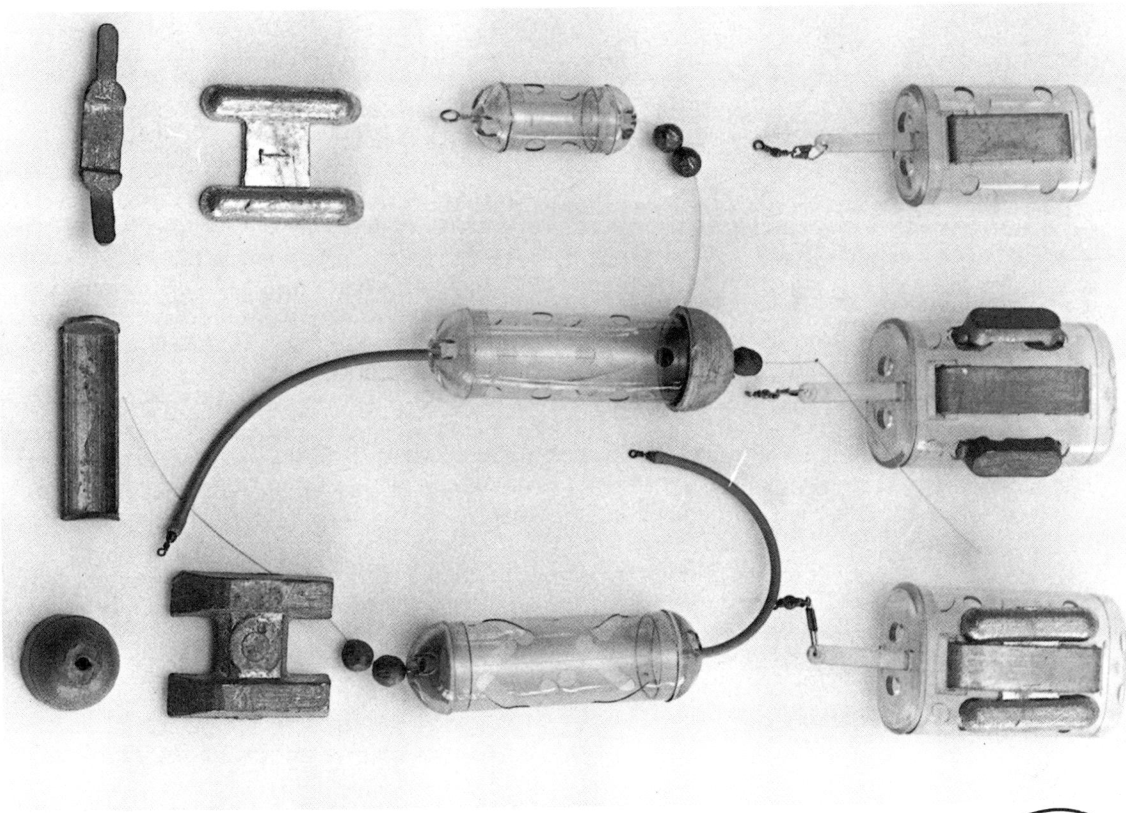

Fig 54 There is a great variety of swimfeeders and weights for the modern angler to use

Necessity brought about the evolution of the feeder. For in those days Londoners always fished their matches to a size-limit rule and bleak were not allowed. Not only were undersized fish not weighed in, but if you had one in your net it was a matter for disqualification. Even non-match anglers were intent on avoiding the hordes of bleak that swarmed up rivers such as the Thames. And the first stage in catching the better quality fish and not bleak was by the use of hemp, which sank more quickly than maggots and was not so attractive to the surface feeding fish.

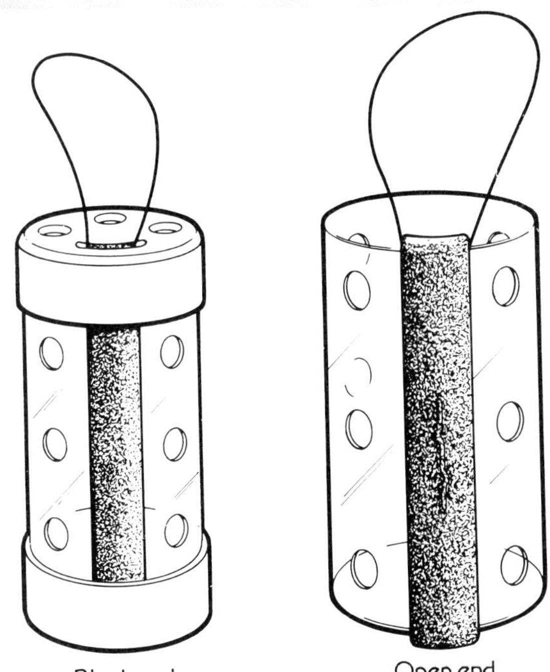

Fig 55 The two main types of swimfeeder. (Left) The block-end, named because it has a cap on each end. (Right) The open-ended feeder, which is plugged at each end with groundbait. There are other types, but all are based on these two patterns

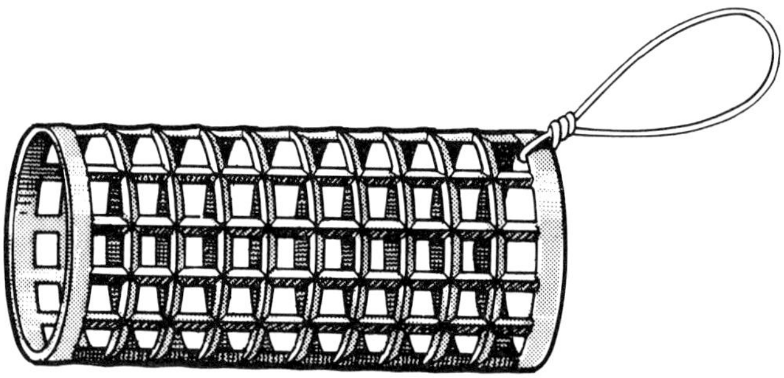

Fig 56 One of the first ever swimfeeders – a hair-roller. These were used in the London area before World War II

Then someone had the idea of using a metal hair curler to hold groundbait. This was cast a great distance to get to fish in mid-river where the float anglers had difficulty in feeding. It sank straight through the bleak shoals and allowed a little cloud of groundbait to lie on the bottom very close to the hookbait. But the hair curler didn't hold much groundbait – it had to be pressed in through the holes; so the next idea was a plastic tube with lead down the side to make it sink quickly. That was how the first real swimfeeder was born.

Eventually maggots were used in feeders, placing them in the middle with each end plugged with groundbait. So the development continued. Dry groundbait was next to go into the middle of the feeders. This gave off a cloud that proved deadly for roach when fished in conjunction with bread on the hook; it's a trick that still gets results today. Then came the greatest time saver of all. Someone thought of stapling a shot-box lid to the end of the feeder tube. Then maggots were placed inside the feeder and groundbait used to plug the open end. Finally this was improved by caps being fitted to both ends with holes in the feeder and caps for maggots to crawl through.

At first anglers outside London looked upon the method as crude, but as southerners started to fish more and more matches in the north – and perhaps more important, winning – feeder fishing continued to grow in popularity. Barbel took over the river Severn and the feeder proved to be a winner with this powerful fish. Huge bags made the headlines and feeder fishing had arrived in a big way. But why use a swimfeeder? It is a fair question from anyone who has not seen them in action.

If we take the example of fast water on a big river such as the Severn, Trent or Wye, putting in bait on its own is just not going to work. It will be carried away downstream out of range of either float or leger tackle.

You could try mixing it in hard balls of groundbait, but it takes an experienced angler to do this well and it also takes a lot of groundbait and time spent moulding it into balls. A feeder is the perfect answer to the problem for it regulates the amount of bait put in with each cast according to how fast the fish are biting. If you get a lot of bites you'll be casting more often, so more refilling of the feeder will result in a constant supply of feed. If bites are slow, the fact of fewer casts limits the free supply.

For the novice angler it is the best way of

Fig 57 Basic rig for attaching a swimfeeder

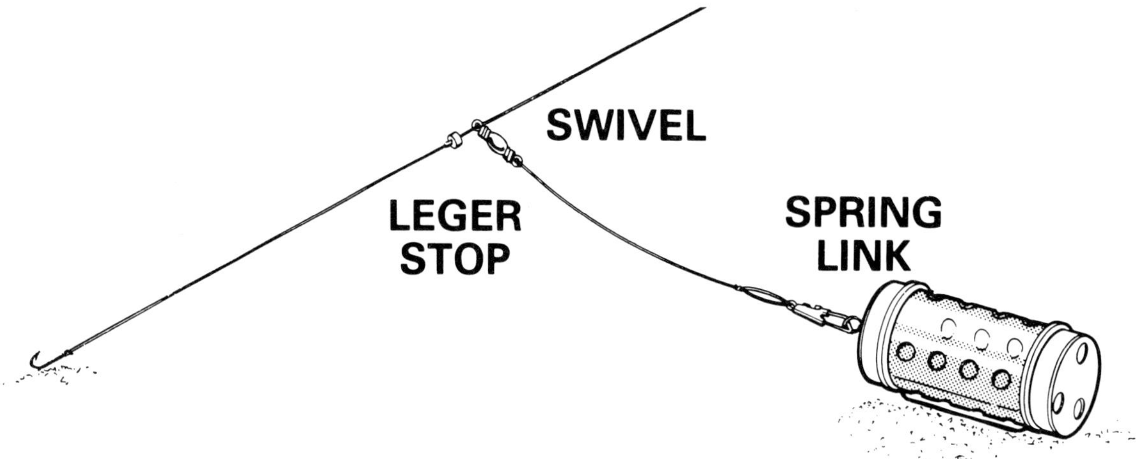

ensuring correct feeding and that the hookbait is always close to some groundbait. Even if you cast badly and your tackle ends up out of position, you will still get some feed near the hook. As a general rule the average angler would probably get overall better results by using feeders than by trying to use cereal groundbait with a straight leger, especially if either casting or throwing accurately is a problem. However there are certain disadvantages with using feeders, particularly in stillwaters. There the feeder limits your strike and it is better to use an Arlesey bomb, casting to a groundbaited area.

On moving water the secret is to get exactly the right amount of weight for the feeder to just hold bottom. Then you can ease it downstream or hold it so that a bite will dislodge the feeder, giving a good indication on the rod tip. A good feeder for running water is the Drennan flat feeder. These hold bottom with a little less lead than the conventional round type. Certainly it is easier to add extra lead to them as they seem to be much sturdier.

With feeder development, more and more waters have become fishable. Anglers are now fishing fast, tidal waters that until recently had been considered impossible. Even so, the need for modifications is still there, the most common being the addition of lead for extra weight. With feeders such as the Drennan smoky-grey type it's simple – all you need is a piece of strip lead of the kind used for roof flashings. It's easy to cut with a pair of scissors and it can be fitted to the feeder as shown in the diagram overleaf.

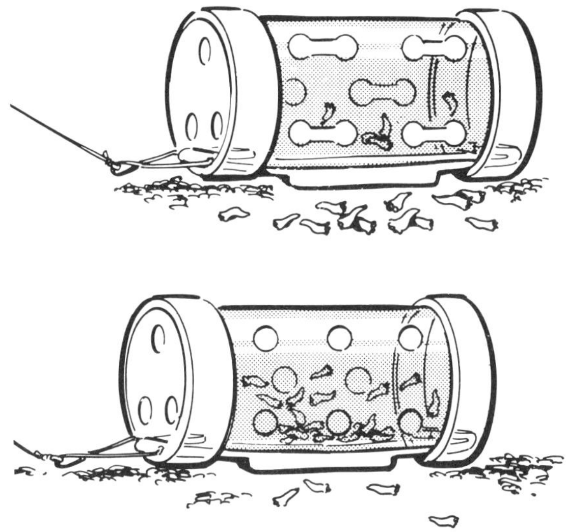

Fig 58 Enlarging the holes in a plastic swimfeeder will enable the current to wash the maggots out quickly (top). The smaller the holes the longer it will take (bottom)

Fig 59

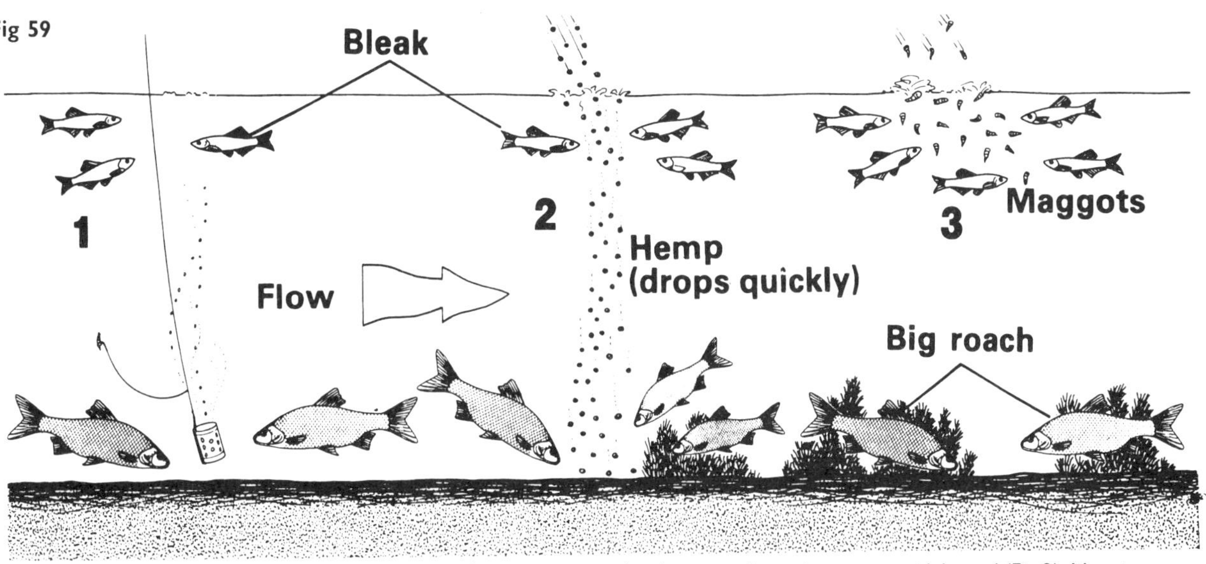

Fig 59 Using a swimfeeder quickly takes a bait, and accompanying groundbait, to the bottom, without attracting the attention of small, surface-feeding fish like bleak. (Fig 1).

The use of hemp is another way of getting bait down quickly. This was a popular tactic on London rivers a few decades ago, and is the reason hemp became so widely used (Fig 2). Now it is also used for barbel and chub on fast waters.

But maggots will always attract bleak as they fall through the water. And their rate of fall is not so easily judged as that of hemp (Fig 3) which should be used generously.

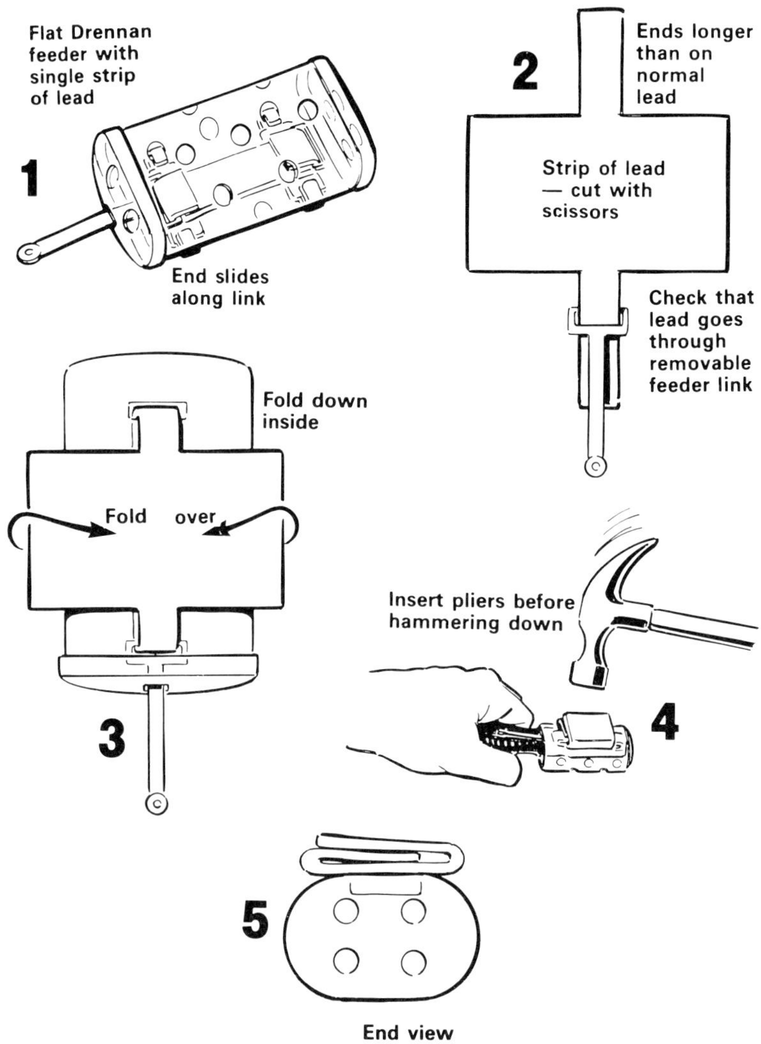

Fig 60 This is the way to add weight to a flat Drennan feeder

Having looked at the basics of good feeders and how to modify them to suit local waters, the next stage is to master the art of fishing them. As a general rule a feeder is cast directly in front – we are discussing rivers, where most feeder fishing is likely to take place. The rod is then pointed downstream and parallel to the bank in the same way as you would with a quivertip.

Sometimes this may not be convenient, for instance if high vegetation is in the way, or maybe a high bank close behind. In such cases rod rests may have to be set with the rod straight out over the water, remembering to keep an angle as close to 90 degrees as possible between rod and line. And in really fast water the rod will have to point very high into the air to keep as much line as possible out of the water; this reduces line drag. The more line there is in the water the greater will be the pressure on it, and the more lead you will need to hold bottom.

When you cast, leave the bale arm of your reel open until the feeder hits bottom. Then tighten up slightly, but remember the faster the water the bigger will be the bow formed in the line.

Remember, too, to always strike across the current and never upstream when fishing a feeder in fast water. If you strike properly the current will both pull, and keep, the hook in your fish. To strike upstream is to place unnecessary strain on your tackle as the current hits the feeder and then the fish. Striking against the flow pulls the feeder off bottom and the current does the rest.

Having got the striking operation clear in the mind, the next stage is to take a look at how best to actually get a bite that is easy to spot. Thankfully most feeder-caught fish are bold biters and in many cases the danger is that the rod gets pulled off the rest. Of course every angler has his or her own way of working out bite detection but with fish such as roach and chub – which can both be very delicate – a short, stubby quivertip about 6in long is a good indicator which clearly shows up the 'drop back' bites which make up some 90 per cent of all feeder bites in fast water.

Line is tightened so that the quivertip has a real bend in it. And if the feeder has been loaded with the right amount of lead, so that it just holds bottom, you can witness a minor miracle. Picture the scene: a chub takes the bait, either moves to one side or rises in the water. This dislodges the feeder and the current swiftly takes it downstream, pulling the hook into the fish's mouth. Meanwhile the tension is momentarily removed from the line and the quivertip springs straight, showing the bite – from a fish that's already hooked.

Yes, it really is that simple, although some bites are still, inexplicably, missed. But then that's what makes fishing so much fun. Even if the fish doesn't actually move the feeder but just touches the bait, the force of the current acting on the hook length is often enough to register some form of bite. Again this is where getting just the right amount of lead plays such a big part.

Finally, but perhaps just as important as the previous operations, is how best to play the hooked fish. Keep your rod upright and remember that even though you may have 5lb line on your reel the hook length is probably a lot lighter and will break if you make a mistake.

The first few times you wind in the tackle while fishing fast water you may think there is a fish on. That's because the feeder swings about in the current and pulls hard on the rod tip. But when there really is a fish on you'll know all about it. It will feel much heavier and bigger than it actually is.

Fig 61 A swimfeeder doesn't have to slide along the line – it can be fixed in place with a shot either side of the feeder link. But a knot in the line, or a loop, is normally better

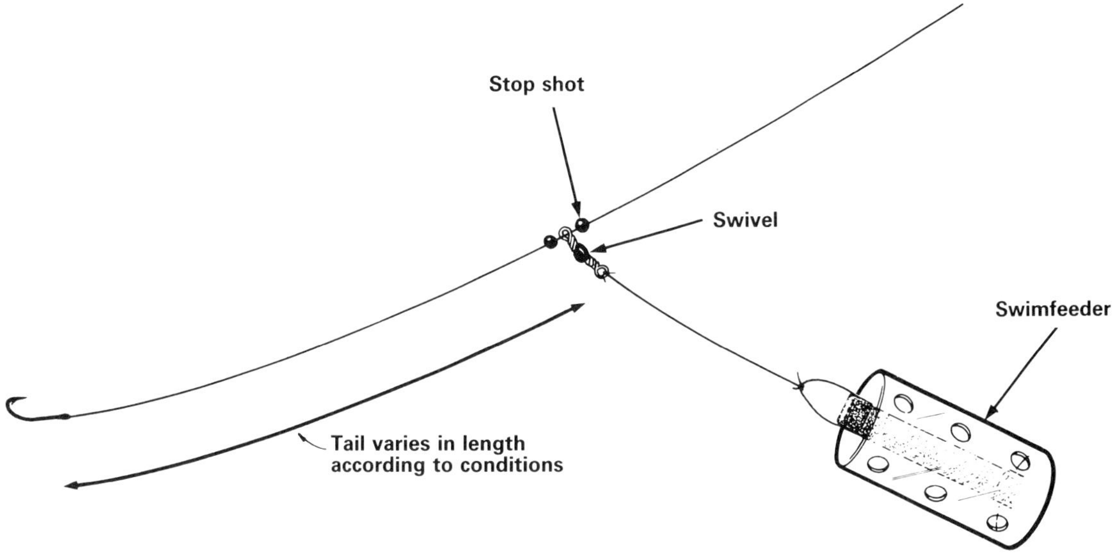

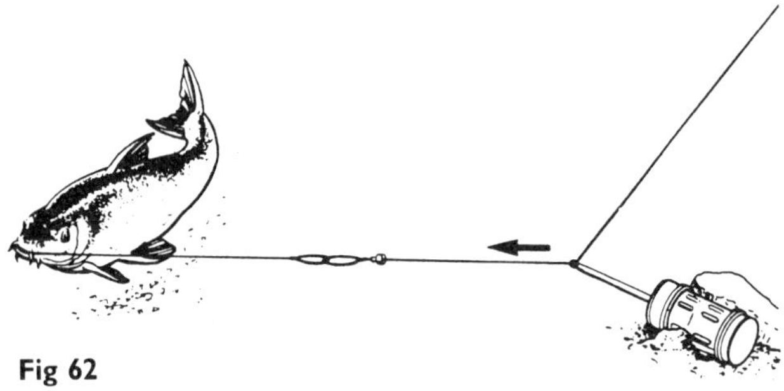

Fig 62

● THIS angler still has a good chance of landing the fish, even though his feeder is jammed between two stones. He is attached to the fish by the line running through the swivel.

Another little trick to use when fishing a water with a snaggy bottom is to always attach the feeder through a running swivel. Then if the feeder is jammed between stones as in Fig 62 the fish can still be played. Had the feeder been tied direct to a fixed link the chances are that the line, or more likely the hook length, would be broken.

Once you are in full swing and catching regularly, be sure to keep up the concentration. All too often anglers scare fish off without realising exactly what they are doing. This state of affairs happens in matches, and starts as a result of casting too far down the swim. The first effect is that the falling feeder scares the shoal as it bangs down on top of them. Secondly it leaves the space upstream of the feeder unfished. This means you are utilising only half the swim and that fish at the head of it will be pulled upstream into the next angler's feed.

In the diagram (Fig 63) the middle angler makes the mistake and casts too far down. Half his fish now have nothing on which to feed and move off upstream. Meanwhile our unlucky angler is fishing farther away for only half the number of fish, and will probably miss more bites because striking is more difficult.

A special feeder

Anglers are inventive people, and are usually willing to share their secrets with others. Matchmen are particularly good in this respect, and have frequently told *Angling Times* of little tricks

Fig 63 The angler in the middle of these three anglers has made the mistake of casting too far down his swim. His swimfeeder is landing on feeding fish which will move upstream, and he is now fishing only half of his swim

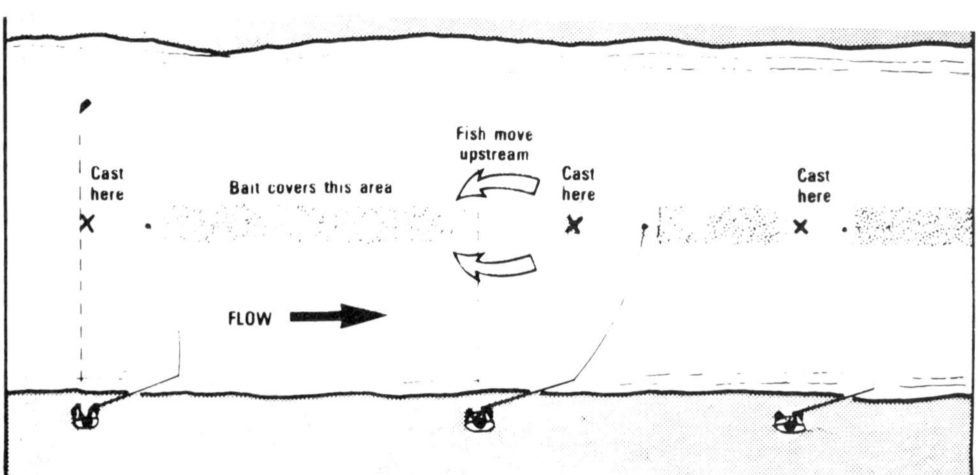

they hold up their sleeve. One of these came from Stan Jeffries, a Leeds DASA National angler, who uses swimfeeders without any holes down the side.

It is used as a normal open-ended feeder, and plugged with groundbait at each end, while casters or maggots are sandwiched in the middle. The advantage is that when retrieved it comes straight towards the surface, instead of tending to stay close to the bottom. So if you have a snaggy swim this feeder won't become snagged.

You don't have to fill it with maggots or casters – it will work with sweetcorn, worms or luncheon meat inside – anything, in fact. Make it from a clear sheet of flexible perspex or any other tubing. It's the principle that is important. There's more water resistance without holes, so the feeder rides upwards on the retrieve.

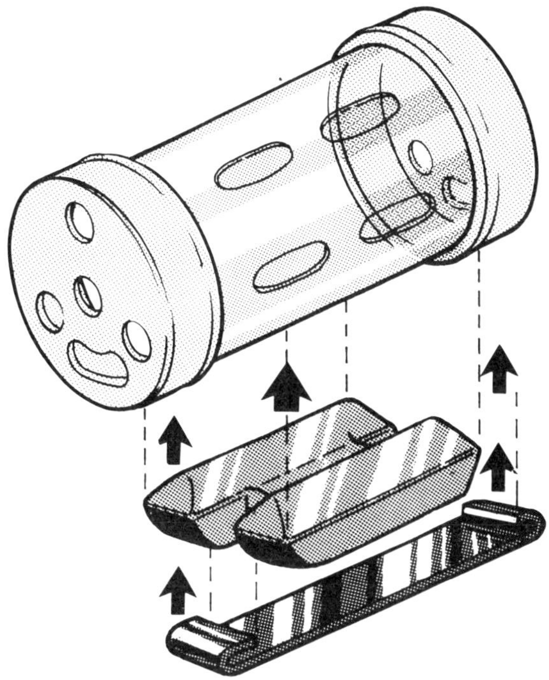

Fig 64 One of the newest feeder ideas is the ski-lead, which runs up to 4oz. To fix it, remove the original lead strip and use this to hold the ski-lead as shown. It is safer to use Araldite to stick the whole lot on, rather than leaving it unglued, as it tends to work loose

CHAPTER SIXTEEN
POLE FISHING

An introduction to the pole

Pole fishing began in this country many years ago on the river Thames where the locals fished with very long heavy poles that have no comparison with the carbon and boron models of the present day. As international matches became more frequent, so British anglers gradually moved towards the pole as an alternative method on most types of fishery. In particular canal anglers realised the advantages of fishing with very tiny floats and very fine lines. The delicate presentation of the pole was also a big factor in helping to improve catches on these very hard venues.

Pole fishing however is not just a method for catching small fish from difficult waters. It can be put to very good use on even the most prolific fisheries such as those found in Ireland and Denmark. Speed is essential if the angler is to compete in the big weight matches for which those countries have become famous. And it is this need that has turned so many to the pole at the very highest level.

Coping with difficult conditions can certainly be made easier with the pole. For example a strong downstream wind on running waters can be tackled with a pole and short-line rig. Such a method will produce a greater percentage of hooked fish. Certainly much higher than the alternative quivertip leger that would most likely be the other option. Master the pole and you will become a better all-round angler. But in order to succeed preparation is of paramount importance. It is impossible to set up the delicate terminal tackle and rigs needed for this style of fishing at the waterside.

The idea is to assemble float, line, shotting and hook at home and then store them on a plastic winder. The pole angler will carry possibly a hundred or more rigs in this manner, enabling him to cope with just about every type of water and weather condition.

Two basic styles should be considered – the short- and long-line methods. A short-line rig will be only a matter of a foot or so longer than the depth of water being fished. This will give perfect presentation with the float directly beneath the pole tip. Long-line rigs will be used for speed fishing with the line about the same length as the pole, enabling a fish to be swung to hand without breaking down joints from the pole. This rig, although much faster, cannot be used to such good effect when wind spoils presentation. However before making up rigs let us consider the actual pole and what makes a good one.

Stiffness is undoubtedly the most important aspect of a good pole and, even with today's standards of technological excellence, you get what you pay for. Today's multi-strand, carbon and kevlar-woven poles are lighter and of a smaller diameter than their cumbersome and pre-historic-looking glass fibre cousins of the late Seventies. The advantages of carbon are obvious. The pole is lighter and more manageable, even at lengths of up to 16 metres. Balance is very important, so poles which have a stated weight which is heavier than others, are not necessarily bad poles. It's a matter of how well they can be handled. Always try to buy the longest pole you can afford. Start by learning to fish with the pole at 8–10 metres and, as your confidence increases, try adding on sections to 12.5 or even 14 metres. You will be surprised at how quickly you will get the hang of handling this amazing piece of tackle.

Telescopic poles have limited uses once they pass 6m in length. The best option is a pole with take-apart joints throughout or with only the first three at the tip telescopic. Joints should be easy to unship and deep fitting. A new pole will need some 'running in' as its joints will need time to 'bed' slightly. One hint to break in a new pole is to assemble a joint with its mate and revolve them to rub off any high spots.

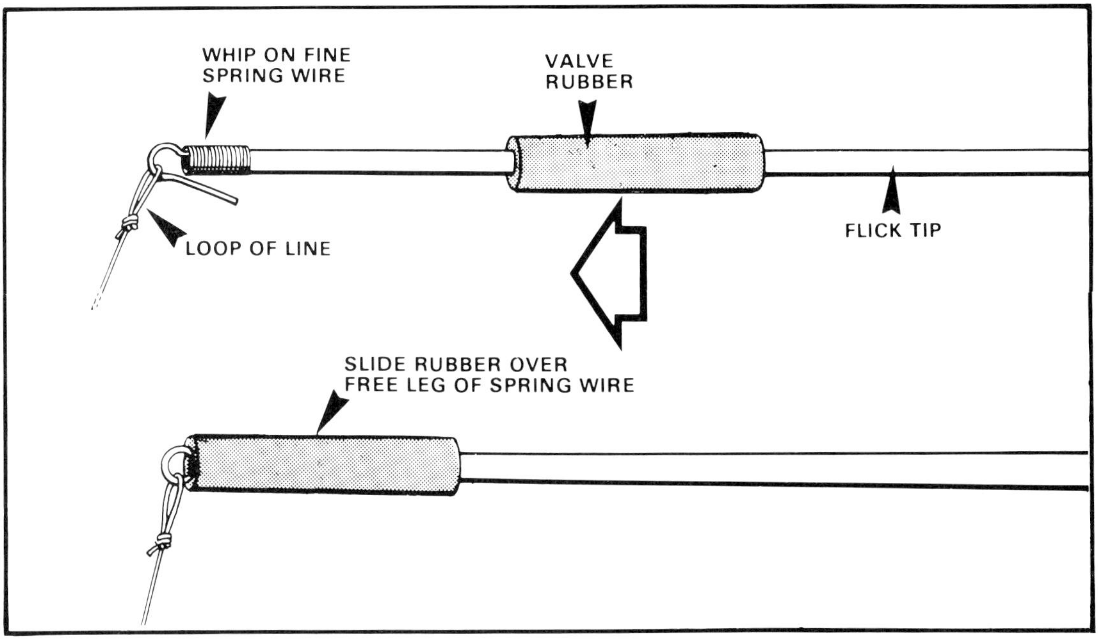

Fig 65 A small eye whipped to the quivertip of a pole is one method for attaching the line

If a good pole can be found with two top sections so much the better. Look for one with a quivertip type top for speed fishing with a long line and a second top of a bigger diameter. This will be used for an internal elastic system which will be described later. The quivertip should be as fine as possible to provide the maximum shock absorption when being used with fine lines.

On the quivertip top a small eye can be whipped to the end or, alternatively, line can be fastened by means of two pieces of fine diameter rubber tubing – float rubbers are fine. Line between the two rubbers is twisted around the pole in spiral fashion. The spiralling will stop any tendency for the line to 'bow' the pole. With the small-eye system a tackle rig can be simply looped through the eye. Another alternative is a tiny hook that all but closes on itself. A small loop in the line can then be slipped into the hook and a length of rubber tubing pulled over it to hold it in place. All three methods work well and the final choice is one best made by each individual angler.

However, there is now a fourth means of attachment which, in years to come, will render these previous methods obsolete. Tackle manufacturers have come up with a micro-bore plastic connector, called a micro stonfo connector, which is glued onto the end of the flicktip. Just like the original stonfo connectors, invented for use with elastic systems on poles, the micro stonfo enables the line to be attached by means of a simple loop knot.

Internal elastic as a shock absorber is by far the best method with short-line fishing. The old-fashioned crook at the pole end into which elastic was slotted tended to tangle and required far more skill to ensure it operated efficiently. So go for an internal elastic, which you will almost certainly have to make up yourself unless your local dealer will do it for you. The elastic will need to be matched to the fishing you intend to do so select either fine, medium or strong. For most fishing a medium strength is probably the best to start with. With telescopic joints it may be worthwhile threading elastic down both the first and second sections as this will give far more buffer potential if a big fish is hooked.

The idea is to thread a strand of the correct strength elastic through the pole's hollow section and fasten it with a bung. At the tip a small bush, preferably of low-friction nylon type material such as PTFE, takes the elastic over the tip's end. On the end of the elastic goes a small swivel with a link onto which line could be fastened. Some of

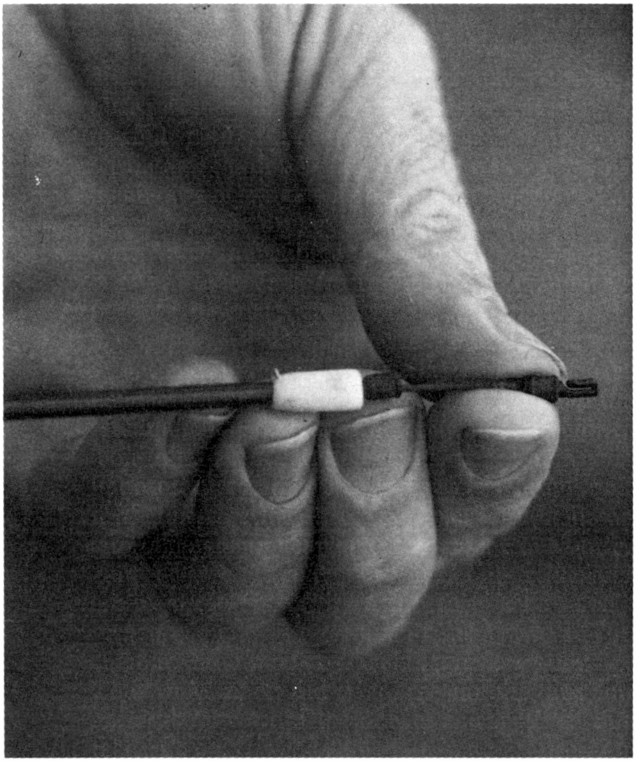

A bush made from PTFE is the best way to ensure internal elastic runs smoothly. The small black hook is a commercially produced system for attaching line

The internal elastic system is held in place with a plug that fits inside the joint end

the smaller swivels now in use may call for a plastic bead to act as a stop between swivel and bush. It also pays to cover the whole lot with a short piece of rubber tubing for extra neatness. There are many ways of achieving the same internal elastic system. Every angler will eventually develop modifications of his own. For example the rather expensive or hard to obtain PTFE bush can, at a push, be substituted by using the brass bush from the end of a ballpoint pen. Simply push out the plastic tube and ball and you have a ready-made bush.

At the other end elastic can be held by a variety of plugs, either the commercial plastic ones or a wood plug made from any soft wood – float bodies are ideal since they come complete with a hole down the centre. What must be remembered is that some form of ejection rig must be included. This can be as simple as a length of strong nylon line left to protrude from the bottom of the joint.

Whenever an internal elastic rig is being made up, the angler must bear in mind what he is trying to achieve. Internal elastic must run freely through whatever bush system is employed. If it does not the fish will be either 'bumped' off while being played or will simply break the tackle. The elastic is a shock absorber and without doubt the most important single item in pole fishing.

Smoothness is something that will need to be mastered throughout pole-fishing sessions. The long pole must be used until it can be passed over your hands without any jerkiness. Joints must be slipped off in the same style – smoothly.

Holding a pole correctly

The first time you pick up a long pole it will feel very heavy and rather clumsy. Chances are you will let the tip crash down on the water surface. But don't worry; an hour or two spent in practice and you will begin to feel confident. Start by fishing with a length you can handle easily, 7 or 8m, and gradually work up to full length.

Most of your pole fishing will be carried out from a sitting position and here it is very impor-

A typical French tackle shop, sporting an amazing and colourful array of pole floats

The French know more about additives and groundbait than any other anglers. This is just a small portion of what Jean Pierre Fougeat, former World Champion, has in his tackle shop in Northern France

DUDULOKOFF
WATER-QUEEN
WATER-QUEEN

MEIN FUTTER
Sensas Z-72 SUPER
Sensas Z-72 SUPER
Sensas ROUBAISIEN
Sensas 2000 spécial gardon amorce de fond
RECORD 515
tout pour la pêche
TIL'T SPECIAL FOND
CHOC
AMORCE X21
SUPER GEANT
AMORCE X21
amorce TESSE
1978 Tiercé gagnant pour l'amorce Tesse avec Guy Hebert
pâte amorce DRICHKO
Rien de meilleur
AMORCE DE FRITURE

tant to position your box so that it sits on the bank solidly. It must be a stable working platform. It must be level and leave you sitting comfortably. Eventually you may wish to purchase one of the superb metal frames with adjustable legs onto which your box sits. These frames ensure that no matter what bank conditions exist you will always be able to sit level and sound in the knowledge that you are not about to tip head first into the water.

Holding a long pole can become very tiring, at least if you go about it wrongly. Start by sitting slightly at an angle to the water so that your left leg is nearest to it. The pole now rests across the left knee, at the same time being supported by the left hand just in front of it.

So far the right hand has not been positioned. This goes towards the rear of the pole, behind the right leg. Its job is not really to support the pole but to act as a counterbalance, pushing downwards.

From this description it can be seen that the thighs and knees serve as a rest for the pole while the left hand gives additional stability and support. The right hand, positioned above the rear of the pole pushes downwards. Done correctly this enables the pole to be released by the left hand yet remain in the correct position. With practice it is possible to fish a long pole and use a catapult for feeding at the same time, but this will take time to perfect.

When joints need to be unshipped during fishing the pole is pulled backwards with the right hand, at the same time allowing it to slide over the upturned left palm. Once the joint to be unshipped is reached, the left hand tightens its grip and the right hand pulls off the joint in a smooth, almost effortless movement. It sounds complicated but you'll soon get the hang of it.

If you are left-handed you will sit with your right knee forward and your left hand on the pole butt.

Setting up the rigs

As stated earlier, pole rigs should ideally be set up

Pole rigs are best stored on plastic winders and marked with the length of line, hook size, etc at home rather than by the waterside. Due to the delicate nature of the operation it is far easier to balance floats in a bucket of water than in a river or lake where so many other factors can have an effect. The idea is to shot each rig so that the tiny bristle tips of the floats are the only thing visible above water. But because they are so sensitive even the weight of a hook can make a difference.

Start by threading the float to be shotted onto a suitable piece of thin nylon and add shot or olivettes as required to cock it correctly. Once the weight has been established it is a simple matter to build them into the required pattern. Try to keep your rigs simple for a start. Far too many anglers get totally bogged down with fancy patterns and strange float shapes.

Continental anglers have always favoured the streamlined olivette leads. These pear-shaped weights come with either a hole through the middle or with a slit down the side which is then closed on the line in a similar fashion to split shot. The holed type need to be stopped on the line with small shots. Use two small ones rather than one large shot as this will provide better holding qualities. The big end of the olivette always goes nearest the hook in order to create the most effective streamlining.

One very good method of shotting a pole float is to select an olivette that is slightly too heavy for the float. Then, after adding all the other shots required to complete the rig, the olivette is filed down until the float cocks perfectly. This is a time-consuming job that cannot be rushed.

As already mentioned, continental anglers invariably use a pattern that incorporates bulk shot or an olivette near the hook. This in itself is not surprising as their feeding usually entails heavy groundbaiting aimed at keeping fish feeding on the bottom.

A day with the pole

The confusing thing is that this bulk-shotting style works equally well when loose-feeding. Yet English shotting patterns nearly always use shots strung out on the line. So which is the best and why?

Effectiveness of the two styles for bottom-feeding fish must be something to do with the greater control enjoyed by the pole angler, enabling him to do what he wants with his terminal tackle and bait. Lakes and slow-moving rivers are where the bulk-shot method scores best. Rivers as fast as the Trent do not help pole anglers, especially when loose-feeding, because the limited amount of line in use cannot follow loose-feed down to the end of the swim.

On lakes

There are two important factors on a lake as far as pole fishing is concerned – the location of the shelves and the bankside cover or weed beds.

Imagine fishing a lake containing roach and bream. The first thing to do is to plumb the depth, for if there is a shelf close in with sufficient weed growth between angler and fish there's a good chance that roach will be caught just over the shelf. For bream you must look for an area in your swim where the bed of the lake is flat – and the larger the area the better. Having determined where in the swim to fish, the next thing is to put in some bait.

For bream it may pay to put in a large amount of bait at the start and leave it for a while, hoping that bream will move in and become confident before you start to fish for them. Mix the groundbait so that it will break up just before it hits bottom. And if a fair number of bream are expected, as much as 2 pints of casters can be put in at the start. There is no advantage to be gained by throwing all your groundbait in exactly the same spot. Try to feed an area about a yard square, for in this way you have more chance of attracting and keeping fish in your swim.

Forget the bream swim for a moment and concentrate on the roach, which means using hemp and caster, feeding a dozen of each every cast. The float should be set so that the last shot is just resting on the bottom (Fig 66). This is a simple but sometimes deadly method. If all goes well you should get bites almost immediately, but remember to let the float disappear before striking to minimise missed bites. Start with a fine-wire, size 18 hook buried right inside the caster.

Depending on how the roach respond, at some time during the session – if you are fishing a match make it during the first half – the bream

Overleaf England's double World Champion, Bob Nudd, selects a pole rig from the dozens in his box

Britain's top match angler in action with the pole at Willow Park in Surrey

BROWNING

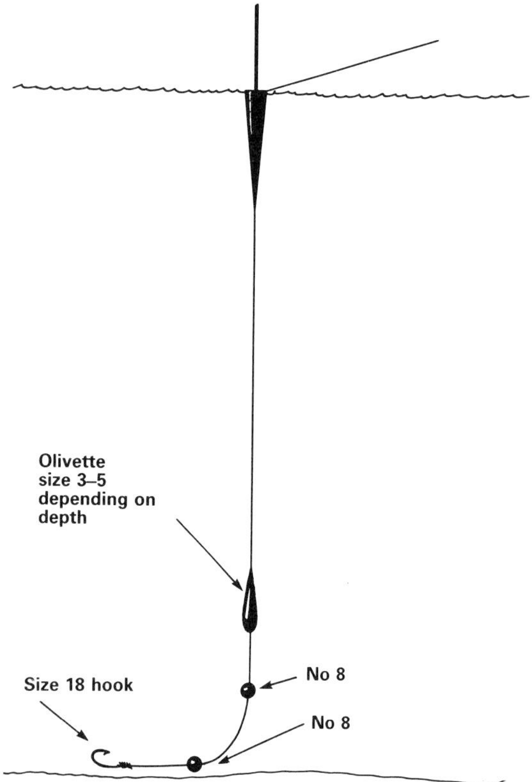

Fig 66 A good rig for roach when using casters. The last shot just rests on the bottom

must be given consideration. Tackle for these fish will be heavier than that used for roach – anything up to about a No 7 olivette, depending on the depth, with a different arrangement of shot between olivette and hook (Fig 67). A short line is essential with this tackle so that the bait can be held as still as possible. Distance from pole tip to float may need to be as little as 2ft.

The float should be set so that the olivette is just a few inches off bottom, which means you will be fishing at least a foot overdepth. If your bait has been taken without a bite registering, it may pay to shallow up slightly. If bream have found your initial feed early on you can expect a bite pretty quickly, but if there is no action to start with, try putting a small ball of groundbait packed with casters in every cast and don't forget to keep ringing the changes with hookbaits.

One of the best baits for bream is the humble worm and a good trick when using it is to lift and drop your float every now and again, which will often induce a fish to take your bait as it moves across the bottom.

River fishing

Tactics for river fishing are similar to those for lakes. If the aim is to catch fish on the bottom, it is essential to find out what the bottom is like – which means plumbing extensively. On most rivers there is probably only one area in the swim that will produce fish, not two or more as on a lake. When plumbing, find out where the shelf is, then look for a flat area at the bottom of the shelf; this is where fish will be caught.

Because we are expecting to catch fish from just one area, we must gamble slightly on what species to aim for. Assuming that we have decided to use bloodworm, with jokers and groundbait as feed, we will expect to catch both roach and bream as well as any bonus perch that may be attracted into the swim.

Once we have found a flat area we must put some feed on it. Different waters will require varying amounts; sometimes a pint of jokers will suffice, while other waters may need half a gallon.

This particular water, let us imagine, holds some bream, some perch but mostly roach. Take

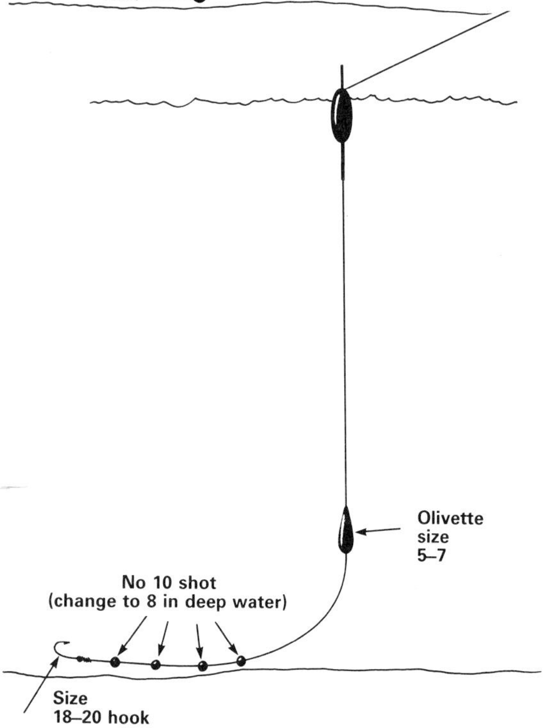

Fig 67 A good pole rig for bream. A number of small shots are laid on the bottom

a couple of pints of jokers and put half of them in at the start of the session. It should be possible to feed a pint of jokers in five large balls of groundbait, bearing in mind that the groundbait must break up only when it hits the river bed. To achieve this it may be necessary to add some fine soil to the usual cereal mix. This initial feed should last some time.

Start off with the tackle described in Fig 68 set to fish a few inches overdepth, but without a shot on the bottom. Drop the float at the head of the swim, let the tackle settle, then ease the float downstream at a slightly slower speed than the current. A quick response from the fish is expected, with confident bites from roach in the 1oz to 4oz class.

Start with two bloodworm on the hook, hoping this will help sort out the better quality fish. If bream are on the cards it may pay to fish more overdepth, overshotting the float with a No 4 shot and letting it move downstream as slowly as possible. For bream change to a larger hook – a 20 or an 18, loaded with four or five bloodworms.

As long as regular bites are coming there is no need to feed any more. When bites slow up we must feed again, either putting in three or four large balls and waiting for the fish to return, or feeding a smaller ball every few casts. If at the end of the session bites are falling off, holding back with the olivette just off bottom should catch a few more fish.

So that's it – a typical pole-fishing session for quality fish. Although bloodworm and joker have been used for feeding and hookbait, more conventional baits such as maggot or caster can work in just the same manner, but they may take a little longer to take effect. And remember what we did with shotting, combining both continental and British thinking into one rig.

Pole floats

As interest in pole fishing grows, so does the size of the pole angler's float box. Certainly the floats needed for this type of fishing seem to hold a fatal fascination that results in a wide, and often strange, variety of shapes and sizes. In truth around six or seven patterns will see you through just about every pole-fishing situation. It is desirable however to build up a range of each pattern in order that swims of different depths and currents can be fished.

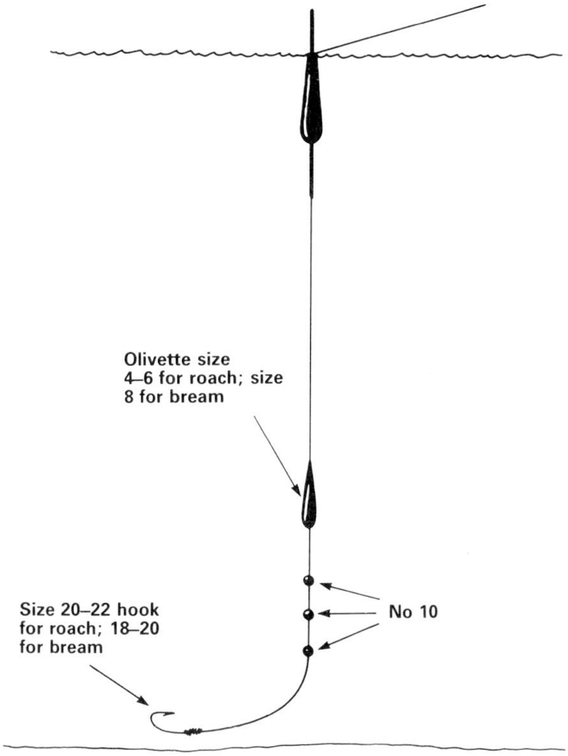

Fig 68 A good starting rig for fishing a river. No shot touch bottom although the rig is set to fish a few inches overdepth

British anglers have gradually weeded out the shapes that work best from the multitude that have landed on our tackle-shop shelves from the Continent. Understanding why each shape works under a specific set of conditions takes a little time, but as a general rule it is possible to apply the same principles that hold good for conventional floats – ie if the bulk of a body is towards the top it is best suited to moving water, if the body is reversed so that the bulk is at the base it will be most stable in still water. The use of a steep shoulder at the top of a body will help prevent a float riding up out of the water if held back hard against a flow. Let us take a look at seven patterns and what they are designed to do:

1 *Bodied float*

This is perfect for running rivers such as the Trent. It will carry a reasonable amount of weight, which also makes it easy to handle in windy conditions. It can be overshotted and held

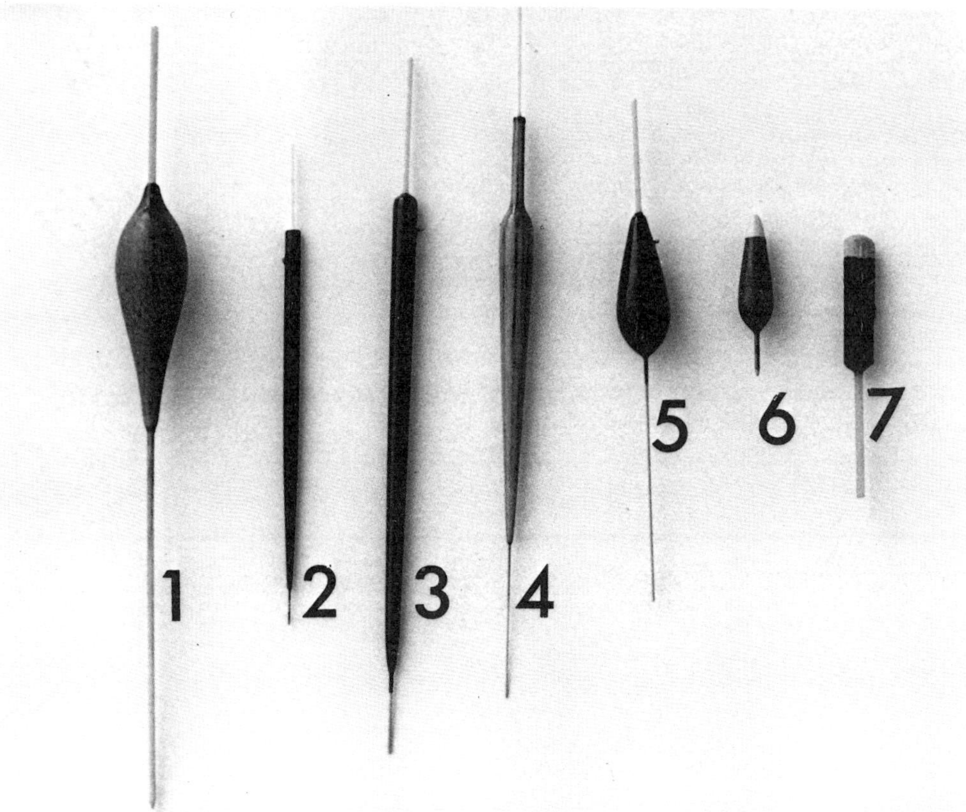

These seven patterns of pole float will enable most waters to be tackled with confidence

back hard, but if the flow is very strong a lot of overshotting is needed to prevent riding up. The trick is to hold back and then keep adding weight until only the bristle rides above the surface. This float shows the typical running water shoulder at the top of its body.

2 *Slim stillwater roach float*

Used in water up to a maximum of about 4ft, and no further out than 3 or 5yd, otherwise it is impossible to see the fine bristle tip. Best shotted with styl weights strung down the line and finished off with one tiny shot about 8in from the hook. Loaded in this manner it is a very good float for catching on the drop.

3 *Larger roach float*

Similar to the previous float and again can be fished with styl weights strung down the line. Lay the rig out on the water in a straight line and bites will register at all depths. It pays to have several floats of the same size in this pattern, but with various thicknesses of bristle. Then if conditions change for the worse a thicker bristle can be used rather than a longer one. Some floats have interchangeable bristles.

4 *Collared float*

A single olivette is used to take this float down to the bottom collar of the body and then a No 6 shot to cock it to the top shoulder. Finally an 8 or 10 will settle it right down to the bristle. It's an excellent float for showing bites in the last 2 or 3ft of water. When the bait has dropped to the bottom, lift the tackle by raising the pole tip slightly and let the bait fall back through that last 3ft again. This is a good float for use on stillwaters.

5 *Stubby stillwater float*

Used on a short line when there is a ripple on the surface or a drift in the form of undertow. Main loading comes from an olivette, with a couple of styl weights to show bites in the last 2ft or so. A very stable float which, unlike the previous pattern, will not ride out if held back.

6 *Miniature canal float*

Takes just two dust shot and is perfect for use with a pole that allows it to be dropped on the far-side shelf of a canal. The thick top makes it easy to see at distance – far better than a bristle. Try it with a caster laid on the bottom. Leave all the tip colour showing and fish it 'top and bottom' in conventional pole-float manner.

7 *Bottom end only stillwater float*

For fishing at range, fixed bottom end only. It allows line to be sunk beneath surface drift. It's also useful for bleak fishing when fish are giving a good bite and you're catching a lot. It's a fairly heavy float and enables tackle to be got back into the water just that odd second or so faster than would be possible with a light outfit.

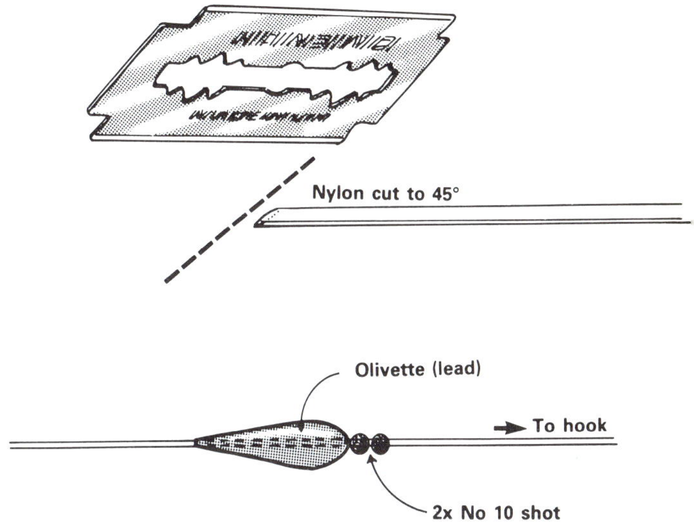

Fig 69 Before threading olivettes on the line it pays to cut the nylon with a sharp blade, giving a clean cut. Olivettes can be stopped with two small shot

Pole anglers on the River Nene at Peterborough. Since the introduction of carbon fibre poles are lighter and stiffer than they used to be, and most anglers can easily handle them up to 30ft in length

Set up winders with these seven floats and you will be well equipped. But in order to get the best results take extra care when balancing them, as described on page 121.

You will have noticed that most pole floats have tiny side eyes through which line is threaded. These are placed in the right position to make the float work in the manner for which it was designed. They also eliminate the need for a rubber, which would upset the delicate balance should an air bubble become trapped. Pay attention also to the small plastic sleeve that holds line to the stem. It must be a good fit, and again tight enough to prevent both slipping, and air from becoming trapped.

A complete rig, line, float, weights and hook are stored on a plastic winder. Mark each winder with all the information you are likely to need. Line strength and total length, hook size, bottom breaking strain together with shot load should all be recorded. Using the different colours of the winders as part of your own personal coding system is another good idea.

The continental approach

Though for many years the top British matchmen knew how the French fished their waters, it wasn't until 1982 that a top continental angler wrote a series in the British magazine *Angling Times* telling his secrets. The articles, by former world champion Jean Pierre Fougeat, intrigued all who read them. What is fascinating about the French matchman is that he has to get everything *exactly* right before he goes fishing, even to the extent of always mixing his groundbait the night before his trip to ensure it soaks up all the water and doesn't change consistency on the bank. Many top British anglers have now started doing the same thing.

The French work on the principle that different sizes of fish stay in different layers of water, even bleak! So they try to get their groundbait to break up at that level, releasing its contents. If it doesn't break up at the right depth it is feeding fish on the wrong layer, fish that you are not fishing for. It follows, therefore, that the texture of groundbait is even more important than its smell.

The easiest place to deposit your groundbait is, of course, the bottom. And because many Continentals use bloodworm they use a lot of heavy groundbait. The item that decides how heavy it will be is clay – *argile* in French, in England sold as 'leem'. Jean Pierre, was unwilling to give the exact mix he used for his own groundbait, but hinted that the amount of *argile* was a key factor.

Anyone who has a pole will inevitably need sets of winders. They are sold in different sizes, each a different colour. And that's not just to make them look pretty in a tackle box – it's a colour code. How each colour is used is a matter for personal preference. Jean Pierre most frequently used red winders to hold lines and hook lengths down to 4oz (!), yellow winders for 12oz line and green for 1lb line; though he had other colours for stronger tackles. Marked on the side was the size of hook.

The length of winder is usually an indication as to the length of line attached, though in Jean Pierre's case he had a multi-layered box with short lines in the top graduating to long lines at the bottom, and the length of float governed the length of winder used. Of course you cannot put a float on a winder which is shorter than the float itself.

The main lengths of lines needed in Britain are 2m for short bleak whips, 4m, 5m and 7m. If you want to use a 6m line you simply break off the end of a 7m one. Some anglers, including England international Bob Nudd, make up all their heavier rigs to, say, 10m, and alter them on the banks as necessary.

With very light floats 6m is the longest you are ever likely to need, since you will almost certainly be fishing on a short line with a long pole.

Anyone who is fumble-fisted is advised to do what Jean Pierre did on the lines he knew he would be using on a flick tip. He kept a short length of plastic sleeving on the line itself to push over the flick tip when it was attached. This makes a neat job of attaching it. However, he always used elastic for bleak fishing because it absorbed the shock of striking and prevented the fish flying off if he struck too hard.

One refinement the Continentals use is to twist their line between finger and thumb before tying a loop. This ensures that the loop is absolutely straight. They do the same thing before tying loops in elastic. Take both sides of the line to be tied between finger and thumb and twist both in the same direction. It will twist itself into a 'plaited' loop. An overhand knot is then tied in this in the normal way, and the loop stands stiff after being tied. This is very important to the

French, who will be plumbing their depth to within 1cm (about ⅓in). Tied in the way most of us do it, a loop tends to retain some of its roundness after being tied. The French way cuts out this small defect, so it stays the same when the plummet is taken off.

When pole fishing on silty-bottomed lakes you should be very careful how you plumb the depth, otherwise the plummet may sink into the silt and give a false reading. So after dropping it in and letting it rest, take the strain again and lift very slowly. If you feel it suddenly come free, lower it straightaway, watching for the slightest slackening of the line which shows you have just touched the silt. Then make any necessary adjustment to the depth of the float.

The French have always been meticulous about their floats. Jean Pierre has his own sets of floats on sale in tackle shops, in four sizes, each size a different colour. So if you want a replacement you don't have to remember the weight needed to cock it, only the colour. The centre of gravity on his floats is towards the bottom of the body, to keep the float stable. For this reason he does not like sight-bobs on the tip, as it makes the float wobble in a wind.

The little wire ring found on most pole floats is very important; it keeps the line below the surface on a stillwater, cutting down on drift. It is better than a rubber ring as rubber may be cut by the line on the strike. There is a rubber ring on the bottom stem, immediately below the body, and another on the bottom of the stem. These have the effect of streamlining the whole outfit by ensuring that the line follows the contours of the float.

A neat little gadget to make pre-shotting pole tackles easy is now on sale in most tackle shops. There is no need to pinch shot onto a line attached to the float, the gadget has neutral buoyancy in water and clips onto the bottom of the float which is then placed in a water-filled bucket. Shot are dropped into the top, and gradually the device sinks. The more shot you drop in the more the float cocks. You add or subtract weights until you get it just right. Then tip them out into a saucer, knowing they will be exactly right for your float. It was 1982 when the first-ever diagram of this gadget appeared, with Jean Pierre's series; it was called the *pèse plombée*. Now almost every pole angler has one.

To return to groundbait, probably the idea of most obvious benefit to British anglers is this ability of the French to make groundbait which will break up at a particular time after being placed in the swim. The French use this trick when fishing for bream; for they agree with the English that bream do not like having groundbait splashing in around them while they are feeding.

The importance Jean Pierre placed on the proportion of clay in the groundbait mix has been mentioned. Gritty soil can also make it heavier, though the ball breaks up more quickly. Since what you add makes a big difference, there is really no alternative to experimenting. To lighten a basic breadcrumb mix there are several items on the market including ground silkworm cocoons, very fine maize meal, a fine bran and powdered egg. And since Jean Pierre's series first appeared, many ready-mixed groundbaits have been imported from the Continent, so there is no need for an angler to make up his own. Nevertheless, there is still plenty of room for the ordinary angler to come up with a mixture of ingredients which, when correctly blended, will form a solid ball that will hold together until needed to release its contents.

Not all the information Jean Pierre gave was of direct use to every angler. But what was obvious was how little the French leave to chance – and how much scope there still is for improvement.

THE MAIN SPECIES

CHAPTER SEVENTEEN
THE BARBEL

Ever tried stopping a runaway train with a length of 6lb nylon line? If you haven't you obviously have never fished for barbel. Barbel are fish that epitomise the reel-screeching 'one that got away' fish we so often hear about. A strike is met with sheer brute force as the fish displays its salmon-like strength.

A bottom feeder, the barbel has an underslung mouth and four large barbules. These hang beside its leathery lips and, because of the position of its eyes, are used as taste and touch cells for detecting food at close range. Some anglers have difficulty in telling gudgeon and small barbel apart. It's easy when you know the gudgeon has only two barbules under its chin while the barbel has four. Barbel average between 3lb and 8lb in size and anything over that is considered to be a very good fish; but double-figure fish are becoming more common every season.

Thirty years ago few anglers in England had even seen a barbel. They were confined to just a few rivers – the Hampshire Avon, Kennet, some Yorkshire rivers and parts of the river Thames were their main holding places. At that time the capture of just one barbel, of any size, was one of the ambitions of most anglers, for they had (and still have) the reputation of being one of the hardest-fighting coarse fish in this country. Now they are to be found without too much difficulty in the majority of our fast-flowing rivers – including those already mentioned and the Dorset Stour – and are within the grasp of any angler who wishes to make the effort to catch one.

Even the Fens holds barbel – some astonishing fish have come from the Great Ouse in Bedfordshire, with odd ones from the Nene and Welland. However, apart from parts of the Wye and Severn, few Welsh rivers hold them.

Two of the most popular barbel rivers are the Severn and the Trent, both of which were stocked by *Angling Times* and the river boards in 1956. The Severn barbel quickly made their presence felt, but the fish on the Trent virtually vanished until five years ago. Now they are thriving there and catches of 100lb are taken from both waters.

A classic barbel swim tends to be a deeper area which shallows up onto a downstream gravel run or hard bottom. Such swims are normally found where the river narrows and the current is faster. However it is always worth remembering that barbel like cover and will never be too far away from weed growth.

A double-figure barbel will put up an incredible fight, taking advantage of the fast water. Because they are such powerful fighters, tackle must be matched accordingly and there is no better method than a large feeder coupled to a 6lb breaking strain line which goes direct to a large hook. Actual hook size will of course need to be suited to the bait being used, but it should always be a forged pattern capable of taking a lot of pressure.

Choice of rod is something of a personal matter but many barbel specialists go for an Avon type, around 11ft long. For close-in work, a steep taper is best avoided since bites can be very fierce and breakages will occur.

Baits are many, ranging from sweetcorn to maggots, casters, luncheon meat, worms and bread. But for the most consistent results maggots or casters take a lot of beating. Certainly they account for a large percentage of the average-sized fish landed every day on the hard-fished rivers such as the Severn and Trent.

Hempseed is one of the favourite baits to include in a swimfeeder. Fished in conjunction with maggot or caster it will hold the attention of barbel for long periods and is well suited to the fastest swims where other, lighter materials would be washed away very quickly. Feeders are often modified to enable the contents to be washed out very quickly. This is done by opening out the

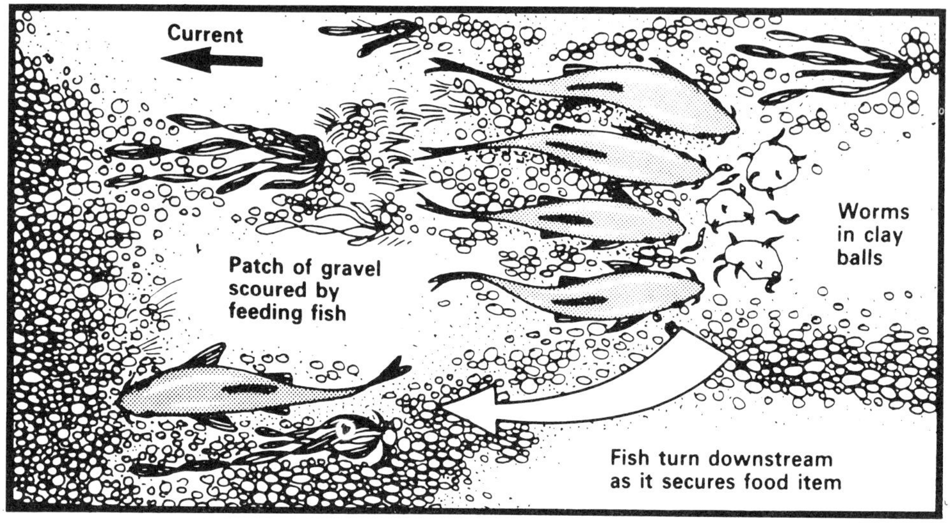

Fig 70 Old-timers used to use worms packed into balls of clay to take barbel. The method still works, and gives good bites as the fish turns and heads downstream once it has picked out its meal, to join the back of the shoal

feeder holes – cutting into slots between the holes is a good method. And in the fast waters the addition of ski leads is often required in order to hold bottom. These extra leads are attached by opening out the original lead strip and then folding it back over the ski to hold everything in place. Feeders such as this can weigh anything up to 4oz, but because barbel demand such heavy gear they do not look out of place.

On rivers such as the Severn the high population of barbel has caused such competition for food that they actually swim towards the splash made by feeders hitting the water. And once on the bottom it is not unknown for the fish to actually attack a full feeder in order to get at its contents. But don't get the idea that barbel are always easy. At times they can be very delicate feeders and some scaling down of tackle, hook and bait will be called for. Usually the later in the year you fish, the more this is likely to be the solution.

As a general rule the best sport is during high summer and early autumn, the best time being late afternoon or early evening. During periods of bright sunshine barbel tend to tuck themselves away even closer than normal to weed beds.

Although barbel are tough fighters they must be handled with extreme care. Having fought so well and given everything in the battle they need time to recover fully. Keepnets can be a problem and unless absolutely essential it is far better to catch and release. Micromesh is by far the best for both landing and keepnets. The fine material will go a long way towards helping prevent the dorsal fin from becoming caught up. The leading edge of the fin is slightly serrated and is easily snagged. For this reason keepnets for barbel are banned in some waters. On no account try to cram a large number of these fish into a net. They are sure to become distressed and may even die if kept for too long. On returning a barbel always hold it upright in the water, facing upstream, until such time that it swims away strongly.

If you must take photographs of your catch get everything ready for the picture beforehand and get the fish back as soon as possible. A better idea, unless you are fishing a match, is to retain just the odd fish for a picture.

Techniques

Spotting barbel

Spotting barbel in rivers can be as easy as finding currants in a bun, or as difficult as looking for a needle in a haystack.

In summer, Wessex rivers such as the Hampshire Avon and Dorset Stour are usually low and clear until mid to late June and finding fish is a matter of walking the banks with the sun behind you on a windless day wearing polaroid glasses.

Rivers carrying more colour, such as the Yorkshire Ouse, Severn and Thames, are a different ball game, and your choice of swim will depend on bankside features and river-bed contours instead of fish sightings. On these rivers follow your nose, trying every bankside feature and change of flow. The Thames in summer hardly flows and the pattern made by the current on the surface gives away the contours of the river bed like the lines on an Ordnance Survey map.

Head for these areas armed with a float and plummet, and find out by trial and error which swims have deep holes and which overhanging trees conceal an undulating river bed.

Fish-spotting becomes easier with experience, but there is nothing magical about the skill, and on the right day you can expect to find fish on your first spotting session.

Always take tackle and some bait on these outings but leave it all in the car. If you come across a really big fish you can nip back for the gear and have a go for it.

Swimfeeder tactics

In coloured water opt for the swimfeeder because it can guarantee that the free samples are positioned around the hookbait.

Use Thamesly or Drennan feeders with the cap at the swivel end in place but the bottom open, plugged with brown crumb to hold the hook samples in, and weighted along one side with a strip of lead. Use a short length of rubber tubing pushed over the eye of the swivel to help prevent tangles. Fish feed well downstream from a feeder, so use a minimum of two feet of hooklength, except at the start of the season, when barbel are bolder. Using leger stops enables you to vary the length of the 'tail' quickly and they also eliminate the need for knots, which are always weak spots in any rig.

In coloured water this rig is lobbed into the spot where the fast water meets the slower-paced area – a line known as the crease. Don't fish in the true slack, but at the point where those two flows merge, and try to draw the fish into that spot. The barbel are at home in the fast water, but presenting a bait properly is often not possible in a strong current.

The thing to remember about these swims is that when you have found a good winter swim, it will be a winter hotspot for good.

Straight leger rig

If you don't like swimfeeders much, and think some fish feel the same way you can use a straight leger rig for summer and winter fishing, and only resort to the 'plastic pig' when the river is too coloured to bait up accurately with a bait dropper.

A good leger rig includes a Drennan bead running freely on the line but tied to a short length of 4lb line that holds the leger weight. The line is 8lb Drennan Specimen or Maxima in summer, and 6lb in winter.

The hook is a size 6 Au Lion D'Or eyed model 1534, or a size 8 Drennan Super Specialist eyed, though in winter use one size smaller.

By pushing the bait above the eye and stopping it from slipping back with a piece of thick nylon through the eye, you will eliminate the chance of the bait masking the hook or a piece of gristle impeding the point.

Try a hair rig for maggots. This is made by tying one end of a very short piece of 1lb, 2lb or 3lb nylon to a size 18 hook. Six maggots are put on this hook, and its point is pinched inwards. The other end of the nylon is tied to the bend of a normal-size 6 or 8 hook. This rig combines a hook delicate enough to carry maggots without bursting them with a hook strong enough to land a big barbel.

The knot to tie hooks is one popularised by the late Dick Walker. It is made by taking the line through the hook eye twice, and making five twists around the main line before taking the line back and making just three turns through the resulting loop. Moisten before tightening.

Baits for barbel are many and varied, but there are two that have no equals – maggots and casters. Luncheon meat is best in winter.

Overleaf In the 1950s barbel were virtually unknown in all except a few of Britain's rivers. Now, following stockings made by *Angling Times* and the river boards they are found in most fast-flowing English rivers, and a few in Wales, though not in Scotland. They are the hardest-fighting British fish, pound-for-pound, except for the salmon. Many clubs have a rule that they are not to be kept in a keepnet because the barb on the front of their dorsal fin catches in the mesh. These fish, biggest 7lb, came from the Severn near Bridgnorth and, like all the other fish shown in this book, were returned alive

A perfect summer's day on the River Kennet, as a hard-fighting barbel comes to the net

CHAPTER EIGHTEEN
THE CARP

The carp has attracted more interest from anglers in the past twenty years than any other species. Thousands of anglers now fish only for carp, having started their fishing career with other species and then found it the ultimate in finned perfection. Once comparatively rare, to be found only in private ponds and lakes in the grounds of stately homes, it is now difficult to find a stillwater that doesn't contain this most majestic and exciting of all freshwater fish.

The carp's fighting qualities are legendary, and even a fish of 4 or 5lb will put up a terrific scrap on ordinary tackle. The top carp anglers, who look chiefly for fish of 20lb or more, pay meticulous attention to their tackle, knowing that one weak link could result in the loss of the fish of a lifetime. But incredibly some manage to land several fish over 20lb each season.

The magic mark for a carp is 40lb. And though only a few waters are known to contain fish of this size, there is always the possibility that fish approaching this weight are cruising around in some long-forgotten farm pond unvisited by anglers for many years. Finding such waters is what makes carp fishing so exciting.

There are three main strains of carp – the common, which is fully scaled (shown in colour on page 138); the mirror, which has large scales either in patches or rows (as shown in colour on page 139); and the leather, which has no scales at all. Dick Walker's famous 44-pounder was a common. It was taken to London zoo after capture, where it swam about 'in state' for many years. Chris Yates's 51-pounder was a mirror and this remains the largest carp ever reported from Britain.

Colours vary considerably, ranging from the almost black of some leather carp, through the typical bronze of commons to the sometimes bright golden of mirror carp.

Two of the best months for carp fishing are December and January. And on really shallow waters you can catch them on floating baits even at that time of year. We often get a big freeze towards the end of January, and it's almost as if the carp have known a last fling, raking in the food to prepare themselves for the worst weather to come.

At the start of the season it is best to fish when temperatures are generally rising, while in the 'dog days' of July and August look for wind and an overcast sky. But in winter you will get better results when it's not so windy. Also avoid the period after heavy rain, which tends to be cold. Nevertheless in both autumn and winter look for a slow, steady drop in temperature, as this seems to spur fish into action.

Techniques

Carp-catching rigs

Carp fishing's mystique and ultra-cult is all part of the fun, but the sport itself is as difficult as you want to make it. Hard-fished waters in which many if not all the fish have been caught, demands an armoury of different rigs to allay the carp's suspicion. On the other hand little–fished lakes and ponds sometimes call for no more than a simple waggler rig or running leger to bring success. Always remember, if you can get away with using a simple rig do so. Only resort to a more complicated one if either you are getting no bites or are failing to hit those you do get. With carp leger rigs an electronic bite indicator is a worthwhile tackle item to employ in order to relieve the pressure required over long hours of concentration.

So let us take a look at five rigs, all of which have proven carp-catching ability:

Running leger rig This is one of the simplest and most effective leger rigs ever devised and has accounted for thousands of carp. The weight is free running on the line and stopped by a swivel, leger stop or single shot. Length of the tail from leger to hook varies but is usually about 12 to 24in.

Link leger rig This is much the same as a standard running leger, but the bomb is tied to a link, between 6 and 9in long. This set-up allows the bomb to become buried in mud or silt without marring the rig's effectiveness.

Floater rig Floating baits that have to be fished at any distance obviously cannot be cast without some sort of weight on the line; this is where the floater rig comes in. The 'float' is usually a piece of hard wood such as mahogany, which has the necessary weight for casting a good distance. The wood is drilled so that line can be threaded through it and a leger stop keeps the float away from the bait.

Fishing with floating baits is probably the most exciting form of carp fishing, for you can actually see the carp take your bait.

Bolt rig The bolt rig is intended for shy-biting fish that merely give 'twitches' on the bite indicator, without producing a full blown and easily hit run. The idea of the rig is that the carp picks up the bait and feels either the hook or the resistance caused by the lead on such a short tail. It panics and bolts with the bait, dragging the lead with it, which partially hooks the fish. A firm strike will then drive the hook home properly.

Hair rig The hair rig is the greatest development the carp fishing world has seen for years. Devised by top carp angler Kevin Maddocks it has proved deadly for otherwise uncatchable carp and can be used for other species too.

The 'hair' comprises a 1 to 3in long length of 1lb nylon onto which is threaded the bait. Alternatively, with soft baits, sharpen one end of a matchstick, tie the 'hair' to the blunt end and push the sharp end into the bait and bury it. This way you can carry a set of rigs ready made up to the waterside.

Carp will feed on those boiling-hot days when the world seems to fall asleep

The idea of the hair rig is to fool the carp into thinking it is picking up a free offering – something which is difficult to do when the bait is mounted on a heavy hook attached to stiff line. A carp comes along, hoovering up the free samples you have thrown in, and sucks in the bait on the hair rig, taking the hook with it. It is a deadly but simple invention.

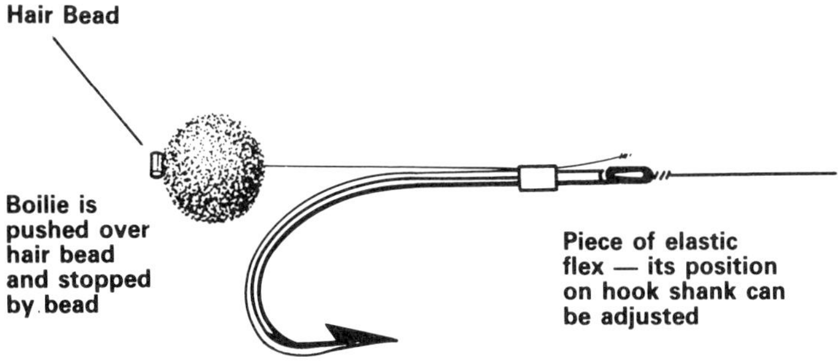

Fig 71 A basic hair rig

Float fishing

Although it's not now widely used by anglers after sizeable carp, float fishing can still be a deadly method, particularly if the fish aren't far from the bank and are finicky. Without a doubt it's the best method of fishing a bait in a small hole in a weed bed, or in a gap among underwater snags. The 'lift' method used by the Taylor brothers in the 1950s is a good method. Just one shot is used, usually a BB, and this is put a few inches from the hook (see above).

Use a small float (one which is partially cocked by the shot) and put it overdepth by a foot or so. Cast out, wait until the shot has hit bottom, and tighten up until only about ½in of the float is visible. When a fish takes the bait it lifts the shot and the float lies flat. Strike as it lifts, and since you will usually be fishing near weed or snags you should be prepared to hit the fish hard and try to get it to the surface as soon as possible.

It is advisable to use some type of hair rig even with a float, since this results in a greater percentage of hooked fish, rather than burying the bait in the traditional way. If the bottom has a film of weed on it a floating boilie will ensure it isn't hidden.

If you're fishing near weed or snags *always* grease the line up to the float so it can't get snagged.

The type of float you use is not very important, so long as it is buoyant. A simple crow quill or piece of peacock quill works as well as anything. However in strong winds you may need heavier tackle, and a float with plenty of balsa at the bottom will hold its position better than a light one.

Surface fishing

Surface fishing for carp must be the most exciting method there is. Even after many years of carp fishing, an angler can still tremble with anticipation when, hidden in bankside grass, he watches that great shape approaching. As it drifts upwards, its back breaks the surface and another flick of the massive tail takes it nearer to the floating bait. Then, as the ripples spread slowly away, its big, thick white lips open as it prepares to bite, every scale on its bronze body clearly visible. You've got to experience it to believe just how exciting it can be. Your heart can be thumping so loud that it seems impossible the fish can't hear it.

Traditionally, floating crust was the bait to use, and indeed there are still many waters where it puts lots of carp on the bank. However, there are many fisheries where carp are now wary of bread. There are also waters where carp stay well out from the bank, and crust just will not stand up to the rigorous casting necessary to get it out. Cooked high-protein cake is the answer in these situations.

Make the cake using a standard high-protein recipe but use double the number of eggs you would use for a bottom bait. Whisk it up to get lots of tiny air bubbles in it. Then pour the mixture into a baking tray, put into a preheated oven on full heat and leave for one minute to seal the outside of the cake.

Turn the heat down to gas mark 6 (200°C) and cook for 45 minutes. When finished the outside of the cake should be tough and rubbery and look like a Malteser. Cut into ½in cubes and it's ready for use.

Remember when making any floating bait that if you wish to add flavouring you should increase the amount of flavour by one-third because up to a third may evaporate during cooking.

The most popular floating baits used now are Pedigree Chum Mixer, Munchies and Dairy Dinner. These are soaked for use both on the hook and as loose-feed. It's an incredible sight to watch carp swirling when these are thrown in, and devouring every morsel in sight.

Whatever type of floating bait you use you will find the reaction of the carp is quicker if the bait is coated in oil. Blended fish oil is the best type to use, but pilchard and soya can both be productive.

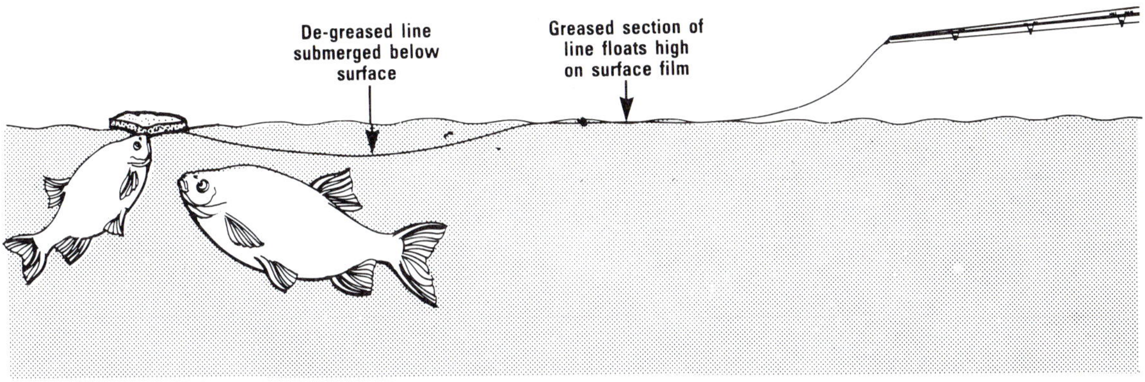

Fig 72 If you fish a floating bait ensure the line immediately next to the bait is sinking, otherwise it will cause a wake in the water when moved

'Beachcaster' rig

Whatever bait or method you use to catch surface-feeding carp you'll get better results if you can keep your line, from rod to bait, off the surface. Carp are keen eyed and will spot any disturbance on the surface caused by you tightening the line or even by the wind drifting it along.

The 'beachcaster' rig (inset below) is best used in shallow water, with few weed beds to snag the tackle as it is retrieved. In deep water, the fish has a long tail from float to leger weight to drag around.

The main picture below shows an adaptation, using a cigar-shaped pike float with whiskers of stiff nylon coming from the bottom to help keep it in place. These whiskers snag surface weed – but are easily broken free. The float is loaded at the bottom with lead to keep it upright. And the long tail necessary with the beachcaster rig is avoided.

The beauty of both these methods is that you can use stronger line than you would otherwise, because the fish cannot see it. Use line of about 11lb right through to the hook.

On the majority of waters it is essential to point the rod upwards to keep line off the surface. A sea-rod rest is useful, though if you are fishing from a high bank this may not be necessary. However, once you realise that fish are in the area

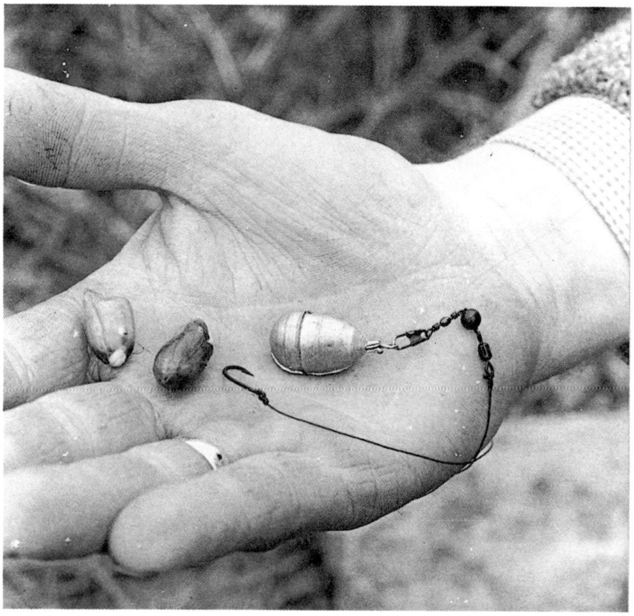

Dacron is a popular line with carp anglers, as it can be dyed and it is very supple. This is a double-peanut hair rig with Dacron hook length

it's best to hold the rod. The moment a fish mouths the bait, drop the rod tip, to allow a little slack line. You'll find that this is a much better way of catching fish than hoping for luck.

The further out you fish, the greater distance needed between the float and the hook length. This is tied to the main line with a grinner knot. Alternatively, you can use a sliding system with a bead and stop knot so that the distance between float and hook length can be adjusted at will.

Note that the hook is not shown to the fish at all. It is inserted into the bait from the top and twisted back without being allowed to protrude from the bottom.

There's no need for a hair rig here, since you actually watch the carp take the bait and can strike at the appropriate moment. The size of hook to use depends on the size of carp but anything between size 10 and size 4 will be adequate.

Getting the best from boilies

Not so long ago boilies were a mystery bait so far as the average angler was concerned. The various recipes and apparently complex mixtures used in their manufacture led anglers to believe the whole business was beyond them. However today there are hosts of ready-made boilies on offer in hundreds of tackle shops. Now the problem is how to get the best out of them.

Without a doubt boilies are best fished on a hair rig of some kind. The two main methods of attaching the bait are with a Dacron 'hair' tied to either the eye, bend or shank of the hook. In the latter case a small tube of silicon rubber can be pushed over the shank to position the hair correctly. With a straight-eyed hook the hair is best coming from the bend, while with an upturned-eyed hook it is best coming from the eye.

The hair rig is usually fished with a fixed lead (known as a bolt rig) or a semi-fixed lead, when a stop knot is put on the line 3ft above the weight. The principle is that the fish, moving off, will hook itself. It is rarely necessary for the angler to

Fig 73 Fishing well overdepth with a leger will allow maggots to float on the surface for a time before sinking. This tactic helped England International Bob Nudd win the 1986 Whitbread Championships, with a top prize of £5000

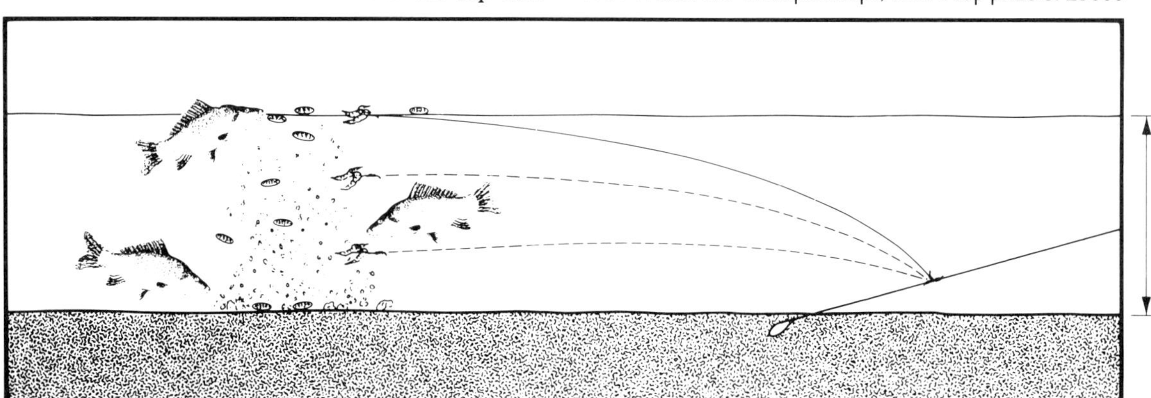

Magnificent examples of fully-scaled common carp

Carp come in all shapes, sizes and scale patterns – including this unusual fully-scaled mirror.

Note the absence of scales on this 40lb 8oz leather carp (*right*), taken from Yateley, Surrey by top carp man Ritchie McDonald

strike – all that is required is for the rod to be gently bent into the tightening line and the hook pulled home.

A good average set-up is with a 9in hook length tied to a swivel. Above this is a large bead, then an Arlesey bomb. Put the line through a snap-link swivel and clip the bomb to this. It is then easy to change it if necessary. Above the bomb is a smaller bead, and above this (the distance is optional) a grinner stop knot.

The matchman's approach

There are times when carp, like any other species, are so shy they can be taken only on the sort of light tackle that matchmen use. And there are other times when, although they will take big baits, many more will fall for small baits such as caster and maggot. Matchmen have developed two special, and rather, spectacular styles to catch these fish in matches.

Method 1

This first method was originally used on Layer Pits, Essex. Basically it involves using a massive, weighted float with no shot down the line. The tiny hook is baited with one or two maggots and the rig is cast anything up to 70yd. Groundbait

consists of balls of breadcrumb containing floating casters, and some sinking casters and maggots. The carp are therefore encouraged to come to the surface or to cruise about just under it, mopping up this groundbait. The hookbait stays on or just under the surface for some time, eventually dropping down towards the bottom under its own weight. When a fish takes the bait it tows the huge float along. Alternatively, if conditions are ideal and the fish close in, the angler may be able to see the line tightening even before the float goes under or moves.

Lines are usually only 3lb, with a short length of shock leader to prevent the line breaking when the float is cast. The floats frequently contain 1oz of built-in weight in the base. But because the fish are so far away when the angler strikes there is an enormous amount of stretch in the line, and breakages are rare. In the mid 1980s a fish of 27lb was landed by London angler, Bob Cheeseman, on this sort of rig.

The reason for the long-distance casting is that in the middle of the day, when matches are fished, carp often make for the centre of a lake where the water may be cooler and more oxygenated, and where they feel safe from any bankside disturbance.

It used to be generally assumed that carp did not feed in the heat of a summer's day, even though they could be seen swimming around. However, the appearance of large quantities of small-particle baits, both sinking and floating, appears to set them feeding. On a windy day it can be dangerous to put in many floating casters, as they can be blown out of your swim and can take the fish with them.

Method 2

The second method, used on Lake Dryad near Portsmouth, Hants, involves legering at distance in shallow water.

This particular lake is only 4ft deep; but it can be tackled with a straight leger and a 10ft tail. The effect is similar to that on Layer Pits – the bait is kept afloat for some time by the line, eventually sinking if it has not been taken by a fish. A bite can come when the bait is anywhere between surface and the bottom. It is signalled in the same way as on a normal leger rig. Fish can be so excited by the floating casters that they launch themselves at the bait, and virtually hook themselves.

Continual feeding is the secret. A small ball of groundbait (it should be very soft) is put out every minute or two. If there is no bite within five minutes, the usual routine is to reel in and cast again. You are most likely to get a bite within 15 seconds of the bait hitting the water.

If you are fishing at close range, be careful not to strike too hard. By the time you see a bite the fish may have hooked itself and you may need to move the rod towards the fish rather than strike, to avoid breakage.

These two styles were each developed for a particular water but they can be adapted to suit any water where there are large numbers of small or medium-sized carp.

Hooks are normally between 16 and 20, according to how finicky the fish are. On a still, hot day the smaller hook may be needed, but if a warm breeze is rippling the surface the fish are likely to be less choosy, and you will get away with using the larger size.

CHAPTER NINETEEN
THE CHUB

Summer chub
Shallow rivers can be a problem, dense weed often reaches the surface and the float angler is forced to walk on in search of deeper, easier fishing. Unfortunately this approach all too often means that the very best – and certainly some of the most exciting – chub fishing is left untouched. Yet a little planning and maybe an afternoon spent without tackle can buy the key to some great sport.

The first stage is to find the fish. Start on a sunny day by watching the river from a high point, for example a bridge or tree. But don't expect to see fish immediately. You may need to sit still for fifteen minutes or so until frightened chub return to their regular spots.

Watch close to rafts of dense weed and rubbish that have built up beneath overhanging trees. These tend to stay in one place for long periods and can become home to a large shoal. Also the

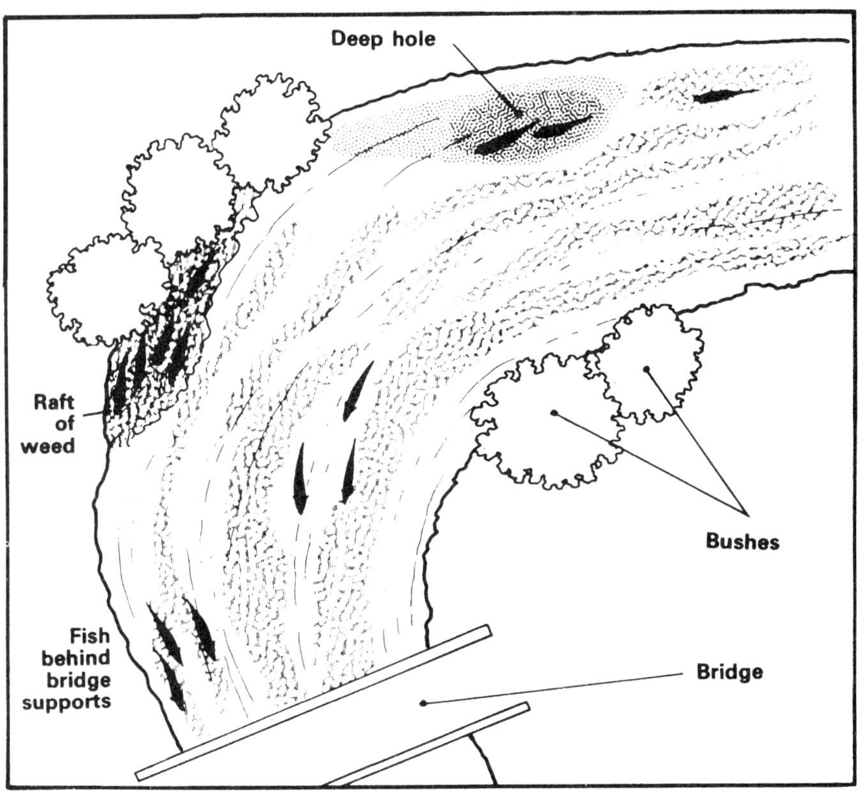

Fig 74 The places you should look for chub – behind bridge supports, under "rafts" of weed and rubbish, over small gravel patches in the middle of weeds, and in deep holes, though they are more difficult to see in deeper water. The fish may be difficult to spot until they move – and then you can see them as they cross gravel patches

There are dozens of waters where you can take a catch of chub like this one. The fish will feed avidly throughout the season. Find one and the chances are you've found a shoal of them

Chub are bold-biting fish, with large and healthy appetites. They can be found in most of our rivers – and some stillwaters, too

ESSEX COU
A.A.

river bed in these places tends to get a good scouring, resulting in very clean gravel over which fish love to swim. The bank in the same spot is also certainly undercut by current action so it will hold even more fish than may seem possible.

At first there may not appear to be a lot to see. This is because fish are difficult to spot as they hang in the current; but once they move across, their outline is more defined. Look also for fish moving against strips of gravel sheltered on either side by trailing weed. This gives the fish an immediate bolt-hole if it senses danger. Other good places are between weed beds and close to bridge supports or any overhead cover.

Another trick is to drop one – or at most two – pieces of floating crust onto the water surface and watch them drift downstream. But if you plan to fish straightaway be sure to limit this feeding to just a couple of pieces. Chub have a habit of taking the first food offerings and then ignoring the rest.

So to start fishing these shallow swims it has got to be the floating crust method. And there is nothing better than seeing the bread vanish in a swirl as a chub crashes on the surface – if nothing else it will boost your confidence to see a rising fish. A catapult may be a handy thing to have around at this stage so that bread can be fired onto the water without the need for a lot of arm waving. Other, small fish may attack these loose offerings but don't worry, the activity will maybe attract the chub too.

Stick a rod rest into the bank so that the tackle can be kept clear of nettles and bankside debris while you are tackling up. Go for a 4lb line and a size 6 hook – yes 6 – anything smaller will make baiting with floating bread very difficult. Nothing else goes on the line, no shot, no float, just a hook and eventually the bait.

Don't throw in other pieces of bread around your bait. Make sure it sails downstream on its own; make no mistake the chub will see it. Other pieces of bread will only serve to split their attention and reduce your chance of hooking a fish. Don't worry about the bait dragging across the current, if you haven't scared the chub they will take it just the same.

Start fishing at the upstream end of the section of river to be fished and keep moving downwards. If you don't hook a fish straightaway after letting the line drift as far down as possible walk 20yd downstream and try again, remembering to make the best use of bankside cover. Keep down with bushes at your back. Never stand up on the skyline or move quickly.

Once a fish takes your floating crust the action really starts, but don't be in too much of a hurry to strike. It's a bit like dry-fly fishing for trout – the fly vanishes in a swirl, there is a slight pause and then the angler tightens into the fish. With floating-bait fishing the principle is the same. The bait is taken, pulled downwards as the fish turns, the angler tightens up any slack in his line and then pulls rather than strikes. A long rod is useful for taking up the slack and it will make landing the fish much easier than a short one. The extra length gives better overall control of both fish and bait.

One handy tip is to always keep a tin of grease handy while fishing a floating-bait method. Greasing the line will ensure that it floats. Left to sink it makes striking difficult and many fish will be missed as a result.

The bait we have selected – floating crust – can be used in a number of ways, but one tried and tested method of preparation is to cut off a 1in square just prior to baiting the hook. Cutting like this at the last moment helps to prevent it drying

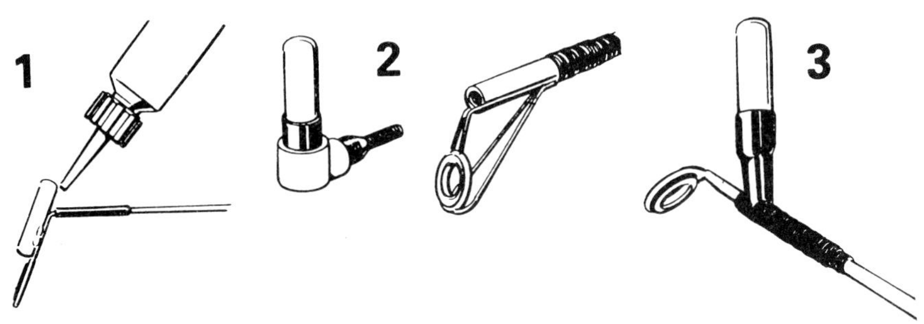

Fig 75 Three different ways of fixing a glowing betalight:
1 Glued on to an extra-long ring on a quivertip.
2 Screwed into a threaded end ring.
3 Pushed into a home-made rubber holder glued on the rod, near the tip ring.

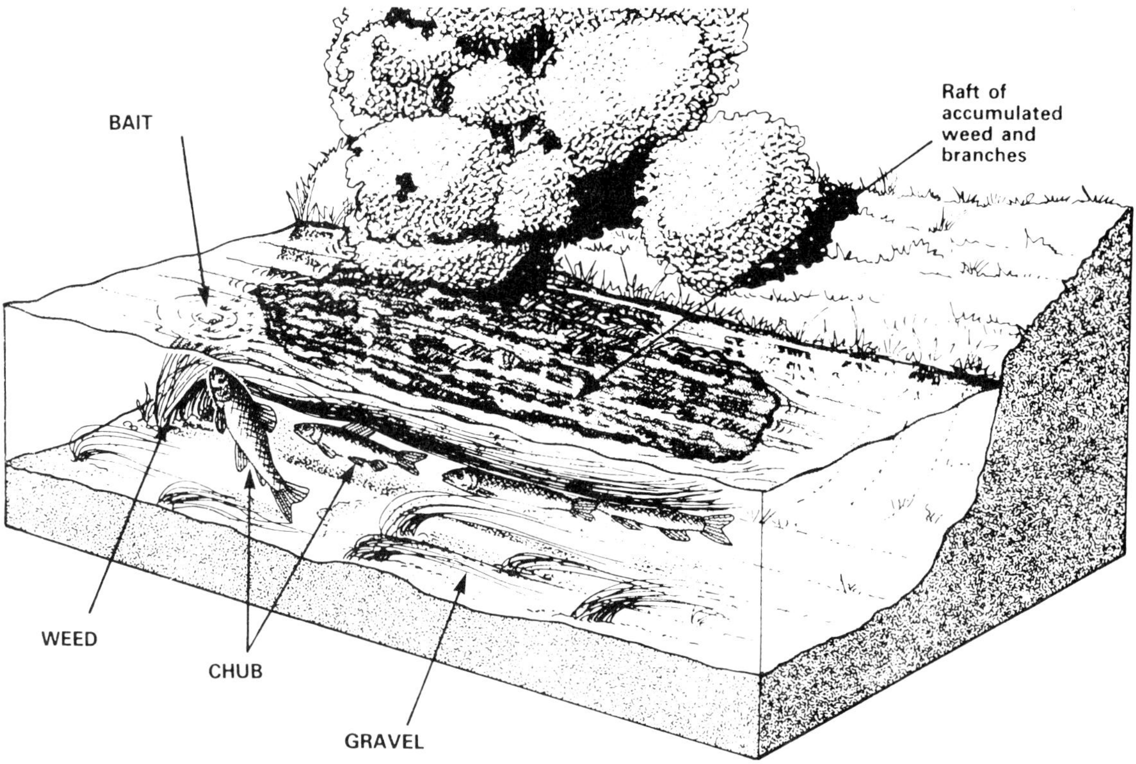

Fig 76 First glance at a raft of weed and rubbish will show nothing special. But take another long, hard, look, and you may see the chub betraying their presence by occasionally drifting away from the shoal. Dave says that, if you see one, there are certain to be others in the same place. Remember that the bank may be undercut, so there is more space than may be immediately obvious. Fish will drop downstream of the raft, or drift sideways, but only rarely swim up in front of it – except to take your floating crust!

(*below*) A typical situation when fishing for chub among heavy weeds . . . the fish dives into a weed bed. Don't keep pulling it upstream – much better to get below it and try again from there, so the current is working FOR instead of against you.

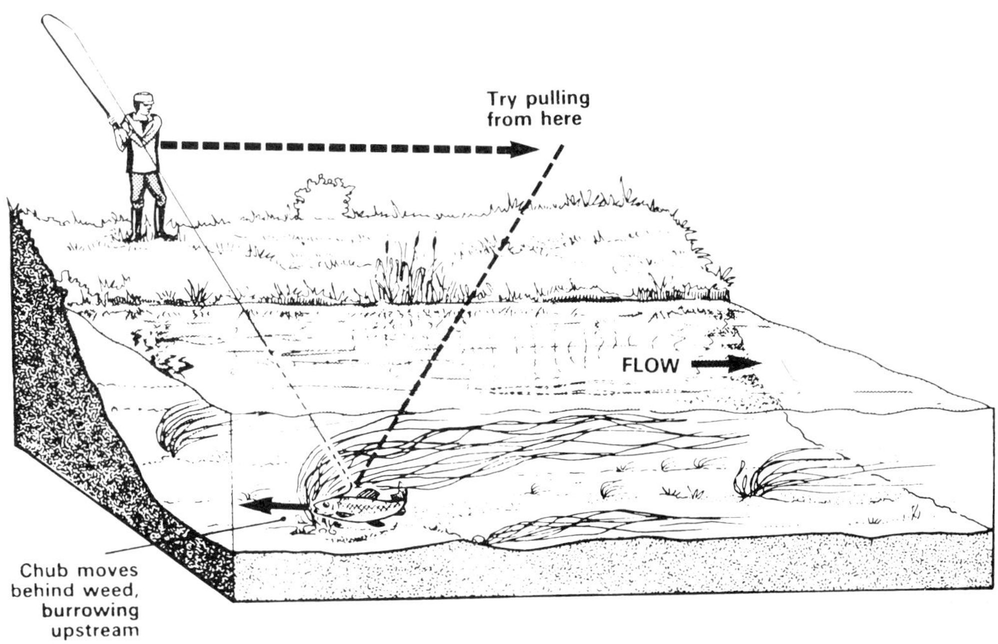

out. To bait the hook pass the point through from the crust side, twist it and pull it back. Done in this manner it will then float white side up and will be much easier to see.

Very new bread will contain more moisture than stale. This makes it heavier and easier to cast than the dry stuff.

Winter chub

Winter fishing can all too often be very hard work for little reward. Those easy feeding shoals of roach and bream will be harder to tempt and the slightest drop in temperature may be enough to leave you fishless. Thankfully chub are the exception, for in many ways they become easier to catch during winter. The hardest part of the exercise may be actually locating them. They will have moved away from their summer haunts, taking up stations in river-bed depressions. This does not mean they will be in the deepest holes, the slowest swims are very often fishless. Look for them instead where the river shelves downwards.

The chub will be in the slacker water but only inches away from the main stream where food will be passing them as it is swept overhead. A big worm or a lump of bread passes by, the fish moves out, gulps it down and returns to its holding position. There's a hook in that food morsel so the fish is yours.

The nice thing about this winter sport is that it is not a stationary occupation. Like spinning for pike there is always plenty to do and any number of swims to fish. But picking the right day is important. If the river is rising after heavy rain fishing may be a waste of time. Get it fining down after a flood and you could be onto a real winner. Aim to catch the river a few inches above normal level but after it has started to clear. Chub don't seem to like a lot of sediment suspended in the current. As to time of day, chub are very obliging. They will feed on and off for most of the time and are probably one of the best of all species in this respect.

This winter method is one that involves moving along the river, baiting three or four swims as you go, returning later to fish them all in turn. But take care not to walk close to the water's edge. For even in fast, coloured water chub will scare very easily.

Baiting the swims is simple enough. Just leave some old loaves in water overnight. Tip away the excess water and mash the bread, squeezing out as much water as possible. Next add a little medium breadcrumb – dry groundbait that is not too fine – to bind it all together. Approach the first swim, preferably from upstream, and introduce a couple of balls of bait. If you are not sure where the deeper holes are, look for the slowest water and then introduce your feed just upstream.

Having completed the task continue to walk downstream and repeat the operation in two or three other likely looking spots. That job over, walk back upstream and start fishing the first swim with leger tackle. Make your first cast to the far side easing the bait back if possible so that it swings across the current. Next cast is to the middle and the third is under the near bank.

If there is a chub in the swim it will most certainly have seen the bait and chances are a bite will result. If you don't get that bite within three or four casts – say about twenty minutes – rebait the swim and move off downstream to the next baited spot. You may prefer to fish with a rod rest or simply hold the rod and feel for bites. Holding the rod and feeling the line is a very enjoyable way of fishing, but be prepared to concentrate very hard. On arrival at the second spot, which is already well baited, repeat the casting pattern just described. When it has been well fished rebait it and move off to the third swim. At the end of the route walk back to the top swim and re-fish all those spots that looked at all promising, particularly those from which you actually caught fish. Chances are there will be others there that by now will have started to feed. Don't make the mistake of stopping in the same swim all afternoon just because you caught a chub there. As a general rule rest the swim after twenty minutes without a chub, but make a mental note to return later.

The good thing about this style of fishing is that the next swim is always just that little more inviting than the one you are fishing. That's part of the attraction and it keeps you warmer than just sitting in one place.

Because you will be roaming the banks rather a lot during the course of a day's sport it pays to keep tackle down to a minimum. Take along just a rod, a rest and a shoulder bag containing line, leger weights, hooks, shot, bait, possibly a few floats and a landing net – but no keepnet.

Talking of keepnets, or lack of one, an extra tip is that you always return chub upstream of the

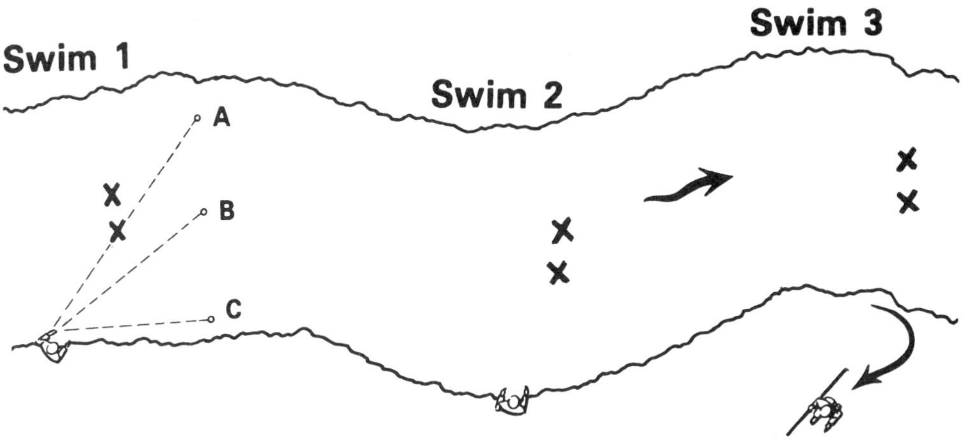

Fig 77 A useful routine when summer or winter chub fishing. Bait in all three swims to begin with. Then return to Swim 1 and try three casts in it (one at point A, one at B and one at C). After 20 minutes without a fish put in more bait and move down to Swim 2. Repeat the sequence here, then in Swim 3, before returning to Swim 1 and starting again

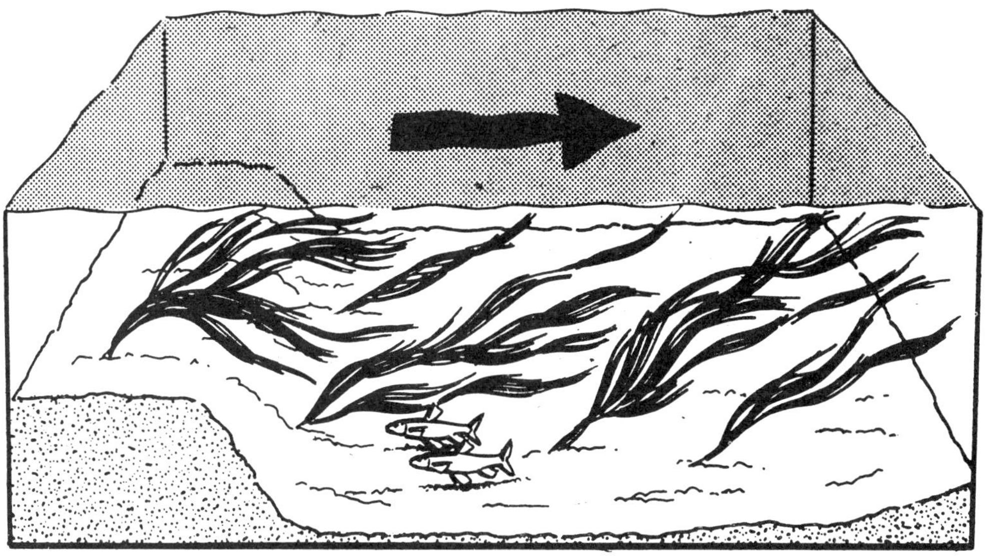

Fig 78 The sort of swim to hold chub in Autumn or Winter. Look for a dip in the river bed and aim to fish at the upstream end. The fish will be in the slack water behind the shelf, moving into the current to take their food as it swirls by. Though there will be the remains of heavy Summer weed, it should not present a problem after the first floods of Winter.

point at which you landed it. It may stay where it is returned or shoot off upstream; but it is unlikely to go back downstream to the shoal immediately, which means you may still be able to catch others before they give fright.

A simple link leger will be ideal for searching your swim in the way described. Say 6 to 8in to the weight and 2ft to the hook. Note that if shot are used as a weight, a leger stop should be used to prevent the link pulling down to the hook. With an Arlesey bomb the leger stop will slip. Use a split ring with a bead above it to prevent the extra weight pulling the stop down towards the hook on the strike.

Although the method outlined is a good one to try with bread flake there are many other good winter-chub baits. Lobworms are one of the best if the water is in any state of flood. And they are easy to collect, cost nothing and can be fished on big hooks which give you the best possible chance of landing a real specimen.

If you plan to fish the breadflake method it may pay to have an extra little trick up your sleeve in the form of cheese spread – the sort that is sold in tubes is ideal. Bait the hook with plain breadflake then add a smear of cheese paste straight from the tube. The tubes come in all sorts of flavours so don't be afraid to try a variety. They all work but the key to consistently good results is good presentation.

CHAPTER TWENTY
THE BREAM

After years of neglect, there's been a growing interest among specimen hunters in the capture of big bream. Massive fish of 14lb, 15lb and 16lb have been taken from a number of waters. And there's no doubt that plenty of other stillwaters hold double-figure specimens, perhaps even record-breakers. Small bream are not hard to find. Commonly located in ponds, lakes, streams, reservoirs, gravel pits and rivers, it's a species many anglers have tangled with. But the bigger fish, still an enigma to most fishermen, can be as wary as the oldest carp. Understandably, therefore, some anglers have become fascinated by those huge, lumbering bream.

Even the bream's admirers would have to agree, however, that it is not the hardest fighting of our fish. A steady 'thump' on the end of the line is the usual tell-tale sign that you're playing one – hence the matchman's term for them is 'nodders'.

And they are not fussy feeders either, if you can persuade them to get their heads down on your groundbait. Once you've managed that then you're in for a bumper catch, for bream will then mop up any bait you care to cast or throw to them.

In the last decade the growing army of Britain's specialist ranks have turned their attentions to the 'unglamorous' bream with staggering results. The magic mark which most specialist anglers aim for is still 10lb. It is a rare water that can turn up lots of bream over this size and more often than not it is the weed-infested gravel pits, rich in natural insect life, which provide the best chance. In rivers, an 8lb fish is considered a more than worthwhile achievement and generally they don't have the necessary natural food to produce a strain of fish capable of growing to double figures.

The fish vary considerably in colour from the beautiful bronze shade for which they are famous to a dark black tint often found in fish from gravel pits and reservoirs.

Practical tips

Two-hook rig

Bream can be finicky feeders. On some waters they will readily take maggots and ignore sweetcorn, while on other fisheries they prefer worm. They will also vary from day to day, at times finding one bait apparently irresistible while the next day completely ignoring it.

Worms, sweetcorn, caster, maggot, breadflake paste – they all have their day. But when you decide to tackle a new water you've probably got nothing to go on at all. What bait do you start with? If you're after big bream there won't be so many in the water anyway, so it's going to take quite a lot of thought to decide which bait will bring success.

A way of doubling your chances of finding a bait the fish will take is to fish a two-hook rig (see overleaf, top left). If the rules allow you to fish two rods you can double-up, and use four different baits at the same time. Suddenly your chances of succeeding have increased fourfold. You could start with sweetcorn, bread, worm and maggot and swop over to conventional rigs once the fish have given away their bait preference.

The basic set-up is exactly the same as for running leger. Bream are essentially bottom feeders, except for some waters where the bait must be placed on top of the weed, and they nearly always feed some distance from the bank. This means legering is the only practical method to use. The running leger rig is the most adaptable, designed to cope with most angling conditions.

Resistance is the key to this method, the more the better, for bream like to feel a steady resistance when they take the bait. The rig itself is nothing exotic. The paternoster link can be altered to any length, though 18in to 2ft is best. You can either use a swimfeeder or straight leger, but the heavier the weight the better.

Some bites are very slow and steady, with the bobbin on your monkey-climber rising agonisingly to the top. Always make sure you wait until it reaches the top before striking, because a bream can mouth a bait for a long time before making up its mind to take it. Even then they sometimes reject it.

The weights to use with the running leger, or any other legering technique, weigh between 1½oz and 2oz. This aids the steady resistance. Line is usually 6lb straight through to the hook for both reel line and paternoster link, with hook sizes varying between 10 and 12, depending on the size or quantity of bait you are using.

Anti-tangle rig

The anti-tangle rig (below left is one way of fishing a bait over heavy weed carpeting the bottom of a lake or pit – the sort of environment bream often make for. A straight leger or swimfeeder rig will be next to useless in a water like this, as the bait is soon lost in the weed or silt. But an anti-tangle

While the bream is not generally noted as a hard-fighting fish it does grow big, well into double figures

boom, which can be bought from specialist tackle shops, will hold your main line above the weed, allowing the bait to remain in full view of the fish. Ungainly it may look, but it works!

Though some shops sell ready-made booms you can make up your own by buying tubing and cutting it to the required length. That can be as much as 7ft in heavily weeded lakes, though 18in is more normal. A 1½oz or 2oz leger weight is tied to one end of some strong line, which is passed through the tubing with a swivel tied on the other end. The reel line runs through this, stopped with a leger stop.

Breadflake is an obvious bait to use with this rig. Another successful ploy is to air-inject a lobworm, using a syringe. This causes it to float or sink very slowly so that it will settle on quite delicate weed.

Bream are hungry feeders and once you've attracted them into your swim, you've got to keep them there. To do this successfully means regularly placing lots of hookbait samples and other groundbait ingredients into an area only a few yards across.

To bait up a swim some 70yd out can be best done by boat (where rules allow) and include several pints of hemp, sweetcorn and maggots, plus some Sensas groundbait. If you haven't access to a boat, the only course of action left open is accurate casting with a swimfeeder rig packed to the brim with free offerings.

This is fine if you're daylight fishing, but casting regularly into the same spot in complete darkness can become a nightmare. Before darkness falls, mark out the distance you want to cast by laying out your line on the bank. If you want to cast 60yd, pull 60yd of line off the reel onto the bank and slip an elastic band over the spool. This will ensure that you cast only 60yd every time.

If fishing with maggots, use a block-end Drennan feeder packed with maggots, hemp, sweetcorn or worms. Use an open-ended Drennan feeder when fishing other baits, normally packing it full of groundbait and hemp with some sweetcorn and maggots thrown in.

You won't necessarily need to concentrate on one tiny spot. Don't be afraid of spreading the bait around a little, for some shoals are quite big, and the larger area your bait covers (within reason) the more chance you have of keeping them in your swim.

You can't beat a lobworm

There's only one bait better than a big lobworm for bream and that's two big lobworms. They can't be beaten, and it's so easy to get them – go on to your lawn on a warm rainy night and you'll see dozens of them. Almost all the big bream taken by Coventry bream fanatic Phil Smith have been taken on lobworm.

Sweetcorn, maggots, breadflake and paste are also obvious bream baits, and even casters have acquired quite a reputation, while Alan Wilson's tremendous bream catches from Startops Reservoir were taken on maggot. River bream will often take a particular liking to the matchman's favourite – the caster.

Because most of your fishing will be done in darkness (this is undoubtedly the best time to catch bream) an audible Optonic alarm is a 'must'. But don't assume that all you do is hear the buzzer and strike; you need a monkey climber or bobbin so that you can watch the bite develop.

A quick burst on an Optonic, followed by no other indication, is probably a line bite, telling you that there are fish in the vicinity of your bait. Don't strike at these twitches. Wait until you get a proper bite.

Playing a bream

There are anglers who claim that bream do not fight well. To some degree that is true, but even so there is a right and a wrong way to go about landing one. Do it the right way and others in the shoal will continue to feed, and you'll probably enjoy a good day's sport. Get it wrong, just once, and the hooked fish will send warning signals to its mates and your fishing will be doomed. So the most important thing to remember, as any experienced angler will tell you, is don't disturb the shoal. Bream in particular take fright very easily. If one fish shoots off scared, it's odds-on the others nearby will follow.

Most anglers know this happens when you lose a bream, particularly if you lose it in the middle of the shoal. If it comes off at the net there is always a chance that it will not return until it feels less jittery. What many people ignore is the other danger time – when a fish is actually being played. The more a hooked fish flashes, or runs through the feeding shoal, the more chance there is that they will take fright. So the answer is to get it out as quickly as possible. And as this will give you more fishing time anyway it's an important consideration, especially if you're fishing a match. The best, and only, way to play a bream is to keep winding once you've got the fish on the move.

The first action is to strike, and continue the sweeping movement of the rod to get the fish moving. Then start winding. The bream should move towards you, more easily than you might expect. They fight a bit like eels with lots of pull, but they come if you pull back at them hard enough.

Chub and pike are more dashing, and will always pull against you. In fact one trick to try when playing a chub that looks like careering into a weed bed is to alter the angle of pull, and attempt to pull it into the weed – often the fish will automatically turn. Then keep light pressure on until it's in open water again. But with a bream it is important to keep it moving towards you in a smooth fashion. Don't pump it. Many anglers do, but really it is a bad tactic. For one thing, the continual changing of pressure can loosen the hook-hold. But the most important reason is that every time you slacken the pressure to wind down to the fish, the latter has a chance to turn away and get its head down. Then you have the job of getting it moving again. And while it turns and twists, it flashes in the water and disturbs the shoal.

The flash of a hooked fish can be seen a long way away by a human, so it must be seen by other fish much more clearly, and that's when the shoal will take fright and swim off. A scared shoal is probably the reason why lots of anglers catch just one bream and no more, if they hook that one before the shoal has really settled down to feed. A hooked fish allowed to flash while the shoal is still making its mind up where to stop is deadly. That's why the first one hooked is always the most important.

Make sure your reel is absolutely free running, for any jarring will upset the fish. Keep winding at a steady pace and don't be tempted to increase speed to save a few seconds, for this may cause the bream to take fright again. With care it is possible to get a fish right under the rod tip before it realises it's hooked. Then it's a matter of turning it over on its side and sliding it over the net. You have to pick your moment, but that will come with experience. The most important thing is to get it away from the shoal.

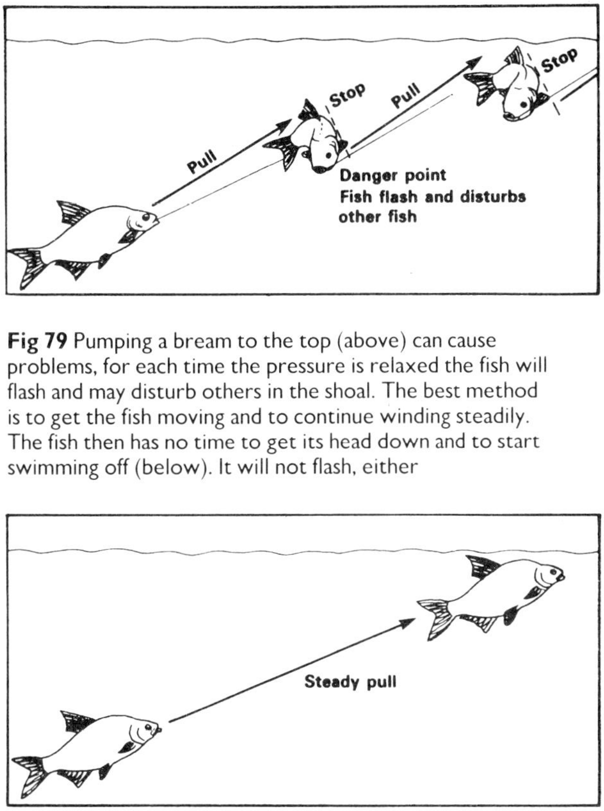

Fig 79 Pumping a bream to the top (above) can cause problems, for each time the pressure is relaxed the fish will flash and may disturb others in the shoal. The best method is to get the fish moving and to continue winding steadily. The fish then has no time to get its head down and to start swimming off (below). It will not flash, either

Roach, can be difficult, and roach/bream hybrids even worse. They will charge all over the river and never give up. Bream don't give that kind of trouble unless they are foul-hooked, in which situation they seem to be able to do just as they like. The same thing happens if a properly hooked fish turns and the line snags beneath a fin.

CHAPTER TWENTY-ONE
THE ROACH

Ask any ten anglers what their main angling ambition is, and it's odds-on the majority will say 'to catch a 2lb roach'.

Catching that magic first two-pounder is something no one ever forgets, for though there are much larger fish of other species swimming around our waters, the delicate silvery-green scales of the roach hold a special place in the affections of most anglers.

There can be hardly an angler walking the banks who hasn't caught one for they are by far the most prolific and most widespread of our freshwater fish. Yet on most waters a 6oz specimen is one to savour, and on 95 per cent of waters in the United Kingdom a roach of 1lb is a very nice catch indeed. However, though most two-pounders, and even three-pounders, fall to anglers fishing specifically for them, there are some waters where fish of this size can turn up unexpectedly, providing some lucky angler with a red-letter day. The Hampshire Avon and Dorset Stour produce dozens each season.

Unlike chub, roach are solid fish, and may well weigh more than would appear at first glance. For instance, the weight-for-length scale given in the *Angling Times* diary shows a 17in chub to weigh 2lb 8½oz, while a roach of the same length would weigh almost 1lb more.

The fight put up by a big roach can be most impressive. Expect to take much longer landing a 2lb roach than a chub or bream of the same weight.

It's hard to generalise about the type of swim inhabited by big roach. In the end you may have to fall back on trial, error and local knowledge. If in doubt about which method to use, start off by fishing a static bait if possible, particularly in winter.

Although big roach can theoretically be caught at any time of the fishing season the best time is undoubtedly during a mild spell in winter, preferably as the river is fining down after a flood. By all means try for roach in summer, but it is a fact that on many waters hardly any are caught until autumn comes.

Identification

Many anglers have difficulty in telling the difference between a roach and its close cousin, the rudd. Here are some pointers (see below).

A roach is silvery green, has rather pale fins and is sleek, though big roach tend to develop a hump back. Generally a rudd is more golden with a slightly more chunky look and blood-red fins.

The mouth of a roach tends to turn down, while the lower lip of a rudd is almost protruding. However the position of the dorsal fin (on the back) should give it away – in the roach it starts almost exactly above the pectoral fins while in the rudd it is set well back from the lower pectorals.

The eye of a roach generally has a reddish tinge while that of a rudd is yellowy. The scales on the

lateral line of both fish are easy to count, as each has a small dot on it. In a roach there are between 40 and 45, and in a rudd from 42 to 45.

The two fish can interbreed, producing a hybrid, but positively identifying a hybrid is a job for an expert, and would entail killing the fish.

Practical tips

Link leger (above)

For a lot of the time, big roach will accept only a static bait so legering forms a major part of the roach angler's repertoire. And the link leger is the most versatile leger rig for fishing rivers (above).

Once you've found a shoal, bites are not difficult to come by, but hooking the fish is another matter. Inevitably you'll have problems, so here are some tips. You'll still not hit every bite but you should hit an acceptable percentage.

Firstly, a rod with a built-in quivertip is a 'must'. Secondly, do not tighten the line completely, but leave a fair bow in it. Next, stay a fair distance from the fish, which will create a larger bow. These last two things will help slow down the indication of the bite, and prevent you striking too soon. Certainly, whatever the reasons, this makes hitting the bites easier.

Float fishing running water

Fished 'double-rubber' and with plenty of shot down the line, this is the ideal set-up for winter roach.

In the heavy flows frequently experienced at

When the river is low and clear this rig comes into its own (see *Hempseed tactics* overleaf)

this time of year you'll need a balsa float taking two or three swan shot. Use 2lb line straight through to a size 12 hook, with breadflake as the bait. Use flake from a fresh loaf and gently pinch a thumbnail-sized piece on the hook, taking care to leave the point exposed, otherwise you will miss bites. The Kamatsu (or Kamasan) 'Specimen Ringed' (eyed) hook, round-bend, No B980 is a well-proven pattern.

For groundbait soak stale, unsliced bread for a couple of hours and squeeze out as much of the water as you can. Mash it up well. For fast water or when you need to throw it some distance mix dry groundbait in to prevent the ball breaking in mid-air. Introduce it in egg-sized pieces, starting with three or four together then adding one every ten minutes or so.

Set it up so that the bottom shot – a BB – is about 8in from the hook and just off the bottom. Then the flake will be tripping the river bed, and you can slow it down by holding back the float.

Alternatively maggots can be used as groundbait and are equally successful especially in really cold water.

Long-range swimfeeder rig

This is the rig which accounts for most big stillwater roach. They tend to stay well out from the banks on lakes and pits, and this rig can be fished at long range. It is still pretty sensitive, and relatively tangle free.

However, long-range fishing is demanding on tackle, so use a 5lb main line and 2lb or 3lb line to the hook. Maggots or casters in a swimfeeder are ideal bait, while the hook should be reasonably small – size 16 or 18. Go down to a size 20 only if the fish are really shy.

It is important to get the hook length right, so start off with one of 3ft, reducing it if you start to miss bites or get maggots shredded without seeing a bite. Gradually reduce it to as little as 4in if necessary.

Ideally pick a swim where roach are seen rolling or 'topping'. Failing that, try to put your bait

Four nice roach – a stamp of fish typical of thousands caught on hemp and tares every weekend throughout the summer

somewhere near an underwater feature in a good depth of water. That's the most likely area to find the big ones. If you're swimfeeding maggot, make sure it goes into the same spot each time. It's vitally important to concentrate the groundbait to draw the fish to your hookbait.

Hempseed tactics

When the river is low and clear this rig comes into its own. This is especially so during summer and autumn, when the combination of hemp and tares, or hemp and caster, works well.

Introduce hemp with a catapult every few minutes, with either a tare or caster on a size 16 hook as bait.

Roach love hemp in warmer weather, but will quickly become pre-occupied with it, so feed it sparingly otherwise they will ignore all other baits.

Driftbeater methods

On large stillwaters where there is a powerful drift, and on slow-moving rivers, the Driftbeater float rig is an ideal set up.

Where sensitivity is important but you wish to retain stability and visibility at ranges of 30yd or more, the Driftbeater will do just that.

The bottom shot acts as your indicator shot, and should normally be between 2 and 12in from the hook – 6in is a good starting point. Normally fish it just off the bottom, using a No 1 or a BB, but if the drift is severe just on the bottom.

The matchman's approach

Roach are a shoal fish, and when you catch one you can be sure there are others nearby. That's probably why they are so popular with matchmen and pleasure anglers alike. When they stop biting freely it's a challenge finding out how to catch them. Yet you can rely on roach to respond even when most other species refuse to feed. Get bait presentation right along with a good feeding pattern and you should catch at least some of those in the swim.

As already mentioned, some of the best roach fishing is in winter, and then you can often pick up quality fish – of 8oz or more – in spots where, in summer, you get only small fish. But whatever time of year you are fishing you'll find a plummet invaluable.

Roach tend to hang around ledges, where food will eventually finish up. So start off by plumbing the depth and noting any spots where the depth changes rapidly, even if only by 4 or 5in. Don't ignore the most obvious ledge of all – where the bankside reeds grow. Often, particularly when the water is coloured, it's possible to catch big roach right under your rod tip, or even closer to the bank.

Though bread is an excellent bait for picking out big roach, maggot is still very reliable. In clear water, caster will work just as well, and this bait has the advantage of allowing you to bury the hook inside it, so you can drag it along the bottom without it picking up too much weed. Former world champion Dave Thomas always uses either one or two maggots, never more. He finds bronze the best colour for roach, believing the fluorescent finish stands out to the fish like a roadworker's jacket. Red maggots are now easily obtainable, and sometimes a bronze and a red together is a good starting combination. If you find fish sucking just one, it will give you a clue to which colour they prefer on that day.

Roach are excited by movement of the bait. That is why loose-feeding is preferable, certainly to start off with. You'll get more consistent results if you can fish a bait either sinking or at least dropping through the last foot of water, rather than placing it straight onto the bottom. Use groundbait only if it's impossible to get maggots to the required spot without it. If you can get roach roaming about after the falling bait they will excite others nearby and you'll get a chain reaction. By not overfeeding you will also get them competing for the bait – that way a roach doesn't have time to make up its mind whether to eat it or not. If it doesn't, the food is liable to be whipped away from under its nose by another fish.

Presenting a bait correctly is a matter of trial and error. If you're floatfishing, start by letting the float go through at the speed of the current, just off bottom. If that doesn't work, put the float higher up the line so that it drags on the bottom. If there is still no response repeat the procedure, but with the float held back to half the current speed, or even stationary. On stillwaters it can sometimes make a difference how much line there is lying on the bottom. With 3in you may not get a bite; but fish 3ft overdepth and bites could suddenly start. Why is a mystery; but it can work.

Britain's most popular species is undoubtedly the roach, which can be found in rivers and stillwaters throughout the country. This fine net was taken from the River Severn

There is some fine roach fishing too in Northern Ireland, where the shoals can be massive. This bag came from the River Erne

AMORCE
Sensas

Fig 80 With a little care it is possible to get the point of a hook protruding through the shell of a caster (left). Even so some roach will bite short and take off the end (known as shelling – centre). It is advisable to inspect the bait closely if you've missed a bite, for what appears to be a complete caster may, in fact, be punctured (right)

In winter it's a good idea to start off on a leger, because often the best chance of a bite is with a stationary bait. In these circumstances take great care with choice of hook. It must be fine wire. This is lighter than the forged hook, and when a fish sucks a maggot in (which it can do from several inches away) the small, light hook allows the maggot to travel into the fish's mouth. A heavy hook may leave it lying on the bottom. Hook the maggot as lightly as you can, so that it wriggles for as long as possible. Use a size 22 if you can handle it, or even a size 24 if you think fish are mouthing the bait but not taking it properly. For a maggot a crystal bend with a whisker barb is a good starting point.

Roach are active fish, and it's almost inevitable that at some time during the day they will stop feeding. But are you sure they have stopped feeding? The odds are that unless conditions have changed – a sudden drop in air or water temperature – they are still in the swim. If you've been loose-feeding regularly it may be the shoal has moved either up in the water to intercept the falling loose-feed, or perhaps a few feet to one side. This is particularly true in running water, when perhaps a slight increase or decrease in current may alter the course of the feed. Alternatively the fish may have dropped back. This is the time to experiment. Don't sit there hoping they'll come back – you've got to find them. Do anything. Move the bottom shot, which will affect presentation, or change depth by a few inches either way. Try farther out or close in, under your rod tip. Or cast to the end of your swim. On stillwater perhaps the fish have moved towards cover. This could be an overhanging tree or a reed bed, or even a submerged weed bed you cannot see. The colder the water the less likely the fish are to have moved very far. So a few inches can make a difference in winter.

There are other reasons why roach will stop feeding, of course. A shoal of roach will have a lot of fish in it, and can easily attract the attentions of a pike. There's little you can do about this until the pike goes. If you can afford to do so it may be worth stopping feeding, as the flashing of feeding fish is the surest way to bring a pike into your swim. Then you'll have to hope you can get the shoal feeding again when old Esox has gone (or when he's had his dinner). On running water, chub can be a nuisance. Often you'll be catching roach when, suddenly, you hook a chub. It may then be half an hour before the roach return. They react to chub in the same way as bream react to eels; they'll swim off rather than attempt to compete.

But if you've been catching roach and they suddenly stop feeding, then, unless you've seen signs of chub or pike, you should assume they are still there and keep working for them.

As a general rule look for roach over gravel swims in summer and over mud in winter. The reason is that gravel usually indicates a fairly fast current which scours the bottom, while mud shows a slower swim where silt falls from the water. One of the most obliging things about roach is that they are usually found in the same swims each year. So a swim which fished well in early season one year should also be a good bet the next year provided it hasn't been changed by dredging or alteration of the flow.

In autumn roach move from the fast, shallow areas to deeper water. In flood they tend always to group together in the same areas each year. And some time in February or March, according to how cold the winter has been, they start massing together in preparation for spawning. If you can remember where these areas are each year you should concentrate on them.

CHAPTER TWENTY-TWO
THE DACE

There aren't many anglers who concentrate on catching specimen dace. But thousands are grateful to these little mini-torpedoes for brightening their sport on rivers.

Look for dace in fast runs; they always hang about in the same areas, and locals should know where to find them. Towards the end of February, however, they pack together prior to spawning, and this is your best chance of making a big catch or getting a good fish. Any dace of 1lb is worth reporting. But as always, take care how you treat them – a 1lb dace will be eight or nine years old.

In summer, bread is a good bait, and when you fish this method keep flicking in a little portion every minute. All round, however, it's difficult to beat caster. Try to leave at least 100yd below you if the water is clear; the fish will keep dropping back during the day. If bites dry up try an extra-long trot down.

Experiment with your presentation, trying a few inches overdepth or at any point up to mid-water. In really hot weather, when little else will feed, they will take a bait on the surface. Anglers fishing flies can do well. At all times the dace likes to come up in the water to take a bait.

A 1lb 1oz dace, caught on wasp grub on the Yorkshire Ure

SBS

When it comes to sheer colour, the rudd takes some beating. This brace of 1½lb fish were taken from a Lincolnshire stillwater

Many anglers travel abroad to fish, particularly during the time the close season operates through most of Britain. Former World Champion Dave Thomas has been enjoying himself here in the River Guden in Denmark. Most of these fish are roach, but the biggest of all is a 2lb rudd – a super fish

CHAPTER TWENTY-THREE
THE RUDD

No one who has ever seen a big rudd could forget that superb shade of gold and its scarlet-red fins.

Although small rudd are easy to catch, the big ones are very shy, and are driven from the bank by clumsy anglers. However, if you are catching small rudd among lilies on a bright summer's day, there is always the chance that you'll latch onto a bigger one. Unfortunately the disturbance made in landing it may scare the others away for a time. But they will probably be back, for although easily frightened, habit seems to overcome the rudd's natural caution.

Of all the methods used to take rudd the most exciting, and certainly the most effective on a hot summer's day, is a floating bait. This includes bread, casters, soaked cat and dog foods, and the many floating carp pastes now on sale. Pedigree Chum Mixer is one of the easiest and cleanest to prepare. Just place the pellets in a polythene bag, add a little warm water, shake well, and seal the bag. The bait absorbs the water, swells and softens, so it's easy to insert the hook. While you're soaking it you can add flavourings or colourings if you wish.

If you've spotted some big rudd close-in, catapult some loose offerings out. But be prepared to wait a long time while smaller fish attack them. Try to go for a particular fish if you can see one cruising around, as this may save a long wait.

Because the rudd is one of the few fish to continue feeding on those boiling hot days when nothing else is moving, most anglers assume these are the best conditions in which to catch them. In fact a warm westerly wind and good cloud cover are much better, as the rest of the shoal will not be so disturbed when one is hooked.

You can fish on the surface even at long range – up to 80yd away – if you use a buoyant leger. These are now on sale in most specialist tackle shops and contain a floating body which rises from the leger weight, ensuring that the bait is not trapped in bottom weed. The length of line between leger and bait can be adjusted, so you can fish a bait just on top of bottom weed or right on the surface. This has the additional advantage of doing away with floating line near the bait – something which always scares fish.

Make sure the reel spool is well filled if you are long-casting. The line should be at least 4lb to take up the shock of casting without breaking. Norfolk all-rounder Dave Plummer uses 4lb right through to the hook. Since fish 80yd away are not likely to have been frightened by your approach they will take baits on stronger line than they might otherwise tolerate.

A soft-actioned rod is preferable to a tip-actioned one as this allows the power in your swing to build up gradually, and avoids casting the bait off. It will also diminish your chances of 'cracking off'. Dave recommends 11ft or 12ft carbons with 1¼lb test curves, and fixed-spool reels. For hooks try a Model Perfect pattern in sizes 10 to 16 according to bait size. You don't have to fish floating baits on a buoyant leger, of course. In fact for close-in work it's best to freeline it if you can, ie to cast it out without any shot on the line.

Unfortunately you won't often have a bait heavy enough to cast without some weight attached to the line. This is where a 'controller' comes in handy. This lies flat on the surface with the line passing through the middle of it. It is there simply to give you weight to cast. Carp anglers use them a lot. Minimum distance from the hook for this is 2ft, but often the tail will need to be a lot longer.

You can also get self-cocking controllers with a fluorescent sight on the top for long-range casting. In this case when the bait may be too far away to see, the controller acts as a bite indicator in the same way as a float. However, instead of being fixed to the bottom of the controller, and there-

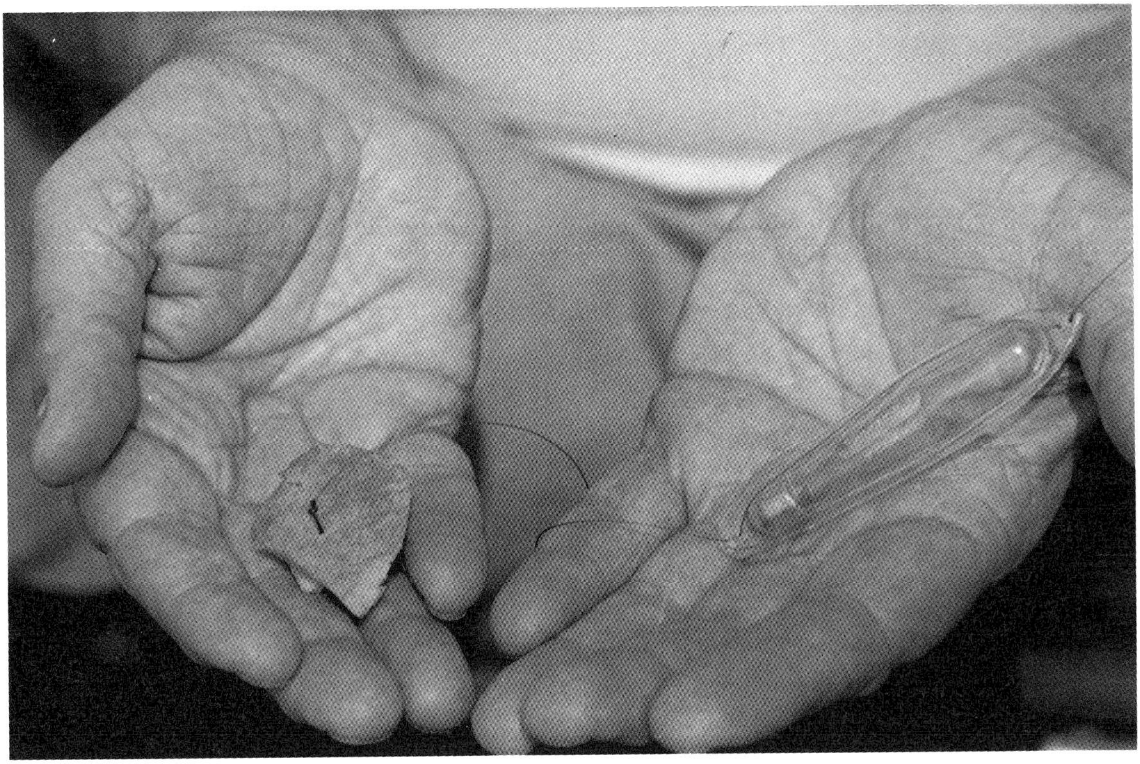

A modern-type controller, slim and neat. This type of hollow perspex controller is partially filled with water to give weight for casting

fore under water, the line can go through the top, which keeps the bait afloat. In very windy conditions when you can't even see the controller, you may need to fix an indicator to the rod to spot your bites.

If your line is sinking, and pulling the bait below the surface, you may need to grease it to keep it afloat. However the last 6in should not be greased, as the wake made when the line is moved is guaranteed to scare any fish about to inspect the bait. For that reason even with the last 6in of line sinking you should move the bait as little as possible. If you are using a controller and the wind gets up, pulling your bait out of position, you may be able to continue fishing with the anchored rig already described.

The most exciting method of catching rudd is by fly fishing. And in fact this is good practice for trouting, the main problem with both methods being the wake made by any floating line. However, the angler flyfishing for rudd almost certainly has an advantage over the trout man because he's probably fishing on a smaller water, which is less affected by the wind. If there are big rudd in the vicinity and you can leave a dry fly motionless on the surface it's odds-on he'll have a go sooner or later. Then the fun really starts, because if you're near lilies the fish is only yards from safety. For that reason don't drop below 4lb line. Best times to flyfish for rudd are in hot, still conditions, and at dusk when the wind dies and the water begins to look oily. Then rudd will give themselves away with huge splashings as they start feeding on insects and flies.

CHAPTER TWENTY-FOUR
THE TENCH

Who can forget the trembling of a float on a still summer's morning as the tench arrive in a swim? No species is more eagerly awaited by the coarse angler starting a new season. For the tench gives everything in battle. And as a species tench are getting larger in waters right across the country. A six-pounder was once looked upon as something very unusual. Today it is a run-of-the-mill fish on many waters.

It's not unusual to find tench and bream in the same water, particularly in old-established shallow lakes. Here they may not be the really big specimens but the average stamp of fish will still make for some great sport. The diagram shows an angler fishing a typical lake holding both species plus some rudd and roach. By making an early start he can expect to find tench in shallow water tight to the reeds. He should sit well back with his keepnet hidden to avoid scaring the fish. You really can't expect fish to feed within a short distance of others being held in a net.

Float fishing is by far the most exciting way of fishing this close-in style and a simple straight piece of peacock waggler or a 'Driftbeater' float is perfect. A long rod of 12 or even 13ft will be handy to keep hooked tench out of the surrounding weed beds.

Having found a likely looking swim about a rod-length out, start by plumbing the depth so that the float can be set with the bottom shot actually on the lake bed. This will be a great help in holding the bait still against any wind that would otherwise cause drift. Two rod rests are essential for this method and the front one should be set in such a way as to put the first 4in of the rod tip beneath the water surface – again this is intended to help beat drift.

Sweetcorn is a particularly good bait but it could be bread, worms, maggots or casters. With corn, using three grains at a time, the hook will need to be a size 8 tied direct to a line that matches

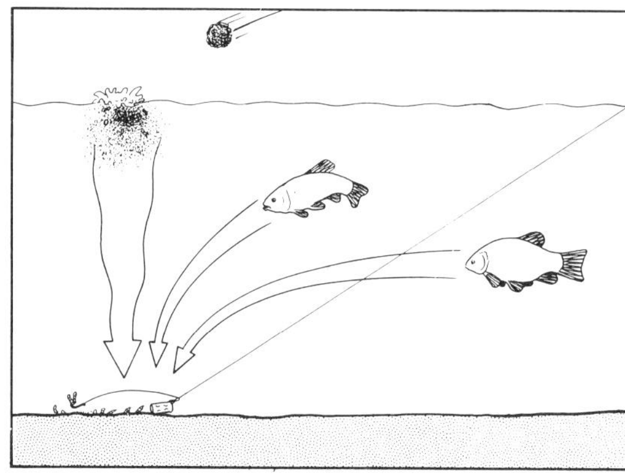

Fig 81 If you are using a swimfeeder there is nothing to stop you putting extra groundbait in. When tench are feeding well on a misty summer's morning the disturbance is unlikely to put them off. This is a useful ploy for getting fish to home in on your swimfeeder rig

the rod; somewhere around 4lb would probably be the minimum for a weedy water holding tench to 5lb.

Start by introducing six to eight grains of corn as loose-feed. Cast, and as the float cocks push the rod tip under the water and wind in a few inches until all the line is submerged. Now the rod goes into the rests.

When a bite develops the float will do one of five things. It may lift then return to its original position and go under; it may lift and move slowly to one side, sometimes sinking as it goes; it may rise then return to its original position several times or momentarily lift; or it may, as is often the case with early season fish, shoot under without any warning. All these situations signal the arrival of a tench and should be struck.

Fig 82 A typical lake swim on a summer's day. Look for tench in among the reeds, right under your feet

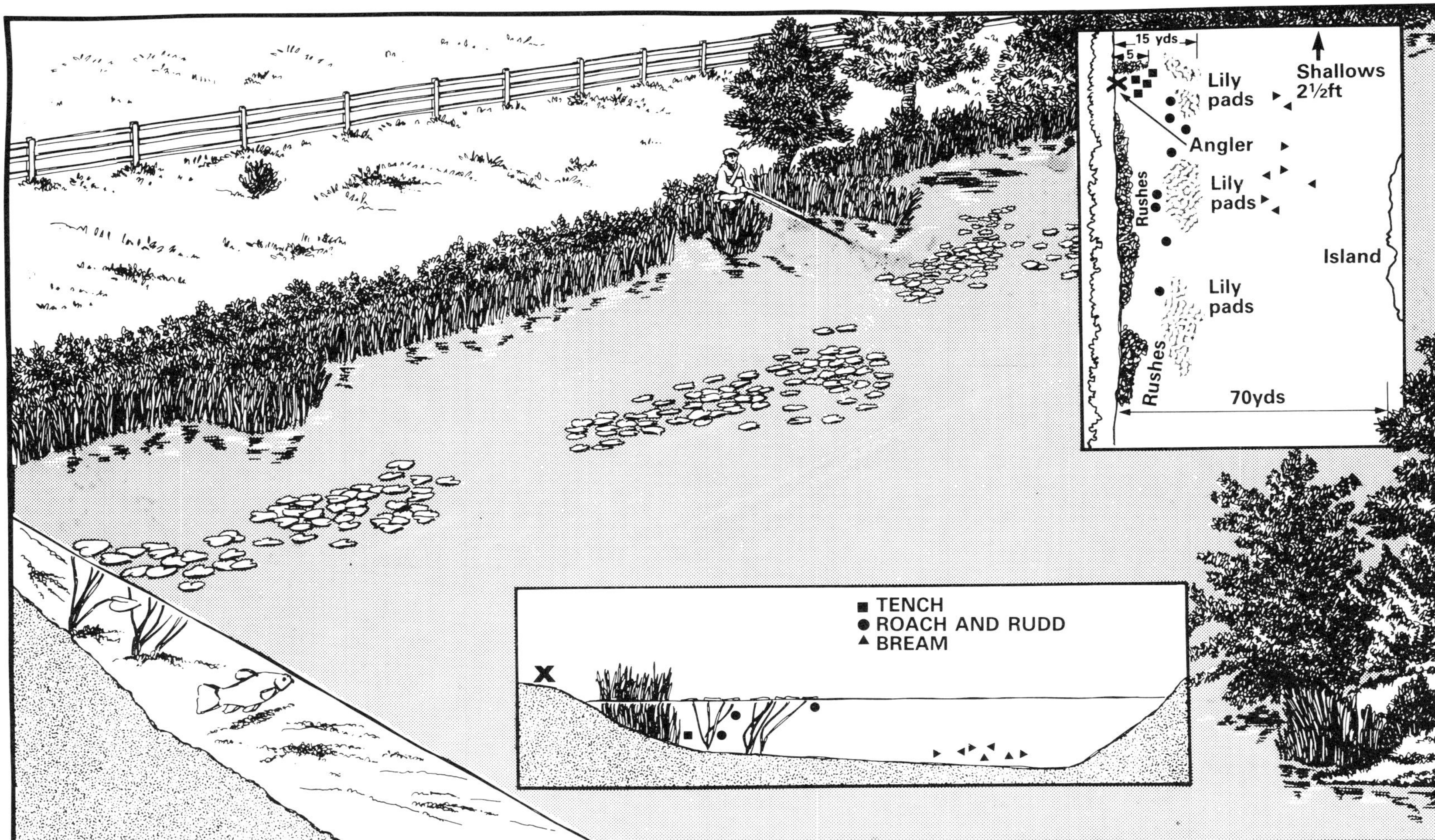
15 yds
5
Lily pads
Shallows 2½ft
Angler
Lily pads
Rushes
Island
Lily pads
Rushes
70yds
TENCH
ROACH AND RUDD
BREAM
X

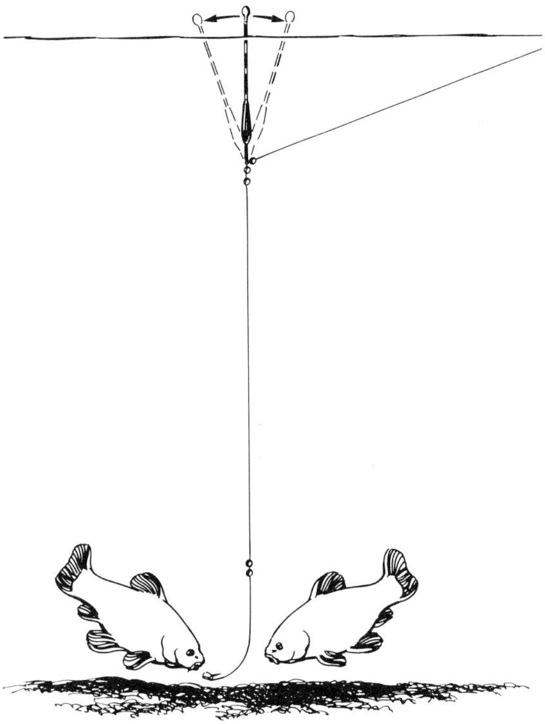

Fig 83 Tench will make a float do all sorts of things before it goes under. One reason is the power of their fin action, which swirls the line. A sight bob will help you see when the float has really gone under if you're fishing some distance away

Sometimes the float will keep lifting and moving to one side. This is caused by a tench browsing around the bait but not sucking it in. If this happens, introduce more hookbait samples – just to keep the fish interested – and then fish just one grain on the hook. Should these 'false bites' continue, try slowly turning the reel handle; this often results in the tench making a mad grab at the bait.

Another good early season method is crust or lobworm fished in conjunction with a peacock quill. The weight is either one or two SSG shots positioned close to the hook – 6in for crust, 15in for lobworm. The set-up is shown in Fig 83. If you decide to try crust it will also pay to introduce some cereal groundbait at the start of the session.

Fig 84 The basic sliding paternoster rig. Note the use of a leger stop instead of a split knot in the top inset. These can be bought from any tackle dealer

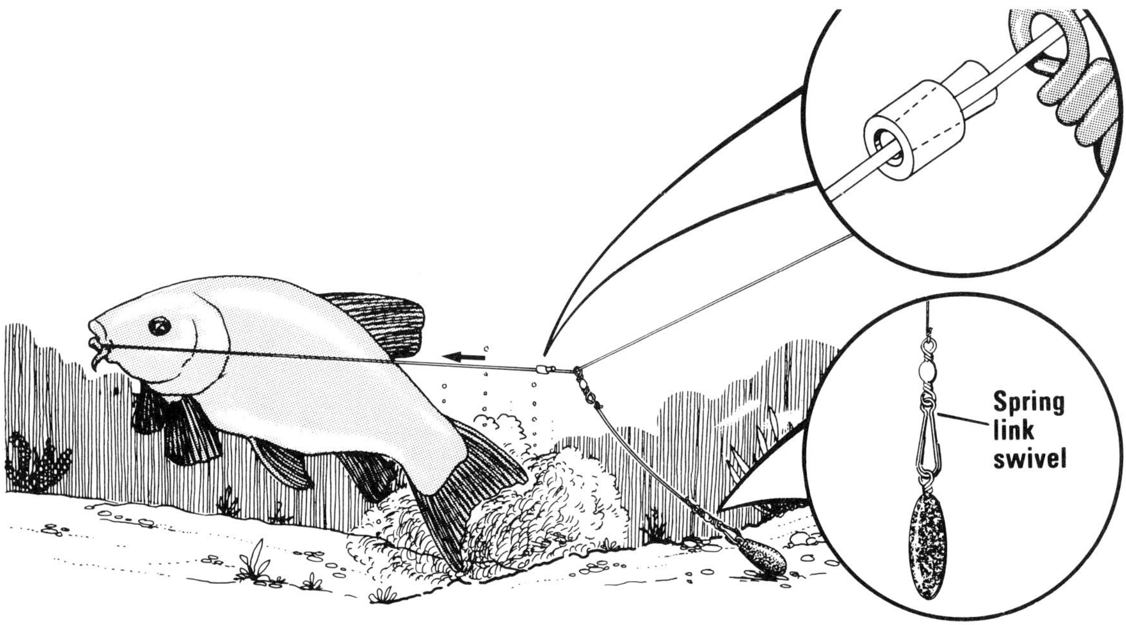

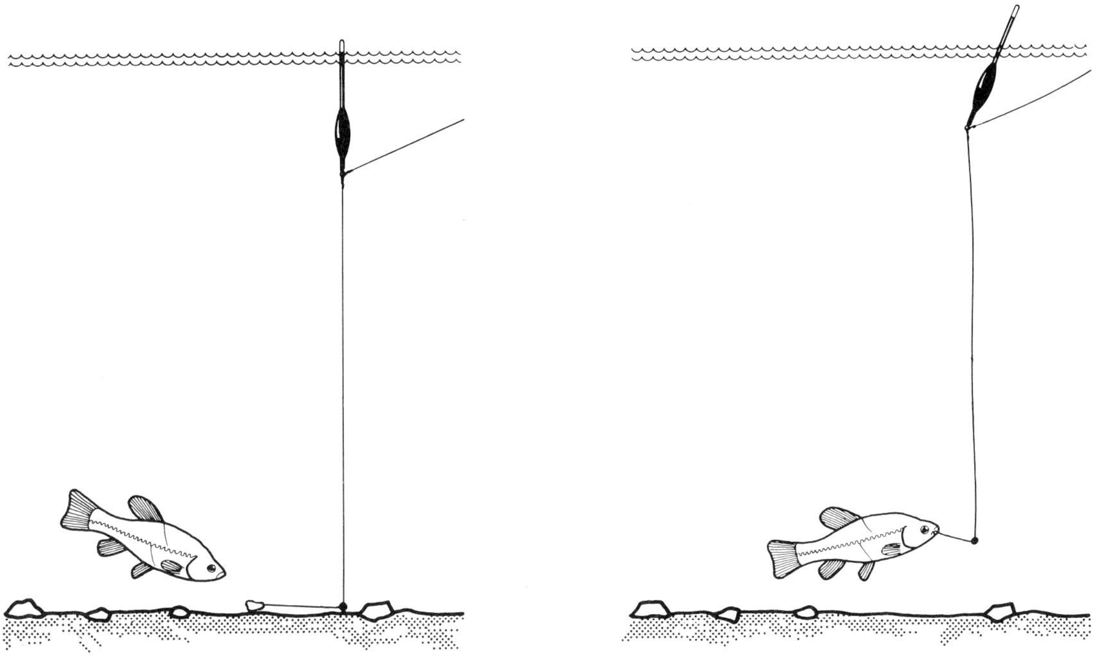

Fig 85 The correct setting on the 'lift' rig. When the fish takes the weight of the bottom shot by lifting the bait off bottom the float will lay flat

But the key to this rig is getting the depth just right so that the shots sit on the bottom. Very minor adjustments may need to be made to get everything in order. And if bites are missed be prepared to lengthen or shorten the distance from hook to shot, but still keeping the shot-to-float distance exactly the same as before. If bites are not very positive and the bait comes back sucked, the hook-to-shot length should be decreased. On the other hand a longer 'tail' will make the bait more likely to lift and look attractive if a fish passes close. It's all a case of a little experimentation as the day progresses.

Fig 86 If you have the bulk of the weight under your float then a fish picking up the bait will cause the float to rise in the water (right). But don't expect it to lay flat as it would if you were using a true lift rig

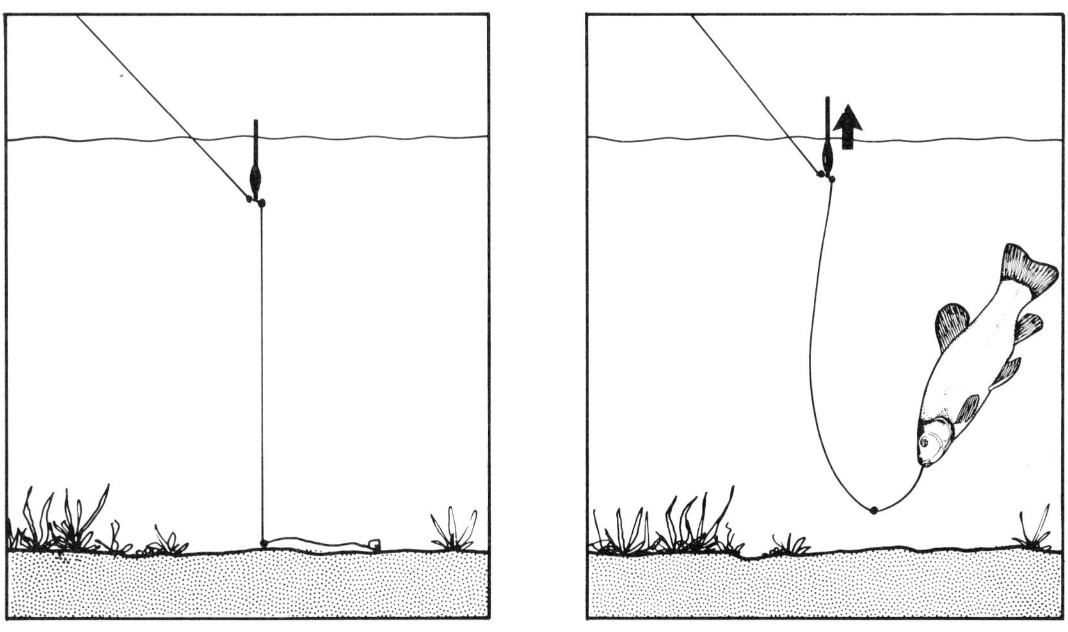

The tench is the traditional fish of summer. This fine catch was taken on opening day, 16 June, from Bainton Pits in Lincolnshire

Wilstone Reservoir in Hertfordshire is noted for its double-figure specimens. This one fell during the opening week of the season

BEACHCOMBER

CHAPTER TWENTY-FIVE
THE PIKE

Making a start

The pike is probably the subject of more legends than almost any other living creature. Though the British record is over 40lb, there is no doubt that much bigger fish have been caught in the past. Their exact weights are, however, a mystery.

According to Fred Buller's *Domesday Book of Mammoth Pike*, the biggest rod-caught pike came from Ireland, taken from Lough Derg in 1862 by John Naughton. It was recorded at 90lb 8oz, was 5½ft long, and took a brass lure. It took two hours to land. But as with so many fish it has been impossible to establish its true weight.

Pike will take anything when they are small – worms, insects, and fry; and even when larger they often fall for a bunch of maggots or worms. But the favourite bait of anglers is a real fish, either legered on the bottom, pulled through the water to make it look alive, or suspended beneath a float. Both dead sea fish and coarse fish will attract a hungry pike.

To many anglers, however, spinning a lure through the water is an even more attractive method of catching pike. In cold weather, when the pike is at its best, this allows a certain amount of movement to warm the angler.

Recently matchfishing for pike has become the rage, particularly following the highly-successful *Angling Times* British Pike Championship series. The Pike Anglers' Club of Great Britain is the organisation to join if you want to learn more about this fascinating fish. The club is open to everyone and has done much to educate the average angler on the subject of pike and pike fishing. Through a chain of local organisers it keeps its members in touch with each other and even publishes its own magazine. If you are new to pike fishing, the club will help you progress quickly.

Pike to 8lb are abundant on most waters, while the first ambition of most pike anglers is to catch a ten-pounder. A twenty-pounder is considered an excellent fish, and anything over 30lb a memorable catch.

Years ago the average pike angler was likely to be equipped with nothing more sophisticated than an old sea rod and a huge centrepin reel loaded with thick line. End tackle too was crude. Rusty Jardine snap tackles and a big bung float was the usual gear. In recent times things have changed. The tackle trade caters well for the pike enthusiast. Specialist rods, whole ranges of streamlined floats, high-quality fine-wire traces and sensible hooks are all easily obtainable at any worthwhile tackle shop.

Rods suitable for pike fishing have a test curve of around 2lb to 2½lb. The more powerful rod is best suited to casting big deadbaits long distances. Reels need to have a capacity of at least 100yd of 10lb line, and beginners are advised not to drop below that strength. In fact Norfolk's pike-fishing expert Dave Plummer never goes below a 12lb line when fishing the Norfolk Broads – just in case there is a really big fish around. Waters with a lot of weed growth also call for a stronger line, and a big deadbait that's needed to be cast a long way may even require a shock leader.

One item that hasn't changed over the years is the need for a wire trace. But no longer is the wire of stiff and unmanageable material; it is thin and flexible. Go for the braided, multi-strand wire as this does not kink easily. Like all line it comes in different breaking strains and it pays not to fish too fine.

A recent introduction to pike fishing is the electric bite alarm. The idea is that you will always know if a pike is taking a bait, even if your attention is distracted. Certainly this development prevents a fish being accidentally deeply hooked. A good bite alarm will register drop-back bites, and like a carp alarm, can be adjusted to combat high winds which would otherwise record as false bites. If you plan to fish with two rods it may be worthwhile buying two alarms with different tones, so that you know immediately which bait has been taken.

Once the fish is on the bank you will want to weigh it. This is best done in a special pike sack or weighing sling that supports the whole body weight along its length. Never, ever, insert a spring-balance hook under the gill covers of a fish.

As for pike rigs, these too are undergoing a lot of change. There has been a revival of interest in wobbling deadbaits – an active and exciting way to fish. Use a fresh deadbait with the swim bladder intact so that it remains buoyant. Mount the bait on a two-treble rig with one hook passed through both lips and the other towards the tail. Bending the bait slightly gives it an attractive side-to-side movement.

On weedy waters a sunken float rig can be deadly. This method uses a float under the surface to keep the rig from lying on the bottom. An ET boom is employed – a neat device that allows line to run through a swivel without becoming tangled. A bait goes on the end of the line and a leger weight is tied to the swivel like a normal leger set-up. By making the distance from swivel to bait shorter than from swivel to weight, the bait can be presented off the bottom. Use a bite alarm to signal a take.

With all this new technology and a much wider spread of knowledge over far more pikers, your chances of catching a twenty-pounder are better than ever. For many of Britain's top trout waters throw open their doors to pike anglers during winter, and these are the waters where pike grow fat on a diet of trout.

The days have long gone when pike were killed as a matter of course. The modern angler, who hates needless loss of wildlife, has carried his thinking over to pike fishing. Virtually every pike taken these days is returned alive and unharmed to the water.

Methods for pike

Summer plugging

One of the most exciting sights in angling is the bow wave made by a big pike as it follows a surface plug on a summer's day. As the lure gurgles and plops across the surface you wonder whether the fish will make up its mind to attack before it reaches the bank. In desperation you stop retrieving for a few seconds, wind down with your rod pointing directly at the plug, then sweep the rod back as fast as you can, so the plug surges forward again. Just when all seems lost the water explodes in a frenzy of snapping jaws, and the fight is on. It's heart-stopping stuff.

But many anglers miss out on this sort of action because they are still concentrating on tench, carp and bream, and don't turn their attentions to pike until later in the season. If they tried summer plug fishing they'd find pike in the peak of condition, tailwalking when hooked, and at their fighting best – a far cry from the tame, lethargic fish so often encountered at the end of the season.

There's a fair choice of plugs on sale in the UK, many of them designed in America for catching large-mouthed and small-mouthed bass. They include the Sputter Bug, Jitterbug, Trouble-maker, Sinner Spinner, Chug Ike, Plunker, Torpedo and Crazy Crawler. Some have propellors at both ends, while others have one just at the tail. Some designs have a vane at the front, or a scooped-out face that digs into the surface and causes the plug to dive when you are retrieving it. The Jitterbug has a metal spoon that makes it wobble as it is pulled along the surface – a real pike-catcher. The Crazy Crawler has metal arms that make it look like a miniature swimmer crossing the water.

Each year new designs are introduced, but whatever you use you'll find the fishing best in shallow water with a flat calm surface or just a gentle ripple. Surface plugs aren't quite so effective in water with waves on it.

Look for a weedy swim, anything from 1ft to 8ft deep. It doesn't matter if there are reeds poking above the surface, as you can work the plug round them without fouling the line. Many have weed guards on, anyway. You can catch surface-feeding pike in any depth of water, but plugs tend to be more effective in water up to 8ft deep. Perhaps it's because in shallow water they bring pike up from the bottom.

Look for a clear space in the weed, cast out and let the ripples subside before you start working the lure. First just agitate it, without drawing it far. If it has landed on a pike's nose this will often bring an immediate response. If not, draw it very slowly a couple of feet at a time. You'll often see a pike following it, fin out of the water like a shark. That's the time to use the trick described at the beginning of this section – winding down and sweeping the rod back steadily. The sudden change of speed seems to galvanise the pike into action.

Keep tackle small and neat. Large links and swivels can affect the plug's action. Traces made from 15lb to 20lb PDQ wire work well, with a small snap-link on the end to enable you to change plugs quickly, and a tiny diamond-shaped swivel on the main line. This is the lightest rig possible; you can fish even the smallest of plugs on this tackle. It helps to grease the last few yards of line to avoid it sinking and impairing the action of the lure. It will give more direct contact than if the line were to sink.

Shorter rods are easier to use than long ones; up to 9ft are adequate for almost all circumstances. And though fixed-spool reels are suitable, multipliers are better – after all, they were designed with lure fishing in mind.

River fishing

Paternostered deadbait Although there's a float on this rig it stays *beneath* the surface, ensuring the swivel to which the bait is attached is held well off bottom, allowing it to flutter attractively in the current.

When you've cast out, tighten up to the float (so you can feel it pulling in the current), put on the anti-reverse and back off the clutch. Stern drag is obviously preferable on a reel. You'll hear the clutch sound when you get a take, but there will be virtually no resistance to the fish.

As soon as the clutch goes, open the bale arm, take off the anti-reverse, tighten the clutch, re-engage the bale arm, then, keeping the rod well up, strike immediately.

Legered deadbait Keep a stock of smelt and sardine in the freezer and you can go piking at a moment's notice. Both have a smell which seems to attract pike.

Legering with deadbait tends to take a smaller number of pike than other methods, but the average weight is definitely higher. Fish a 7in pencil pike float slightly overdepth, tightening the line so that enough of the float shows for it to be easily spotted when it's cocked at an angle. Stay close to the rod and strike at the first indication.

It pays to leger deadbaits near the margins of rivers, as pike tend to hang about the weed beds. If one takes the bait into the weed bully him out immediately, before he realises what is happening. It always works.

Spinning Start spinning only after you have tried a known swim with bait and not had much luck.

A large silver spoon put though a swim which you are sure should hold a pike can often produce a take after only a few casts. Try to get as slow a retrieve as possible, often stopping the retrieve for a second to vary the depth at which it is fishing. The average size of fish taken on spinners is usually smaller than those on bait, but on a cold day the sport can warm you up as you search various swims.

Stillwater fishing (below)

Paternostered deadbait This is an ideal lake rig, for it can be dropped into a known pike hotspot and left there until the pike find it. As with the river rig, use tubing on both main line and the

trace to prevent tangling, the trace tube being about 3in long and the other just a little longer.

A sliding float is essential to allow easy casting. The front treble slipped loosely into the skin around the deadbait's mouth allows early striking. The treble hook in the flesh near the bait's dorsal fin takes the weight when you cast.

Distance legering This rig can be fished at distance even if you don't know how deep your swim is. The sunken float keeps the line off the bottom, preventing it getting caught on underwater obstructions. The distance you set it from the float is optional (above).

The bait for these big waters is a smelt or mackerel tied to the trace with PVA string after it has been hooked with two trebles. This string dissolves soon after hitting the water. For longer casts half a mackerel, cut at an angle, will give you a better aerodynamic shape.

Use Optonic or drop-off indicators with this method, which is very much a waiting game. On really big waters it may take many visits to discover a hotspot.

Dumbell float The dumbell float (Fig 88) is universally popular because it tells you exactly what is going on under the water, and it can be controlled easily.

It helps to prevent any tangling, and because of the increased water resistance on both ends you can lift the line without the float coming towards you, and control the direction of drift. If necessary, you can add a weight below the float in deep swims. But this rig is at its best over weed in shallow swims, when no weight is used.

This float is a favourite of Derrick Amies, who caught a British record pike of 42lb from the Norfolk Broads in 1985. But it's not a new idea;

Fig 87 Typical deadbait rig incorporating the ET anti-tangle boom

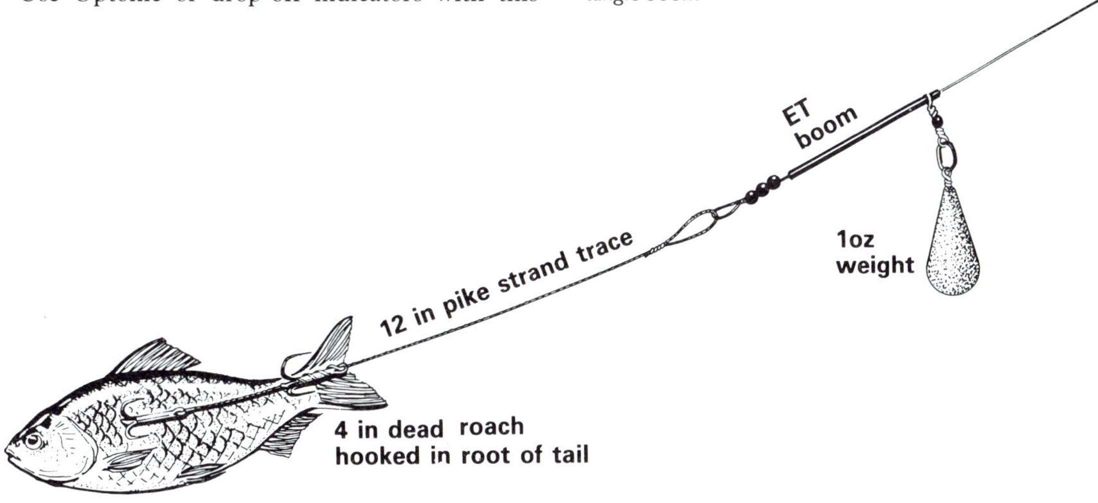

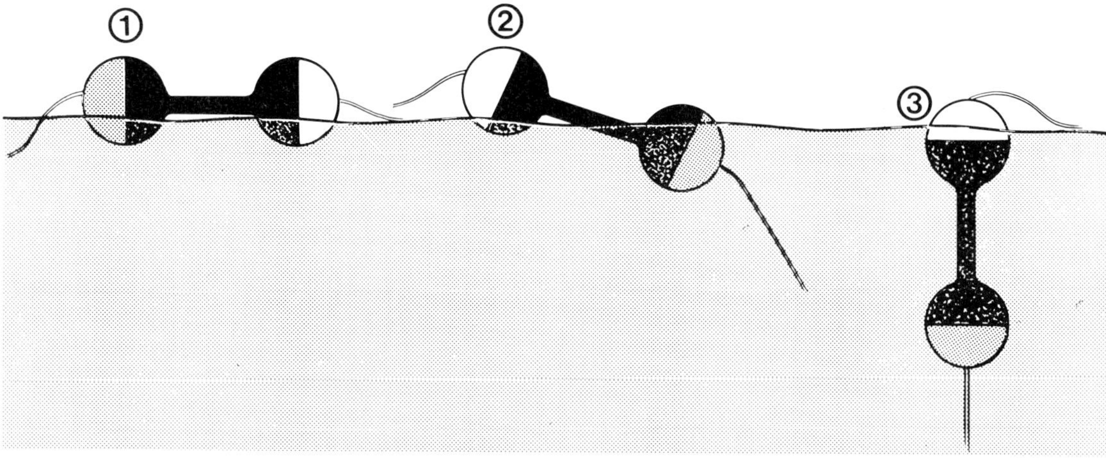

Fig 88 The Dumbell float at rest (1), when a pike is mouthing the bait or swimming slowly away (2) and when the pike has finally taken the bait properly (3)

the late Dennis Pye, who took hundreds of double-figure pike from the Broads in the 1950s and 1960s, used it many times.

The float is simply two 1in cork pilot floats joined by a hollow peg. The best overall length is 4½in. The line goes through the centre of the float and the hollow peg is then plugged. Alternatively it can be used as a sliding float, in which case a large leger stop is placed on the line at the required depth.

Each end of the float is painted a different colour so that you can see before you get a run which way a pike is (or has been) swimming, or even whether it is moving round in a circle – something which may not be immediately obvious with a standard cigar-shaped or bung float. Also having two different colours gives you a better chance of being able to pick it out if the light is bad. There are no protruding ends to catch on reed stems.

Derrick Amies used it with livebaits, in which case the float tips slightly when the bait swims in one direction. But when a pike takes the bait the float stands up on end. This float will, in fact, show that a pike is at the bait before a normal float will register the fact.

Used with a deadbait the wind acts against the float's considerable surface area, blowing it against a gentle flow towards the weed beds where you think your pike will lie. If you then tighten up so that one end dips, the air resistance is less, and the amount under the surface is greater. At this point the flow starts taking effect again, and the bait goes in the opposite direction.

Conditions won't always be ideal, of course, but this float will enable you to control your bait to a greater extent than with other pike floats.

Wobbled deadbait This is an exciting method of catching pike, and produces a lot of fish. In fact it's surprising more anglers don't use a wobbled deadbait. It's an excellent method over weed, allowing a very slow retrieve.

A lot of big fish fall for moving deadbait. The secret is to keep it moving all the time, dipping and jerking, as slowly as the depth will allow.

Use an 18in wire trace with a large snap-tackle rig for instant striking. One hook goes through both lips, the other into the bottom of the fish – ideally a small roach – in the centre of its body.

Landing and unhooking

The fact is that many anglers are frightened of pike. But that's no reason for treating one any differently from the way you would treat, for example, a 3lb roach. Indeed it's your duty not to do so and you shouldn't go pike fishing if you're not equipped to unhook them quickly and painlessly.

Some anglers still use gaffs, despite the fact that almost all over the British Isles their use is illegal. And even used properly (which was never easy) the fish will still go back with a hole in its jaw if gaffed. No – use a net. The modern piker goes armed with a king-sized landing net. This is the

Weighing Derrick Amies' record 42lb pike. Fish should always be weighed in a net or special weight sling. This fish was caught from the Norfolk Broads in 1985

Derrick poses with his magnificent fish before returning it to the water

BRUCE &
WALKER

Pike expert Mick Brown cradles a superb 30lb plus specimen, taken from Bainton Pits in Lincolnshire

An idyllic pike water – beautiful Fin Lough in County Clare, Southern Ireland

A pike thrashes the surface just before being landed. Pike fishing has grown in popularity during the last few years and is one of the most exciting branches of the sport

safest way. The only disadvantage is that if you're using a barbed treble hook, one of the exposed hooks can catch the net if the fish twists and struggles when it is landed. Even that danger can be minimised if you use barbless trebles. Land small pike by hand, and if you're going to use a net play the fish so that it is that much more tired, then hold the net to your body when the fish is on the bank to prevent it spinning. It's better for the pike that way.

Always have some sort of protective covering to lay the fish on. Wet it first, for damage can be done if the fish loses a lot of its mucus slime. A wet pike sack will be ideal.

Once you've landed a pike the next thing is to unhook it as quickly and safely as possible. For this you will need a good pair of forceps fitted with very long stems. If you must use a gag, be sure it is not too strong and that the ends are well masked with tape to prevent injury to the fish. In fact a pike can often be unhooked by wearing thick gardening gloves to protect fingers and then holding the jaws open.

The following is the procedure adopted by top pike angler Derrick Amies from Lowestoft, Suffolk.

> The area where your fish is to lie must be clear of all other objects. Holding your fish, move the rod away and direct the trace away from the pike's head. You don't want the trace to go behind a gill cover when you lift the pike's head up for unhooking. It may cut the gill rakers – a common mistake for beginners to make. If the fish tries to jump or kick, wrap matting around it, or enfold it in the sack it is lying on. Covering the head usually quietens it down, and even the liveliest of fish won't move much in complete darkness.
>
> With the pike lying with its belly towards you – right-handed anglers will find it easier with the fish lying from right to left – slip your left hand, palm outwards, under the pike's chin, just inside the gill cover. If the belly is towards you, you can see what you are doing. Allow your fingers to slip towards the pike's head into the V-slit under the chin. Don't put your whole hand in at any time; there are small, sharp teeth inside the cover itself. But your hand will now be into the fleshy part of the chin.
>
> Now lift the head of the pike up, and its mouth will open. Be confident; it cannot close its mouth against its own weight. I like the tail of the fish to be just touching the hooking mat, and this also steadies the fish. At this stage a friend can help by holding the trace taut with an upright pull. If you are alone, hold the top of the trace or the line in your teeth. Now you have a tight line to the hooks and with the pike's mouth open should be able to see where they are.
>
> With your free hand wield a sturdy pair of forceps or, in my case, a good back-up hook remover in the shape of an old-fashioned football lacer. With the top sawn off it makes an excellent tool, as the solid handle makes it easy to get a strong grip. I always free the second treble first (the one nearest to me), and when this is free tension will stop it getting a hold again.

Lay the pike in a wet sack or something similar. Covering its head for a moment will stop it kicking

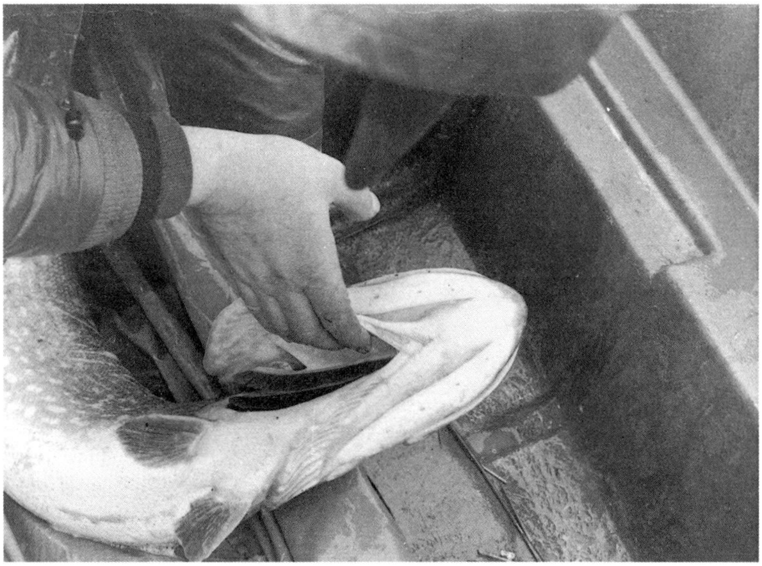

Slip the fingers under the pike's chin, just inside the gill cover

Allow your fingers to slip up to the chin and, holding the fish in the left hand, extract the hooks with forceps held in the right hand. Get a friend to hold the trace taut, or hold it in your lips

If you have been been unfortunate enough to let one treble disappear down the pike's throat, a gentle pull, slow but firm, should bring it into sight. Then the forceps can be slid in through the gill rakers and the hooks freed one by one. You'll need to keep tension on the line to keep the hooks in view. Once they are out, throw the hooks well clear. If at any time the fish does kick, steady it with your unhooking hand and start again. There's no need to panic.

If you are going to weigh the fish use a wet sling, and if you are going to take photographs put the fish in a carp sack or keepnet, making sure the fish is in an upright position, until you are ready. Wet your hands before lifting the fish, and hold it firmly. Cradle it for the photograph, and do not extend your arms towards the camera, or you may end up dropping it. You can also take the pike under the chin in the same way as when you unhooked it, and its tail in the other hand, lightly supported on your thighs. Keep kneeling; then if the pike happens to leap out of your hands it doesn't have far to fall.

Pike take twenty years to reach between 20lb and 40lb, so treat them with care.

The grayling is undoubtedly the most elegant of all Britain's coarse fish. This specimen was taken from the Derbyshire Derwent at Whatstandwell by local angler Peter Hall

Eels may not be every angler's favourite species but they grow big, fight hard and can be caught from virtually every stretch of water, large or small. This young angler won't forget the day he landed this massive specimen!

AFTER YOU'VE CAUGHT YOUR FISH

CHAPTER TWENTY-SIX
CARE FOR YOUR CATCH

There is intense pressure on the large fish stocks of this country. For not only has the number of anglers increased dramatically, so has their ability to catch more. Thankfully with the growth in knowledge, there has become a greater awareness on the part of anglers, clubs and fishery owners of the need to protect the fish in their waters.

Sometimes just a few fish in a water are caught so often that they give it a big reputation. This is often demonstrated by pike and carp, but it is also true of other species. Where tagged fish have been released the recapture rate of some individual fish has been very high. So if those few fish were to die, or lose weight, the potential of the fishery would slump rapidly. How then can anglers get the pleasure of catching, weighing and photographing specimens without causing them damage?

First thing to ensure is that tackle is strong enough to land a fish without the need to play it to a complete standstill. With ultra-light tackle it's possible to play a fish until it is so exhausted that it may not recover or may suffer such shock that it loses weight for some time afterwards.

The next step is to have a landing net that causes the fish no harm. For this the best net material is micromesh. All others split fins to some degree, which makes fish look unsightly at the very least. The only problem with micromesh on large landing nets is that they are unwieldy if you want to move them under water. A 'hybrid' net with large mesh in the top half and micro where the fish lies solves both problems and will, hopefully, become standard in the future.

When a fish is carried to the bank, care should be taken to see that it is put down on soft ground and not allowed to thrash around with the possibility of causing damage to its gills which, on all fish, are very delicate. Any bleeding from this area is a sign of trouble.

Artery forceps should be used to remove hooks

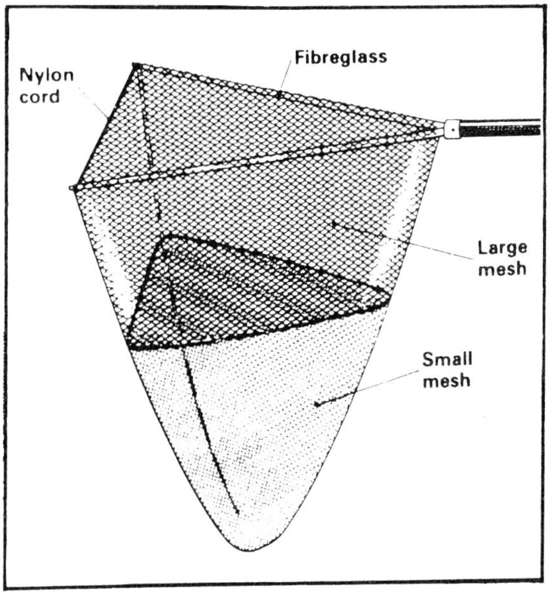

Fig 89 A specially-made landing net with micro-mesh to prevent damage to fish. The top half is made of larger nylon, which will sweep easily through the water

Overleaf Make sure big fish don't jump out of your grasp when you are unhooking them. Keeping them in, or just above your landing net will help

When taking catch pictures, ensure the fish are laid out in the mouth of a wet micromesh net, not on the grass. Always hold the fish with wet hands and ensure that they are returned to the water as soon as possible

MARCEL VAN DEN EYNDE
LOWAAS
5X WORLDCHAMPION

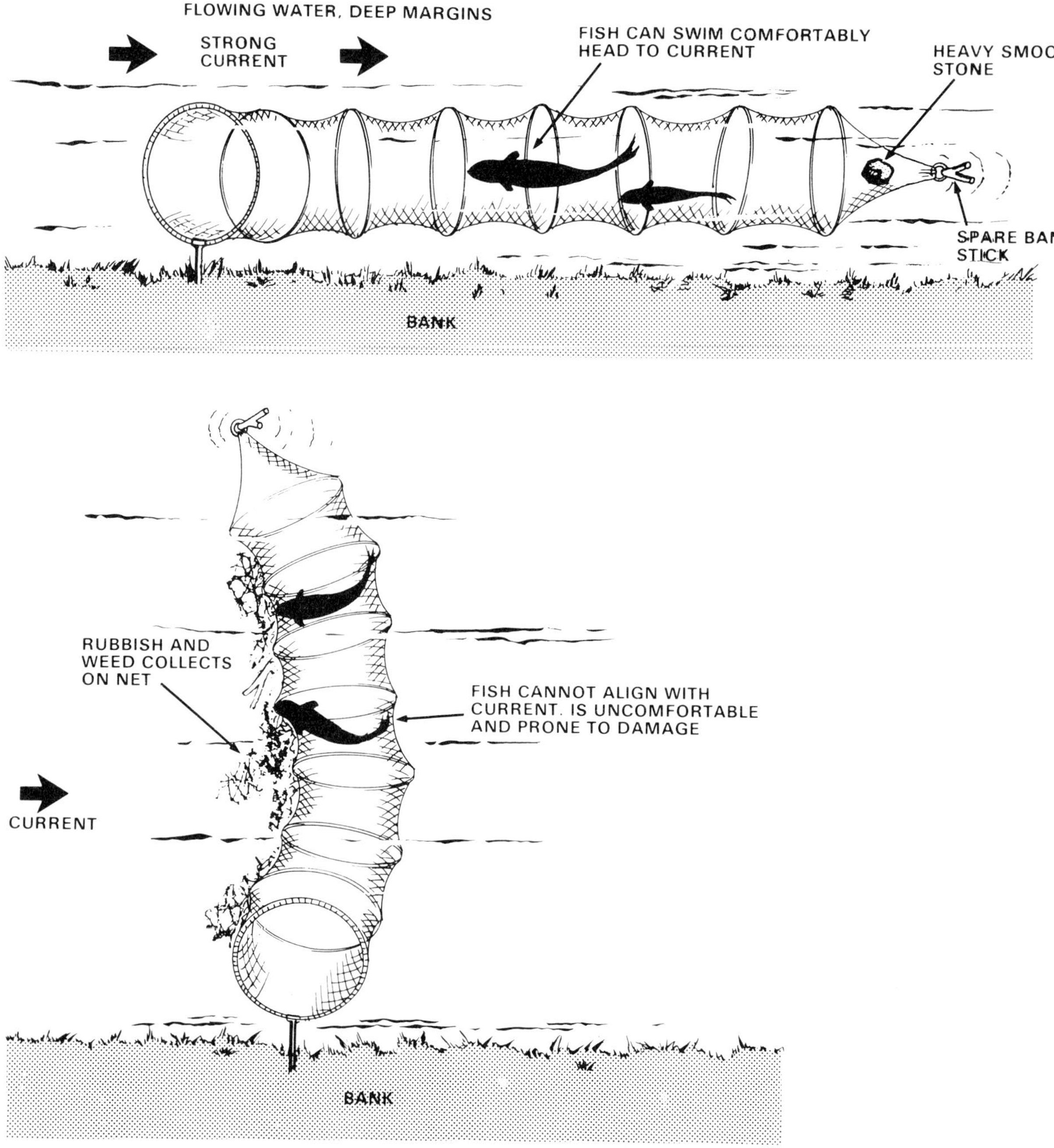

Fig 90 Staking your keepnet out so it lays parallel with the current will ensure a good flow and will allow fish to face the current (top). This is particularly important for barbel. Staking your net across the current (bottom) causes problems as rubbish can collect on the sides, reducing the flow through the net. Also big fish cannot face into the current

even if you can get your fingers to the latter. However if the hook has gone out the other side it is much better to cut the line and pull it through. Deeply hooked fish are a problem so make every effort to remove a hook, but leave it in if all else fails. The fish should be rested in the water for several minutes before attempting to disgorge it. At night it is often better to cut the line off, leaving a couple of feet, then hold the fish in a net until daylight when the problem will be much easier to sort out.

As for keeping big fish, the golden rule is – don't! Many fisheries now insist that all fish are returned immediately after capture, but even on waters where this rule is not applied the sooner fish go back the better. Most fish are kept only through force of habit. Most youngsters, for example, usually get a keepnet before a landing net. Again micromesh is the only material to use as it doesn't cause split fins or descale. Keepnets should be wide and long so that they go deep into the water where it is cooler and well-oxygenated. Fish can then rest and recover as there is plenty of water circulating in a big net with rings. Also if the oxygen level is low at a certain depth, a fish is free to move to where it is more comfortable.

This is where the danger comes with using carp sacks. They are a cheap and easy way of retaining fish but they are dangerous if used carelessly.

When it comes to weighing, there are several good slings on the market tailormade for the job. These don't cause any harm if wetted first and used reasonably. And they weigh practically nothing when dry so are no trouble to carry in your tackle box.

Photographing fish is dealt with in the next chapter, but a few points need stressing here. Photographing can take a long time so it is best to rest the fish for a few minutes first so that it can get its breath back. Then take a couple of shots of each side in a suitable pose. Again if the film needs changing, give the fish a break in the water first, or better still, make sure you have plenty of film loaded before you start. Never hold a fish high off the ground, or too far out from your body, unless you are standing knee deep in the water because if it falls to the ground from waist height it will be damaged.

At whatever stage a big fish is returned to the water make sure it is fully recovered. Don't launch it into deep water. Place it in the shallows to make sure it can stay upright and swim off on its own accord. If it can't, don't leave it. Keep it propped upright until its strength returns.

Finally remember that, although it's your moment of glory, it wouldn't be possible if the last chap who had caught that fish had treated it badly – whatever the size.

CHAPTER TWENTY-SEVEN
GETTING IN THE PICTURE

Photographing your best catches is a great way to ensure there is a permanent record of those memorable days that make angling such an exciting sport. It's a simple enough task, but one made easier if you follow a few golden rules.

Preparation

At all times welfare of the fish is most important; that goes without saying in a country where virtually every coarse fish taken is put back alive. So unless there is someone with a camera all ready to take pictures as soon as a fish is landed, and unless the location is planned, you're probably going to have to pop your catch into a net or sack until you're quite ready to take the picture. On waters where nets and sacks are barred, five minutes working out exactly what is going to happen if you get a big 'un will be time well spent.

Carry a 12ft square sheet of thick polythene, because with the best will in the world fish do kick and may roll across the ground. If the angler holding the fish (or net of fish) is in the middle of the polythene, no matter what happens a fish will not get grit or earth on its protective slime. Most specimen hunters carry a carp sack, which can serve the same purpose.

You must decide where you're going to be and where the photographer will stand. If there's mud around it may be better to walk 20yd to a grassy spot – but decide on this before taking the fish from the water.

Check that your hands are clean and wet before handling the fish. And if the ground is wet it may pay to pull on a pair of waterproof trousers if you're likely to be kneeling. If you are to be holding just one fish, make sure there aren't any buckles or zips around to damage it. For best results a bright jacket or jumper is preferable to a dark one.

The photographer should make sure not only that there is film in the camera, but that he's got enough shots left. Next check the exposure, if the camera is one on which it can be altered. Tips for the photographer follow shortly.

Poses

With one large fish, such as a carp, the easiest pose is kneeling, with the fish on the sack or polythene at your knees. With a pike the tail can be on the ground while you hold the fish off the ground and across your body. At all times make sure the photographer is taking a picture of the side of the fish – so prop it the right way up, placing your hands behind its body as support. If you are confident of being able to control the fish, hold it in your arms just above the ground.

With one medium-sized fish it should be possible to hold it across your body, above the waist. It's best to kneel, so that if you have to lower the fish to the ground you don't have far to go. Spread your sack, polythene or a wet net in front of you in case you have to put the fish down. As before, keep it side-on to the camera. Make sure the tail isn't hidden by your hand or one of your arms.

Photographing a big mixed catch of fish is not easy. In most cases a decent picture is impossible, and it may be better to take out just the best fish. Wet the landing net, having unscrewed it from the handle, and put the fish in there. Modern landing nets are knotless and kind on the fish, and you can hold it just off the ground (still kneeling) until the photographer is ready. Then lower it to the ground, smile at the camera, and hope for the best.

The correct way to hold a big fish for the camera, low down with a plastic sheet as a safety net. Note how the bankside foliage has added to the atmosphere.

To take a picture of a catch in a keepnet shake the water from the mesh first, so that what's inside can be seen. The larger the mesh the better the results.

Colour or black and white?

Few anglers use black and white film so the question doesn't usually arise. But unless you are a reasonably experienced photographer it is probably better to use black and white, because more can be done in the printing stage to correct mistakes than with colour.

Laying the pike on the ground towards the camera, as here, will form a vertical picture. In this case the photographer has turned his camera on its side, which will enable him to move closer in. Sitting down, and resting your elbow on your leg, will help beat the photographer's worst problem – camera shake. Wind and poor light both accentuate this problem

Tips for the photographer

If the camera is a 'point and shoot' model, with no adjustments possible, the main point to watch is choice of background. Avoid sky or water at all costs, as this will affect the automatic exposure and the angler and fish will probably appear dark and under-exposed. Better to use a hedge or bushes behind the subject.

If the camera has symbols for 'bright sun', 'hazy sun' or 'light cloud', the same advice applies. If you're using print film (as opposed to slides) it's as well to take a pessimistic view of the weather and put the symbol to the next dark one down. If it's hazy sun, put the camera on 'light cloud'. The reason for this is that with both black and white and colour print films it's better to over- rather than under-expose.

If you have some photographic experience and maybe a 35mm camera, you will know you can alter the exposure as you wish. Again, with print film, err on the side of slight over-exposure. It's not a bad idea to set the dial on 'plus one stop' if you shoot on automatic. Then you may get away with having water or sky as a background. However, it's always better to bracket two stops either side of what the meter suggests.

Framing the picture

A common mistake is to take pictures from too far away. Don't be frightened of getting in close; what you see in the viewfinder is pretty well what you get on the print. In the case of a person kneeling with a fish in front, turn the camera on its side, to get in closer.

In sun or shade?

Nearly always it is better to have fish and angler in shade. The main exception is if the light is very bad, when you need all the help you can get. But always try to avoid putting the subject in bright sunlight. If it's a hot day find some shade, or get the sun behind and a little to the side of the angler. This reduces contrast and will make a much better print. But remember, if possible, to adjust the camera's exposure. If it's an automatic camera it will do this itself.

Moving in close will produce dramatic pictures like this. Here the photographer has completely filled the frame. Note the sheet under the angler's hands

How many pictures?
Never be afraid to take several pictures. Even the professionals don't pretend they can get it right first time. The angler may have a silly expression on his face in some – if you take only one you can bet it will be that one!

If you can adjust the exposure, take some with the exposure both greater and less than the meter shows. If your camera carries symbols, take one on each symbol – you're bound to get one right in the end. Film is cheap, and costs only a few pence per frame. Once angler and fish are properly posed it takes only seconds to get another shot.

Focusing
You may not be able to focus with your camera but if you are able to do so, and if you're taking a picture of an angler with several fish, focus on a point one-third in from the front of the fish going towards the angler. The closer the angler is to the fish, and the less they spread out towards you, the better chance you have of getting angler and fish all in focus. The poorer the light, the greater the problem.

Taking a picture of yourself
A 35mm camera will probably include a self-timer. This will allow about eight seconds to get back from the camera to pose with your fish. Some specialist angling shops sell stick-adaptors which enable the camera to be screwed into a bank stick. Alternatively, put the camera on a

Congratulations, mate! Putting a big catch on a sheet of polythene with helpers grasping the sides will ensure the fish are unharmed. When you've taken your photographs take the sheet to the water's edge and let the fish go. This particular catch came from the Middle Level Drain near Upwell, Norfolk. There were an estimated 100lb-plus of bream here. But to help ensure the safety of the fish they were not weighed

tackle box; but this is not ideal as you may have to wedge it so that it points slightly downwards.

Keeping the fish moist

A garden hand spray which emits a fine mist of water is ideal for keeping fish moist in hot weather, and gives them an attractive gleam.

Getting your pictures published

The first requirement is that they must be sharp. The most common cause of blur is camera shake, so make yourself comfortable before you start clicking away. If it's windy, you've got wobbly hands or if the light is bad, try to rest your arm on something – even a friend knelt down by your side. Hold the camera steady and gently press the shutter. Don't stab at it.

The picture must show the fish well. That's why a single fish should be upright, not lying belly towards the camera. If there is more than one, taking a picture from slightly over the top will show less of their bellies.

There should be as little wasted space as possible. That's why a person with, for example, a 4lb tench, should try to hold it well above his waist. That way there isn't too much human body in the picture. The picture is about the fish and the captor's smiling face, almost everything else is irrelevant.

The exposure should be reasonable, and in the case of a colour slide it must be spot-on. There is a little more leeway accepted in the case of black and white prints and colour prints (which can also be reproduced in black and white), though a magazine or newspaper may need the negative to work on to get an acceptable result. Most published colour pictures are taken from colour slides, though occasionally high-quality colour prints can be reproduced. However, because the cost of publishing a colour picture is much greater than for a black and white, magazines will use only the best colour pictures.

You don't need an expensive camera to take a picture that's perfectly acceptable. But always try to be quick off the mark. Old pictures have little worth in the publishing industry.

THE SEASONS

CHAPTER TWENTY-EIGHT
SUMMER FISHING

Summer is one of the best times for all coarse anglers. Because the water is warmer than in winter, the angler has a realistic chance of catching most of the different species of freshwater fish.

Certain fish, such as tench, carp and barbel, feed more regularly during the summer months, and surely there is a no more romantic image than a pleasure angler floatfishing for tench at dawn in the margins of a lily-covered lake as the sun slowly rises.

Summer fishing also means longer hours of daylight and the angler can fish at any time of his choosing between the hours of 4am and 10pm. Catching fish is much easier as most species are more active, more eager to feed at certain times of the day and much more likely to pull that float under or put a real curve in that quivertip.

As with all aspects of fishing, there are certain hints and tips which can make summer fishing all the more successful and memorable.

Stillwaters in summer

Stillwaters have a magic of their own. There's nothing quite like watching the dawn mist rise from a lake on a hot summer's morning, when the damp air contains the promise of a net of hard-fighting tench or bream. But, to make the most of your sport, choose the right time of day to fish if you want to increase your chances of a bumper haul.

Just because match anglers tend to fish between 10am and 3pm doesn't mean that this is the best time of day – these hours are probably the worst of all! Species like tench, carp and bream tend to feed more actively early in the morning, or in the evening when the powerful rays of the sun are not directly on the water. Roach can be caught throughout the day, despite the heat, as can small eels, but the better specimens tend to be less active during this period.

If you study a water carefully you can often see tench and carp lying under the lilies, basking in the warm water of the margins. But when the water cools, or the sun disappears behind the clouds, a basic urge to start feeding is often triggered. Humid, overcast days can also be excellent times to fish for tench, while carp are totally different. This species, more than any other, is heavily influenced in its feeding habits by barometric pressure. While they will often feed as avidly on hot, sunny days as on wet, windy ones, they tend to feed heavily only if the weather has been settled for several days.

During the summer, carp, bream and tench love to forage for tasty morsels in the margins of the lakes, so you don't need to cast huge distances to locate feeding fish. It's not until the onset of colder weather that they retreat to deeper and warmer water.

Rivers in summer

Rivers represent a different challenge but, like stillwaters offer the prospect of superb sport. Unlike stillwaters they also provide shoals of fish which are prepared to feed throughout the day. Species like roach, dace, chub and barbel are the angler's quarry and can all be caught in good numbers if you choose your swim with a little thought and care.

At this time of year river fish tend to inhabit stretches where the water is shallow, weedy and well-oxygenated. Look for a gravel glide between beds of streamer weeds. It is here that you'll find roach, dace, chub and barbel. If your river isn't of this classic 'Mr Crabtree' variety, never fear. Look for any places where there are near or far bank features – a bend in the river, a far-bank bush, an overhanging tree under which a raft of rubbish has collected. Swims such as these are always likely to be home to a shoal of chub or other species.

Barbel are another good target species and these beautiful fish, with the fighting qualities of an

Atlantic salmon, can be most obliging during the warm months, although the cream of the sport usually peaks in September when, it seems, they sense the coming of autumn and feed with renewed determination. Dace, roach and chub will often feed throughout the day, particularly if the swim has some form of cover to which they can retreat.

Summer baits

During these warm months just about any bait will catch fish. But some work better than others. Seed baits, hemp and tares, are particularly effective, as is sweetcorn. Hemp can be an absolute killer when water temperatures are high. On days when you can't get a bite on a size 26 hook and single squatt, you can slip a single grain of hemp on a size 16 and watch the float disappear time and time again as the roach go berserk.

Tares are the perfect complement to hemp. The size of a garden pea, they tempt the bigger roach and will often produce 30lb nets of specimens to 1lb or more. Sweetcorn is an amazingly versatile and inexpensive bait which will catch anything from gudgeon to barbel. Chub, roach, tench and carp all love it, too. It can be fished with either float or leger tactics, but always remember to use a reasonable-sized hook. If you try to cram a couple of grains on a size 20, the chances are they will fly off when you cast. Match the hook to the size of the bait. Sizes 16, 18 and 20 are fine for tares and hemp, a 14 or 16 for sweetcorn.

Maggots are a super all-year-round bait, and few anglers would fish a summer session without them. Colour can be of vital importance, however. For stillwaters, where carp, tench and bream are the quarry, red maggots can be deadly as hookbait, even though you may be feeding the swim with white or bronze samples. For some reason these species love that red colour. Conversely, on rivers, most species seem to prefer bronze-coloured maggots!

There are days, however, when the river is low and stale, and other baits will produce more fish than the maggot. Casters are one of those change baits which can dramatically bring a summer swim to life. They always seem to produce the better fish. If your local river is full of troublesome minnows, which grab every maggot, caster is the answer. It is important to use the freshest possible casters – stale ones will quickly be rejected.

Another effective summer bait is bread – tench, carp, bream and chub will take it avidly. It's cheap, easy to obtain and simple to use. You can use it with floatfishing, legering and freelining tactics. Although hi-tech carping methods seem all the rage today, there's nothing to match the thrill of freelining a piece of crust in the margins and watching as a hungry carp sucks it in! Bread has been a standard summer bait for centuries and the fish still like it as much today.

The joys of summer – beautiful surroundings and plenty of fish!

Another often neglected summer bait is stewed wheat, especially in waters which are bordered by wheat fields. It's cheap, simple to prepare, and a little goes a long way. It's a great bait for most species, particularly roach, dace, chub and bream, and like other seed baits, will often sort out the larger specimens.

Don't overlook the humble worm either. Redworms and earthworms will often produce fish, and big ones too, on days when other baits fail. Their only drawback is that they often attract the unwanted attentions of eels, a species which most anglers would prefer not to catch! Still, it's always worth taking a few worms with you – they can be deadly for tench, bream, chub and big roach.

Every angler's dream summer swim

Winter on the beautiful River Wye at Symond's Yat

Irish international, Jack Tisdall, lands a hybrid on the River Bann at Newferry

CHAPTER TWENTY-NINE
TACKLING AUTUMN

As the days shorten, and long chilly nights cool the water, natural foods like insect larvae, water shrimps and daphnae become scarce, and fish have to start working harder for their food. This is good news for the angler because at this time of year fish, like all wild creatures, feed heavily in order to withstand the rigours of winter. Even notoriously hard summer waters will produce good fish at this time of year. And because the sun is less bright at this time, fish are more willing to feed through the day. In addition heavy weed growth, which will have restricted many anglers fishing for tench on lakes, or barbel and chub on shallow rivers, is starting to die away.

There is one problem – when leaves start to fall they foul the water. Avoid the areas where they collect. Fish will tend to keep clear of these areas anyway, because the rotting process sours the water.

Carp and tench are often considered to be only summer fish. Yet they, also, feed heavily in autumn, and many swims will now be accessible for the first time since the season opened. The fish won't roam about quite so much, and can be concentrated with a bit of prebaiting.

Autumn fishing tactics, in general will not differ much from those used in summer, except that there will be fewer opportunities to catch fish from the surface. But you will find fish in slightly deeper water than in summer. On lakes long-range swimfeedering is likely to pay off, to get your bait to the medium-depth swims where roach will start massing before they move off to their winter hideouts. Given mild, overcast conditions they will feed all day, but on a bright day the two hours before and after dusk will be best.

On rivers, the eel menace will have diminished, and some of the best barbel bags of the year are reported in autumn. It is easier to spot the fish now that the weed is dying, but you will need to be extra careful as you approach the water to avoid scaring them. Look for deepish swims running close to the banks.

For roach and chub make for a shallow swim leading to a deeper glide. This is the opposite of summer, when you are looking to take them running a bait onto the shallow areas. Fish tend to shoal up in certain sizes at this time of year, so if you catch a quality roach or chub it's worth trying a piece of breadflake for its brothers and sisters.

For pike a moving bait will work better than a static deadbait. Wobbling a deadbait near the surface is an exciting and fruitful tactic. You can get a rig on which to mount your bait from any good tackle shop. Both perch and pike need a fair amount of light in which to hunt, so generally midday is the best time, though they will feed avidly for a short time towards dusk on a clear day. Perch are making their way to deep holes in autumn, and a leger is often necessary to place the bait in exactly the right spot. You can't beat worm as a bait, particularly if the waters on both lakes and rivers start to colour up.

Bream are the problem fish in autumn. A slight drop in temperature will be liable to put them off feeding. But on a river, extra water will revive them provided it is not fresh and cold. Best time is on the third day of a mild spell when the water level is dropping after a slight colouring up. They always appear in the same swims, so local knowledge is a 'must'.

This is the time when you will reap the rewards of having either your own wormery or at least a place to keep your unused worms when you've brought them home. Even anglers who normally take only maggots with them should have both bread and worms in autumn, because this is the time when the 'ordinary' angler is most likely to suddenly find himself catching big fish.

It's probably the best time of all to go fishing.

CHAPTER THIRTY
WINTER FISHING

General advice

The majority of British anglers fish in a similar manner to match anglers; they choose a spot they think will produce fish and then settle in for the day. They will take whatever comes along as opposed to the specimen hunter who will set his sights on one species or even a single fish. In winter there are special problems for the all-rounder. Time is limited to daylight hours and he's unlikely to have a tent in which to stay warm. The winter all-rounder must be an opportunist, ready to take his chances as they arrive.

Winter fish are less active and more likely to accept a still bait than one they have to chase. But because they are less active, once they are found it's a good bet they will be present for the whole day. And because of their stationary lifestyle they make choice of tactic easy. A leger rig is always a reasonable method on which to start a winter session. If the leger produces bites quickly, it may be worth running a float rig through a few times. But don't waste time on the wrong method. If fish are not caught on the float go back to the leger and take what fish are feeding. It's all too easy to have your interest wane on a cold, biteless day. If that happens you will fish badly and may even be better off at home.

Former world champion, Dave Thomas, has a system for winter fishing. If he gets a bite on leger tackle within 30 seconds of casting – which means a fish has taken the bait as it is still falling or immediately it reaches bottom – he assumes fish will go for a moving bait presented on float tackle. So get well prepared and set up a float rod just in case. Don't expect a huge catch. If one comes along so much the better, it's a bonus, but start by fishing for a bite. Two or three quality roach on a hard winter day can give as much pleasure as a big bag made on a warm summer evening.

And from the moment you arrive at the waterside take care. Fish can be scared just as easily in winter as during summer. They may not be as easy to spot, but they will still react to a basket being thumped down hard on the bank. And because there is going to be more flow they may be closer to the bankside than usual, which calls for even more care.

Picking the right swim is possibly more important during the cold months than in summer. As a general rule the medium-to-deep swims offer the best chance if you're working 'blind', without local knowledge. So in a deep river, say up to 18ft, water around 12ft to 13ft deep is a good starting point. The really deep areas are so often disappointing. If there is a sudden mild spell, fish may move into swims only 6ft deep even though they have been feeding for a month in the other depths.

Consider also the state of the river. If there is a lot of flood water rushing down, it will bring with it suspended dirt and silt. Fish will move away into slacks where this rubbish can settle out quickly to the bottom, even if these areas are only 2 or 3ft deep. An added bonus for the fish is that this shallow spot may be warmed by the sun slightly, if only for an hour or so. To the angler this temperature rise will be unnoticed except perhaps for the increased number of bites.

Winter will narrow the choice of productive swims but finding one can be easier than in summer. Every year the same swims will become hotspots as fish move off the shallows. The local tackle shop is always worth a visit if you are a stranger to the water to be fished. The tackle dealer makes his living from people catching fish and he's unlikely to send you to the wrong place. Certainly it pays to ask for advice. Once at the waterside don't ignore the water close in under your feet. Fish will come in very close if the water is coloured. And under flood conditions the slightest cutback in the bank may be enough to house a small shoal, sheltering from the current.

Since their introduction to English waters in the sixties, zander have spread like wildfire. Although they have been blamed for the decline in fishing in East Anglia, they are prized for their sporting abilities. This 13-pounder was taken from the Ramsey Forty Foot drain in Cambridgeshire

(*opposite*) Trout waters, like Bough Beech in Kent, contain many specimen pike. This 30-pounder was taken from the water by Rob Milford

Having picked a swim the next stage is to decide how best to feed it. In winter it is far too easy to ruin your chances by overfeeding. And for this reason it's a good idea, if possible, to loose-feed. Even then take care. Half a dozen maggots every two or three minutes may be all that's needed.

On fast waters a swimfeeder may be needed to get bait down to the correct spot. In this case a Drennan feeder that has been cut down will work nicely. By cutting it down in size it will take no more than about a dozen maggots and prevent overfeeding. A simple, but often overlooked, tip for winter is to always tie the feeder or leger link direct to the main line via a knot. This set-up will collect far less rubbish than a rig that includes a swivel.

Quality fish will usually respond best to the loose-feed method, so in any case it is worth trying to fish without cereal groundbait. However, on waters noted for small fish, a tiny amount of cereal may get roach and small bream feeding. But if you start catching small fish on maggot it is still worth trying a caster on the hook from time to time. This bait will, at times, sort out a bigger fish; but don't waste too much time. Give it a couple of minutes and if nothing happens revert back to the maggot, maybe trying caster again later on. Another good winter bait is a small portion of redworm. Use a piece just a little longer than a maggot and on a small hook.

In winter, concentrate hard. Bites will not come thick and fast and you need to make the most of every one you get. Fish may come in short bursts.

Get one and others may follow soon after. Keep up the pressure until bites stop. Then is the time to relax a little and maybe have a cup of coffee so that you're ready for the next good session that may begin an hour later.

Fishing the colder weather calls for some mobility. Give a swim half an hour before even thinking of a move and possibly an hour before setting off for a new swim. The days are short and the best time is usually between midday and 2.30pm. After that the air temperature will drop rapidly and bites will slow or stop.

One way to cut down the experimental time is to fish two maggots on the hook, each a different colour. After a bite, inspect the bait to see if just one colour has been nipped. That way you will be able to sort out which colour is the one to fish. Pink is generally accepted as a good colour when the weather is bright and cold.

If the double-maggot trick eventually results in a decrease in bite frequency, that's the time to drop down to a smaller hook and a single maggot. A size 24 will not be out of order if the going is hard, but be sure to take some ready tied to the waterside – your hands may be too cold to tackle tying on the bank.

Winter floods

Bait

Some of the best fishing of all comes on those glorious winter afternoons when the wind blows warm and the river is flowing fast and coloured. For in flood conditions fish tend to congregate in the deep or slack swims where the angler can easily find them.

In a highly coloured river, fish rely heavily on their sense of smell to help them root out their food. So one of the first requirements is to use a bait that has a good 'pong'. Also, because the water will be moving faster than usual, a large bait tethered to the bottom will appear more natural than, say, a single maggot lying stationary. Maggots will work, of course, but generally you need a steady swim, and one which is not too dirty. On the whole floods are a good time to pick out the larger than normal fish, which have less opportunity to inspect your bait than they would in clear water. Finally, if you hook a good fish which tears out into the main current, you'll be happier playing it on a size 8 hook than on a size 20!

All of which adds up to the fact that you won't go far wrong in a flood if your bait is big and smelly. Here are four which meet all those requirements:

Cheese Once a very popular bait, but now not used as much as it should be. The easiest way of using it is as paste, and if you're trying it for the first time, use Dairylea. It's soft, and can be moulded easily to whatever shape you require. It hardens a little in cold water. Use hooks of size 10 or larger – specimen hunters will happily mould the cheese round a size 2 hook. One tip is to give it a flat surface which will naturally hold bottom.

Cheese can also be cubed. You'll need a hardish type like Cheddar or Red Leicester for this. These can also be mashed up and moulded into a paste, but you'll need to do this at home. The soft cheeses, like Dairylea, can be used on the bank straight from the wrapper. If you use harder cheese make sure the hook point is showing.

Lobworms Lobworms are the 'classic' winter bait for big roach, though all species, including pike, will take them. They are now a 'must' for chub anglers fishing the Trent in winter. Collect them by going out on a mild winter evening when the ground is moist, and not frozen. Although all books say the best place to find them is the lawn, in fact it's easier to gather them from flower beds. They will lie on the bare earth, right beside the path and sometimes even on it.

The collar of the worm contains no vital organs, and some anglers recommend hooking them here. One trick is to hook the worm through the head, thread it up the line and hook it again through the tail. Then place a small shot on the line below the head to prevent it slipping down the line. Chub will approach the tail, sucking in your hook first. Do not use line of less than 3lb with this method, as a chub can damage your line with its hard teeth if it takes the worm very far into its mouth.

Sweetcorn This is another easily obtained hook-bait; but don't use just a single grain, use three on a size 8 hook. These will hold bottom more readily, and will be spotted by a fish in coloured water more easily than a single grain.

You can put sweetcorn in groundbait or loose-feed it. Its main advantage is that it is used straight from the tin. It's easy to dye, and in the

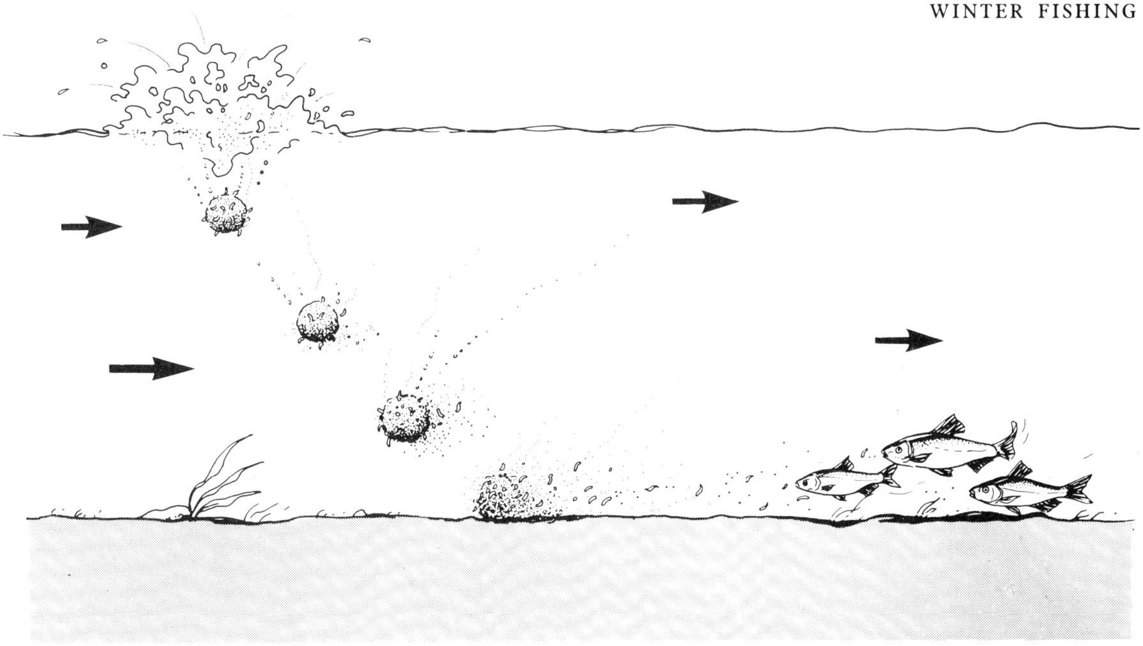

Fig 91 Make sure your groundbait is solid enough to get to the bottom breaking up and releasing its contents. Then remember the fish will tend to be downstream of the spot where it lands

1980s red became the 'in' colour. It will attract most species of fish. And though you can use it straight from the tin it's advisable to open the tin at home and take it to the water in a maggot box, as many clubs do not allow tins or polythene bags to be taken to the water.

Don't be caught out inadvertently breaking the rules.

Luncheon meat This is probably the most popular winter bait of all for chub. Cut a slice ½in thick from the side of a chunk of meat, cut this into strips, and finally cubes. Although you can do this on the bank (remember tins may be barred) you'll finds the meat is very soft. It's better to put the cubes into a fridge overnight. In the morning they will have gone slightly darker and will have become leathery. These are just as succulent to the fish, but will stay on the hook better.

To hook them on, push the hook right through the cube, then twist the point round so that the meat won't fall off the hook. Use big hooks – a size 14 isn't large enough to hold even a small cube of meat, and the bigger the cube the less likely you are to break it apart when you put it on the hook. Large hooks are also easier to handle, particularly if your hands are cold. So use size 8, 6 and 4 hooks.

Groundbaiting

Because fish are likely to be holed up, finding them is the most important part of fishing a flood. So you're not going to need to use a lot of groundbait to attract them to your swim – you've got to go to them. Nevertheless there will be many times when you'll want to get at least some bait out to start them feeding and to give yourself confidence. The secret is to ensure that in the fast water every scrap of bait you put in gets down to the fish.

Forget about light groundbaiting with cloud groundbait. You'll only need that in clear, slow swims such as sometimes exist in the mouth of a feeder stream or culvert. The rest of the time you've got to attack the river. And the place you want to get your bait is to the bottom, where fish will be taking advantage of undulations in the river bed to gain respite from the current, yet where they will be near enough to the main stream to dash out for food if it comes by.

Swimfeeders For years the 'feeder' has been gaining in popularity, and now most anglers have some in their basket. This is certainly the easiest and most popular way of groundbaiting a swim in winter. Apart from anything else it is self regulatory in that, because you fill the feeder with groundbait each cast, the more fish you catch the more bait goes in. And when bites slow down, so does the amount of groundbait you use.

If you're using maggots you won't go far wrong with a block-end feeder, where the maggots crawl through or are washed out of the holes. In moving water you can also use casters like this. Otherwise use an open-ended feeder, ensuring that the groundbait plugs in either end are rock solid. It's better to err on the side of having them too hard rather than too soft in floods. The last thing you want is for your luncheon meat to be released just under the surface to possibly end up in the next swim down.

This is a particularly useful way of getting worms out to your swim, either chopped or whole. But follow the rule of not mixing your cereal groundbait and your loose offerings – always plug one end of the feeder with neat groundbait, fill the middle, and plug the other end. Then press both ends with finger and thumb to ensure it's firm before casting. Cast with a gentle swinging motion, or the contents may be released as you punch the tackle out.

One exceptionally good tip is to bait your swim with a swimfeeder even if you are intending to floatfish. It's easy and accurate, and it does away with the possibility of making a ball of groundbait too light, so that it breaks up before hitting bottom.

Cereal groundbait This is an excellent way of getting samples of your hookbait to your swim, provided you can make it hard enough. There are now so many proprietory brands of reliable consistancy in the shops that this is now easier than it used to be.

Ensure that the groundbait is well soaked. If you can't make it up overnight, leave it for at least half an hour before using it. If you need to stiffen it, but have no leem or heavier groundbait, add earth from the river bank. Another way is to mash up slices of bread, minus the crust, drain them, and add dry groundbait. This makes an exceptionally stiff mixture. Use a ball the size of a cricket ball for feeding swims near your own bank. When it enters the water it should make a distinct 'ker-lump' sound and go straight to the bottom.

For baiting swims under the far bank or more than 12yd from where you are sitting, a catapult will probably be safer. In this case don't make the balls too big; err on the smaller side. Use too much at a time and you risk them flying off-course. You can include almost anything inside, including worms, sweetcorn or casters. But beware of using maggots, especially pinkies, which are active and may break up the ball in flight or when it hits the surface.

Loose-feeding

You may be able to get worms, sweetcorn, cheese or luncheon meat straight into your swim without the use of groundbait or a swimfeeder. But you'll need a reasonably slow swim to do it, and you may still need to put in your bait several yards upstream of where you are fishing.

Luncheon meat may float however; test it before putting it in. The cheaper brands tend to contain less fat and are better for loose-feeding. Scalding it at home with hot water helps disperse some of the fat. Sweetcorn and worms should only be put neat into slow swims unless you're absolutely certain where they will end up. A lobworm is, however, heavier than a redworm, and a catapult is useful for putting it out some distance. It will still sink rather slowly, though, as it has a large surface area for the current to catch. Cheese can be made up into hard balls and sinks fairly quickly.

You'll be able to loose-feed maggot or caster only if you're fishing in the mouth of a feeder stream, or in an eddy where you can be certain they won't get swept into the main current. In all cases watch the speed of the current and, if it starts running faster, put your bait in farther upstream, or be prepared to alter the place you are fishing by shifting it downstream.

Hempseed This is a useful standby because it sinks fairly quickly, and has a small surface area for the current to catch. It is used particularly in conjunction with maggots and casters – you can be certain it will lie on the bottom once it gets there, in all except the fastest swims. It's also an excellent bait for putting into a feeder with almost any other bait.

Most tackle shops sell hempseed either frozen

or packed in preservative. Wash any unused seed at the end of the day before putting it back into the fridge.

Hempseed can be prepared overnight by washing a cupful of uncooked seed, placing it in a vacuum flask to no more than one-third full, and filling the flask with boiling water. The seed will expand and crack to show the white kernel.

Techniques

Float fishing Unless you are experienced in casting heavy float tackle a long way, you'll probably choose to fish close to the side. And you'll get a lot of fish like that.

It's likely that the length of your swim will be short – perhaps down to an overhanging bush. And at some time during the day you'll want to fish a stationary bait. In fast water, however, when you hold a float back it rises. The answer is to overshot. Trial and error is the best way, but the faster the water the more shot you will need 'downstairs'. Generally you will be bulking your shot together a foot from the hook. In the average swim expect a 4 AAA float to need 6 AAA when held back, and in really fast water it may take almost double the normal amount of shot.

A gentle underarm swing should be sufficient to place it in position, but you won't be able to trot it down to your chosen spot because it will sink.

Swimfeeder rig The simplest rig of all is with line running through the centre of a block-end feeder, with a leger stop or shot on the end of the line to prevent it falling off.

If you're using an open-ended feeder you'll need some kind of a link from the line to the feeder. But remember that if there is a lot of rubbish coming down the river, the more swivels you use the more weed will collect on your line. By far the simplest set-up is to use a knot and to fish a fixed link.

Legering The simplest rig is with the line running straight through the swivel on the leger weight, or a coffin lead with the line through the centre. For both legering and swimfeedering, the leger bead, with a hole through the centre and a place to tie the leger link, is a boon. It is stopped by a leger-stop or shot. Disadvantage of a shot is that it may move on the strike.

You'll need stronger lines in floodwater than you'd normally use. You may find yourself hooked into large rafts of weed or lumps of rubbish. Alternatively, if you've hooked a good fish it will take advantage of the current, and it will take much longer to land than normal. All

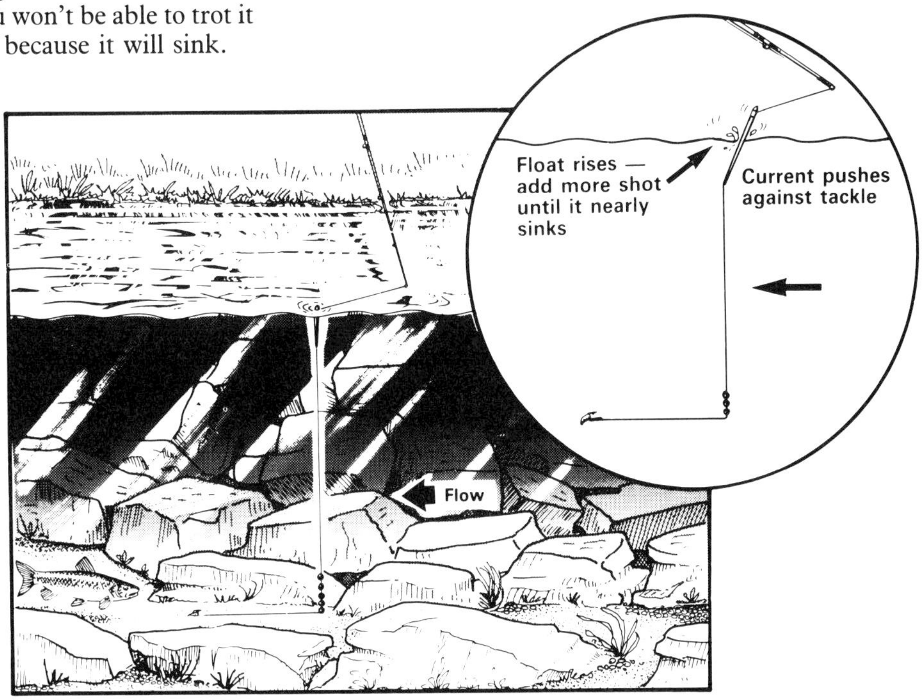

Fig 92 Fishing under your rod tip with an overshotted float is a useful ploy in floods, when fish tend to come into the side out of the force of the main current. Bulk your shot a foot from the hook. In fast water you may need almost twice the normal amount of shot to get the float to stay with just its tip above the surface (main picture)

this time line is under considerable strain. Also you'll be using heavier swimfeeders than normal, with extra weight attached because you need to hold bottom. Experienced anglers will realise that in coloured water fish aren't able to inspect the bait so minutely, and will start thinking about 5lb line if they are expecting big fish.

Don't think about using hook lengths of less than 3lb in a fast-flowing flooded river, and it's better to use an 'all through' set-up if you can, with the hook tied to the end of the reel line. The absolute minimum for fishing in a flood, even if the river is clear of rubbish, is 3lb.

Other tips

1 Push a piece of stick into the bank right on the edge of the water when you get to your swim. Keep an eye on it, and you will see whether the water is rising or falling. Almost always the fishing will be better as it falls.

2 Remember the banks may be slippery if the river has been well up. Take care not to stand on a piece of bank which has been undercut by the current.

3 If you see a piece of flat wood on the bank as you walk to your swim, pick it up. It may be useful to support your basket on mud.

4 As the water is likely to be coloured, don't ignore the first few feet of water out from the bank – they may be crawling with fish.

5 Never fish a flood without worms. They can be deadly in coloured water.

6 The nicest glides are not always near the bank. Look for them also in the middle of the river.

7 There's usually a deep hole where two rivers meet, made by the scouring action of the tributary. The same applies where there is a pumphouse on the bank. If it is working, watch where the water rushes, and when the pump stops try the deep spot.

8 To get more feed into an open-ended feeder, use one with one end capped, plugging just the open end. Make this the end which hangs down when you cast.

The stringer

Do you know what a 'stringer' is? Well actually, there are two.

The oldest definition is that it's a piece of string or twine pushed through the jaw of a pike so that it can be tethered in the water instead of putting it in a keepnet. However, the use of carp sacks in which to keep big fish, including pike, has meant that the use of this type of stringer has largely died out.

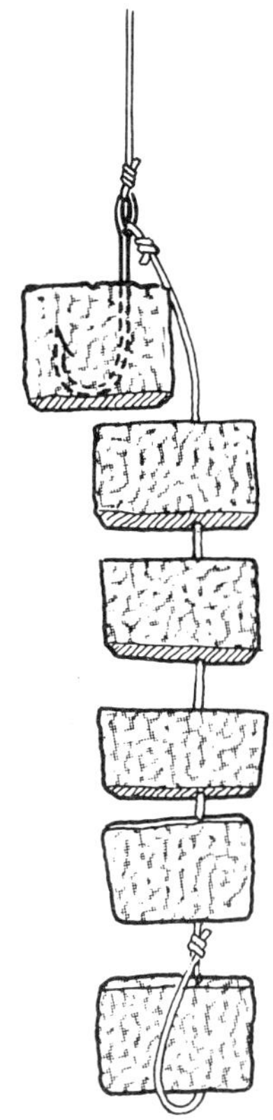

Fig 93 A 'stringer'. One piece of bait (in this case luncheon meat) is placed on the hook. More pieces of bait are threaded onto a piece of PVA string, which dissolves on water, leaving them loose to attract fish to the baited hook. The bottom piece of meat has simply been tied to the string to prevent the others slipping off on the cast

The newest type of stringer is a form of groundbaiting – and very ingenious it is, too. It consists of several portions of bait threaded onto a piece of PVA string which is tied to your hook. Then the hook is baited as normal, and cast out.

But PVA string dissolves in water, so very soon you are fishing with just your baited hook while the loose samples lie nearby. This is an ideal way of introducing luncheon meat into your swim, though you should check that it won't float before using it.

It's also possible to thread sweetcorn or even worms onto the string.

MATCH FISHING

CHAPTER THIRTY-ONE

YOUR FIRST MATCH

Fishing your first match can be an exciting, even daunting, prospect. But with a little care and thought given to selecting the right venue you could be well on the way to becoming a star. If you've decided to give the match scene a try chances are you've already had a fair bit of success as a freelance or 'pleasure' angler. Don't throw the knowledge gained out of the window. In a match you will be trying to catch the very same fish that you caught as a loner. Be prepared to use tactics you know work and have confidence in; but above all keep your eyes and ears open as you fish.

For your first match, pick a small one fished on a water close to home and which you know well. Maybe you will want to join a local club that can offer perhaps one match a month. For the first season or two it is best to forget the big open events that are costly and will match you against anglers of much greater experience. Far better to go along to them as a spectator, pick out a well known angler who has drawn well and see how he tackles the swim from start to finish. Store the little tricks you see away in your mind, ready to be put into use when the right situation occurs.

Having chosen your match – or small match series – begin by finding out what has previously won similar events on that water. The local paper and a few enquiries at your tackle shop will help. Keep an eye on river reports featured in *Angling Times* and read these reports to find out the latest results. Knowledge is possibly the best piece of equipment you can take to your peg. Without some target at which to aim you will be fishing blind. For example it's no good fishing hard for 5lb of roach if at least six pegs are in with a very good chance of producing bream.

But be careful not to aim too high. Match fishing can be a hard game and too often a forecast of 10lb to win is, in fact, likely to be optimistic with half that weight being enough.

If the club you join is new to you, find out who are the top anglers taking part. Then if you are pegged next to them you can see where, and how, they fish and perhaps remember it for the time you draw that swim. Always keep an eye on the top men and learn from them. Most are only too happy to talk about their fishing, tell you how they caught and how they didn't, what they did wrong and how they would tackle the same swim again. If the club you choose has a star who wins match after match, don't join the band who despise him. Someone has to be top dog and you should be making it your aim to beat him; he'll enjoy the competition and you'll be a better angler for the experience.

Once the match has been selected and the appropriate club membership paid, you'll start to worry about your tackle – don't. It goes without saying that it and your bait must both be in perfect order – a match is no place to find you have no small hooks or that your reel handle is stiff. But if it's good enough to catch fish on a pleasure session it will be good enough to get you going in the world of match fishing. Smart, expensive rods will not catch more fish than the one you're using. And the tackle you fish with week after week will be well known to you. If you must invest in more tackle buy a second rod and reel of the same model as the ones you already have. That way you can switch around without having to readjust during the match. It is very important that line is in good trim. Match fishing takes a lot out of line and it will need to be changed frequently. You may find a need to scale down on breaking strain and hook sizes to cope with the extra pressure of having to catch fish at the most difficult times of day. The disturbance of the match will also make fish just that little bit harder to catch too.

All this knowledge can be stored away but above all – keep it simple. Far too many new-

If you catch fish like this while you're pleasure fishing there's no reason why you shouldn't do it in a match

comers to match fishing get carried away and go to a match loaded with every bait under the sun, three or four rods, a couple of poles and enough tackle to see them through the season. End result is they spend half the match switching around from rig to rig and never really get down to sorting out one method on which to catch enough fish to figure in the result.

Match day

On match day you will pay an entry fee and perhaps invest cash in a pool – pools are usually optional and for a start may not interest you. But as success is earned they do help pay for the extra bait, tackle and travel that match fishing involves.

Having made your draw don't rush off to the peg. Ask a few questions of the other anglers. Few can resist telling another angler what a good peg he has drawn or how it should be won from such-and-such a spot.

If you arrive at your swim in good time keep off the skyline and sit down, watch the river or lake and try to decide what you have in front of you. Try to pick out weedy areas and possible changes in bottom contour – anywhere that could hold fish. At this stage you may want to ask the advice of the anglers drawn on either side of you. But let them get tackled up first, then they will be more likely to give you their time. Don't however take every bit of advice as gospel. They may know little about the area either.

Finally make your own judgements and tackle up as you think best. Eventually the starting whistle blows and you're off. Take your time and plumb the depth properly. It may be fashionable to find the depth by trial and error but you should not be taking shortcuts yet.

Having got the depth sorted out, wind the float to the rod tip and make a note of where the hook is in relation to one of the rings. Later if you break off or need to re-tackle you will be able to go back to the correct depth without having to plumb again. Keep an eye on the men either side and let them make the first moves. If they both opt for fishing down the centre of the river you may be better off fishing either just short or just beyond the same range. By going for a different range you effectively give yourself a much longer clear run, up which fish can be attracted by your feeding.

Don't rush into a heavy feeding pattern. At most follow the lead of the anglers near you. And keep an eye on them for the first hour. Try to estimate how you are doing in relation to their catch rate. If you are holding your own, stick with your plan, if not start thinking about a change.

If you've struggled all through for bites it may pay to switch to the inside, fishing light over a few loose maggots. That little patch of weed just downstream may hold enough fish to put you back in the race. And a change of pattern will also rest the main swim long enough for a few fish to move in. Be prepared to scale down hook size and use a smaller bait. Often a pinkie on the hook will get a bite from a swim that has produced nothing to a big maggot.

On hard-fished match waters it may be worthwhile starting the event by fishing close to your side of the water, while feeding a main swim further out. As bites become harder to find keep moving out until you eventually reach the main feed area. This approach is usually better than one that starts close to the far side and works back. In match fishing it is usually the inside line that dies first.

Keep an eye on your watch and try to pace yourself through the four or five hours of the match. Work out a plan – how long you will stick with a method before a change, perhaps switching from float to leger for example.

Keep in your mind the target weight you worked out to win the match. But be prepared to make late changes if all is not going well. If two pegs away, bream are being caught, it may pay to switch to a suitable method in the hope that they move. An old dodge is to put in a lot of groundbait, in the hope that the angler sitting on the shoal will panic and follow suit. If he does there is always the chance the shoal will move away. It's then an even chance on it going towards or away from you.

And, when you've finished your first match, perhaps with not as much as you would have liked to show for it, weigh in your catch – you may not be among the winners but you can learn a lot. For a start, having weighed in you should follow the scales, or, better still offer to help weigh in the other anglers' catches. This is the best way to learn about a water. You'll see where the fish were caught and perhaps the chatter at the scales will give you more information as to how they were caught.

If you have been well beaten by anglers near you, ask them what they think you did wrong. You may be told you put in too much groundbait, not enough, or fished the wrong line. Store this criticism away for future use.

You will know how your catch compared to the other results. Jot down some notes in a diary. Record how you fished and how the winners caught their fish, the conditions and state of the water. Making a note of results from as many pegs as possible is also a good idea.

In time you will succeed and perhaps move to the open match scene where things are much harder. But the same rules apply and the best anglers build up a network of contacts who swap information on the waters to be fished. Try to get in on the act and always be prepared to tell all you know.

CHAPTER THIRTY-TWO
MAKING IT TO THE 'NATIONAL'

Any angler who says he isn't nervous about fishing in the National Championship for the first time is either lying or has the most extraordinary self-confidence. It's natural to worry about whether you will let your team down. For this is essentially a team event. And your inclusion in next year's squad may rest on your performance in this year's match.

In the days when the issue was decided on total weight it was difficult to decide on team tactics. But now that each angler's performance in his section gains points, almost all the competitors will be fishing for a reasonable points score, and ignoring the individual crown. That is why team tactics, designed to ensure that every angler makes a reasonable catch, are now so important.

However, the advice of former world champion Kevin Ashurst has always been to treat the 'National' as just another match. This is the last occasion on which you should be experimenting with new tackle or baits, or fishing a method you are not familiar with. You should feel at home on the bank, and taking a load of extra tackle and bait 'just in case' is only going to confuse you. If you normally take just one pint of casters to a match on this venue, then take one only – the fish aren't going to be twice as hungry on this one day of the year. In fact it's nearly always the opposite; it's rare that a National venue fishes to form. Sometimes there's an unexpected frost the previous night, or the match itself takes place on a boiling hot day with no wind, or there's cold water in the river, or it's in flood.

Yet even assuming the conditions will be quite unexpected it's still worth practising to familiarise yourself with the water. Find out how deep it is and how much flow it normally has. Gauge the effect of the prevailing wind, and get an idea of what fish are in the water and how big they are likely to be. From that, work out how many methods will catch fish, the bait which is most likely to produce the fish you are looking for, and the tackle you may need. This includes, for instance, the amount of shot you're likely to need on a float to get it to the farthest spot you'll be fishing.

There are plenty of advance matches on most venues, so there's ample opportunity to practise under match conditions. But the best teams won't be in too much of a hurry to lay down strict team plans, for it's impossible to say what conditions will be like on the day. That's where practice comes in. For this enables anglers to have at their disposal several tactics which may all work. The good teams almost invariably leave it to their men to make the last-minute decisions on the day.

In the past, several winning teams have made a point of not fishing a water on the fortnight prior to the match in case it gave them the wrong impression of how to tackle it. The National Championships fished after the beginning of September are particularly prone to last-minute changes in weather. So remember the reason for practising. It should be to get used to the water, not to formulate some magic method that is certain to win on the day.

The worst thing a team captain can do is to confuse his men by trying to get them to fish in a way in which they are not happy, or to take so much bait that they are totally confused. You can't make an angler catch fish if they aren't there. The job of a team captain is to make sure that if there are fish in front of an angler he's relaxed enough, and sufficiently at home with his tackle, to catch them.

PUMA
INTER ACTION

SPECIALIST
0708

Bream can be relied on to provide both summer and winter sport. This 5-pounder was taken from the Twenty Foot drain, near March, Cambridgeshire

Big barbel are also prepared to feed throughout the season. This sleek 8-pounder fell to tackle dealer Pete Henwood when he fished the River Kennet

Sunset over Cromwell weir on the River Trent – a popular fishing spot

CONCLUSION

Well there it is – several lifetimes of experience rolled into one book and still many questions to be answered.

Hopefully you are a better angler than when you started at page one. Continue to apply the advice each chapter offered, but above all think for yourself. After each fishing trip ask yourself questions. Did I make the best of the swim? Could I have caught more or bigger fish? What would have happened if I had adopted a different feeding pattern? Was the swim the right one on the day? If I fish it again what experiences will I draw on to ensure a better result?

Never fail to ask these questions of yourself and, maybe one day soon a journalist from *Angling Times* will be asking you the questions.

Good Fishing!

INDEX

Figures in italics refer to illustrations